Critical Essays on
Louise Bogan

Critical Essays on
Louise Bogan

Martha Collins

G. K. Hall & Co. • Boston, Massachusetts

Library of Congress Cataloging in Publication Data
Main entry under title:

Critical essays on Louise Bogan.

   (Critical essays on American literature)
   Includes index.
   1. Bogan, Louise, 1897–1970–Criticism and inter-
pretation—Addresses, essays, lectures.   I. Collins,
   Martha.   II. Series.
PS3503.0195Z62   1984   811'.52   83–12801
ISBN 0-8161-8680-4

Grateful acknowledgment is made to Farrar, Straus and Giroux,
Inc. for permission to quote from *The Blue Estuaries* by Louise
Bogan. Copyright 1923, 1929, 1930, 1931, 1933, 1934, 1935,
1936, 1937, 1938, 1941, 1949, 1951, 1952, 1954, © 1957,
1958, 1962, 1963, 1964, 1965, 1966, 1967, 1968 by Louise Bogan.
All rights reserved.

Material quoted from the Louise Bogan Papers at Amherst College
is © 1984 by Ruth Limmer, as Trustee of the Estate of Louise
Bogan.

CRITICAL ESSAYS ON AMERICAN LITERATURE

This series seeks to anthologize the most important criticism on a wide variety of topics and writers in American literature. Our readers will find in various volumes not only a generous selection of reprinted articles and reviews but original essays, bibliographies, manuscript sections, and other materials brought to public attention for the first time. Martha Collins' volume on Louise Bogan is a welcome addition to our list in that it is the first collection of scholarship ever published on this important modern writer. Among the thirty-five essays are comments by many of Bogan's contemporaries, including Allen Tate, Ford Madox Ford, Theodore Roethke, W. H. Auden, and Marianne Moore, as well as an essay by Bogan herself. There are reprinted articles and reviews by Yvor Winters, Malcolm Cowley, Elder Olson, Harold Bloom, and Elizabeth Frank. In addition to an extensive introduction by Professor Collins, there are original essays by Deborah Pope, Ruth Limmer, Diane Wood Middlebrook, Carol Moldaw, and Sandra Cookson. We are confident that this collection will make a permanent contribution to American literary study.

James Nagle, GENERAL EDITOR

Northeastern University

ACKNOWLEDGMENTS

Appreciation is due to Jo Anne Miller and Camille Norton, for their consistently intelligent research assistance; to John Lancaster, for access to the Bogan Papers in the Amherst College Library; and most of all to Ruth Limmer, for encouragement, advice, and illumination, as well as for permission to quote from the Bogan Papers.

CONTENTS

INTRODUCTION

It is difficult, if one is a poet with some interest in formal poetry, to realize how little critical discussion Louise Bogan's work has generated. It is tempting to think that this is the result of recent neglect: during her lifetime, Bogan's books were consistently, prominently, and often intelligently reviewed, and she won most of the major awards for poetry. In fact, however, Bogan's strongest admirers have almost always been poets. The majority of the reviewers and critics in this volume are poets; some of them knew Bogan, some of them learned from her, and most of them admired her greatly. But while Bogan has received much praise from poetic high places, she has not stimulated the kind of critical discussion and controversy that keep a poet alive and well in college classrooms. Until recently, and with some exceptions, Louise Bogan has been something of a poet's poet.

One reason for this is that the body of poetry is small: *The Blue Estuaries*, Bogan's final collection (1968), contains only 105 poems. The work is also, to a large extent, early: only 32 poems in the last collection were added after 1937, and many of those were written before 1940. But numbers are not enough to explain why many people who have read much poetry, or modern poetry, or women's poetry, or formal poetry, have never read Louise Bogan. "Such a poet will never be popular," said Theodore Roethke, in the most widely published and quoted essay on Bogan. Why and whether this should be so is a question which not only the poems, but also the criticism of them—from the earliest reviews through the most recent essays—can perhaps help to answer.

Published in 1923, when she was only twenty-six, Louise Bogan's first book, *Body of This Death*, was the culmination of a considerable period of productivity. "I began to write verse from about fourteen on," Bogan wrote in her memoirs. "By the age of 18 I had a thick pile of manuscript, in a drawer in the dining room—and had learned every essential of my trade."[1] During her single year of college, poems appeared in the Boston University *Beacon*; two years later, after a marriage and the birth of her only child, two poems appeared in *Others*. Magazine publications followed in sufficient numbers that, by the time the book appeared, reviewers could refer knowledgeably to Louise Bogan.

Body of This Death was, as several reviewers noted, a small book: twenty-seven poems, many of them short. Some reviewers found the range as narrow as the book was slim—though it was precisely in this context of narrowness that high praise began to be sounded, as in the review by Mark Van Doren reprinted in this volume.[2]

Several reviewers suggested that the narrow range was somehow defined by the boundaries of love, or love and death, or a woman's experience of love—a point worth making in the context of some later reviews, which would be less certain what Bogan's poems were actually about. Beginning with the third or fourth poem, it is in fact hard to miss the book's emphasis on the difficulties of love, especially for a woman, and one effect of this easy identification of subject matter was the almost invariable linking of Bogan with other women poets. Men and women alike compared her to such contemporaries as Edna St. Vincent Millay, Elinor Wylie, and Genevieve Taggard; Llewellyn Jones, in the discussion reprinted here, was unique in comparing her to male poets (Robinson and Yeats), and even he included her in a chapter devoted to "Four Younger Women Poets."

Despite the ease of categorization and placement, reviewers tended not to understand the poems, which troubled some and pleased others. In a 1924 letter,[3] Bogan cataloged some negative reviews, giving the impression that the book was not well received. One of these, a brief notice in the *Dial*, did castigate the poet as "an inexpert craftsman striving fitfully and inchoately to express that which defies expression," using words which were "often only obscurely significant";[4] but the reviews Bogan cited were brief, and the longer ones were remarkably favorable. What most of the reviewers did share was a sense that, though the general subject might be clear, the poems themselves were obscure. The reviewers included here located the difficulty in the technique; another, though wishing that Bogan would "deliver herself more loosely and luxuriously to her art," found that the poems were difficult "because she has too much to say."[5] Whatever the source, whatever the judgment, the critics struck a note that continues to be sounded today, and one that goes a long way toward explaining Bogan's limited popularity: the poems are indeed difficult.

This would not have surprised the poet, who, to the regret of some recent critics,[6] left a few of her more explicit early poems out of *Body of This Death*—and then, when she published her first collected poems in 1941, removed five more—three of them among her most descriptive, most direct, and, like the poems omitted earlier, most prosodically free. The poet's reticence—discussed by Ruth Limmer in the recent essay in this volume—may have been the primary reason for this. But Bogan was a less severe censor than many poets: in her final collection, she included all but thirty or so published poems, and only six of those thirty had appeared in books. Moreover, I would venture, Bogan knew her strengths, and had her reasons. Reviewing Elizabeth Bishop in 1946, she wrote: "None of these thirty poems gives up its full meaning at once, so it is a pleasure to read them repeatedly."[7] Later in her life, she said, more than once, "Poetry . . . has always been difficult"; "Poetry—high formal poetry—has always been obscure."[8]

The insistence on the poetry of it is perhaps what critics least grasped about *Body of This Death*. Perceptive ones saw the source of difficulty itself in the craft: Van Doren's "packed . . . tightly with pure poetry" foreshadows the title of Marianne Moore's later essay, "Compactness Compacted," and identifies one of Bogan's most distinctive characteristics. Less apparent to even the most astute critics was the gradual shift of emphasis in the book from the difficulties of love to the triumph of poetry. *Body of This Death* begins with several poems which may be read as aesthetic statements, and there are lovely ironies in the play of life and art throughout the book. "My voice, not being proud / Like a strong woman's," actually is proud and strong, asking not "That death disarm her," but remembering, "while there is time." Later, beneath the naiveté of "Chanson Un Peu Naïve," is the address to the song itself, which is given a message double in meaning in its final lines: "Cry, song, cry, / And hear your crying lost." The final two poems focus even more emphatically on poetry: "You may have all things from me, save my breath," begins "Fifteenth Farewell," and "Sonnet" ends with the promise that the mind, metaphorically in flight, and therefore suggesting the poet, will "Seek out the storm, escape the bitter spell / That we obey, strain to the wind, be thrown / Straight to its freedom in the thunderous cloud."

The promise of "Sonnet" seems in some way answered in "Winter Swan," the first poem in Bogan's second book, *Dark Summer*, which appeared in 1929. "Within the mind the live blood shouts aloud," the poem tells us—but the bird here is less clearly triumphant than the freedom-seeking mind of the earlier poem: "Here, to the ripple cut by the cold, drifts this / Bird, the long throat bent back, and the eyes in hiding." It's a disturbing image, and *Dark Summer* was a disturbing book. More widely reviewed and almost as extravagantly praised as *Body of This Death*, it tended to evoke less illuminating comments.

Like the first book, *Dark Summer* was a small volume. Aware in 1928 that she hadn't enough poems for a new book, Bogan wrote: "I have a strong feeling that there should never be too many poems in a book of poetry. Thirty-five is, I think, the greatest number I should wish to publish at one time."[9] The book actually contained thirty-six poems, eleven reprinted, as the third of its five sections, from *Body of This Death*. The second and fifth sections were each comprised of a long poem, "The Flume" and "Summer Wish."

The book was widely reviewed:[10] in the *New York Times* and the

Saturday Review, as well as the periodicals represented here; in news-papers across the country—Chicago, Philadelphia, Knoxville, Des Moines; in small magazines, where, in contrast to the general reception, the book was sometimes dismissed in a few words: Bogan was "over-estimated," her best work was in the earlier volume, and one reviewer failed to see "any ultimate value" in the poems.[11] The reception repeats the pattern of response to the first book: the negative reviews that Bogan cataloged in her 1924 letter did not appear in prominent places, either.

Again, many distinguished reviewers praised the poems; increasingly, they tried to rank them. Yvor Winters' tentative placement of Bogan among the English and American poets was not typical, but several critics made claims: Bogan was "one of the most important women poets of the present generation"; she and Léonie Adams were "the two finest metaphysical poets in America today."[12] But while Bogan was still compared to other women poets, and sometimes reviewed with them, the business of singling her out from others of her sex had clearly begun, and was sometimes made explicit, as in the Untermeyer review included here. More than once, Bogan was compared to sixteenth- and seventeenth-century poets; briefly but astutely, she was likened to the French poets,[13] and to A. E. Housman.[14]

For all their praise, and their sometimes astute placing of the poems, many of the reviews were oddly lacking in substance. Obscurity contin-ued to be a recurrent word, probably for good reason: begun, like *Body of This Death*, during the early years of a relationship that became a marriage, the poems in *Dark Summer* do not so easily reveal their subject matter. Eda Lou Walton's review, reprinted here, was almost unique in making a thematic connection between the second volume and the first. Most reviewers avoided the question altogether; some confessed their inability to understand, or castigated the poet for her lack of clarity.

And yet the poems were said to be exact, accurate, precise. Lan-guage, the word, the phraseology was exact, as in Walton's review; the imagery, the poetry itself, was accurate, authentic. Untermeyer's and Zabel's reviews, in this volume, were not the only ones to make intel-ligent statements about Bogan's use of the exact image. Paradoxically, some of the difficulty of many of these poems may stem from just that precision. As Untermeyer noted, Bogan's images evoke a very living reality—but their aim is to get at "the secret behind appearance."

Rather than attempt to discover that secret, many reviewers of *Dark Summer* were content to point to craftsmanship, a word which began to appear with as much frequency as "obscurity." It is difficult to argue with Zabel's estimate of Bogan's "fine craftsmanship and sure judgment," but one begins to sense, in several other reviewers' emphasis on craft, a tendency to dismiss the poet as merely skilled. In a brief review, Babette Deutsch made the dichotomy between content and form explicit: Bogan's "difficulty seems to be bred of an intense concern with her materials, a concern that makes the hammering of a word, the chiseling of a phrase, supremely important to her. As a result one is more aware of the craftsmanship in these lyrics than of the emotion that impelled them or the intellection that enmeshes them."[15] Deutsch was unusual in her mention of both the feeling and the thought behind the poems, but the terms occur elsewhere, with several critics, like Winters, citing the primacy of feeling over thought—a response Bogan would have approved,[16] but one which is interesting in light of some later criticisms of the poems as lacking in human experience or feeling.

It is of course to be expected that such oppositions as content and form, emotion and intellect should occur in the discussion of any poet's work; what is surprising, in the responses to Bogan's second book, is the failure to note the extent to which opposition governs the poems themselves. Walton was alone in identifying the dichotomous "warfare of mind and heart" which, by those and other names, is intrinsic to much of Bogan's poetry. Significantly, Walton focused on "Summer Wish," the long final poem in the book, which is a dialogue between two voices: one looks out, hopefully, describing with great precision what the eye sees; the other looks "into the breast," relentlessly, "press[ing] sight / Into a myth no eye can take the gist of." The two voices in "Summer Wish" may say more about the way the poems in *Dark Summer* work than any critic has yet done.

But critics tended not to like either "Summer Wish" or the other long poem in the book, "The Flume." A final question to ask about the critical reception of *Dark Summer* is whether Bogan may have been influenced by this judgment. There may have been good reason for dropping "The Flume" from the 1941 collected poems—"the 'facts' are false, at the end," Bogan wrote in 1956;[17] but it is perhaps worth asking whether she was needlessly discouraged from longer efforts by the reviews of the second book.

The third book, *The Sleeping Fury*, was written over a period of eight years, amid considerable difficulty. There was, for one thing, other writing: stories, a number of which appeared in the *New Yorker* between 1931 and 1934, and reviews, which Bogan began to write for the same magazine in 1931.[18] During these years, poetry itself was becoming increasingly difficult to write; following breakdowns in 1931 and 1933, Bogan began to question whether the struggle was worth it. She spoke of her "inability to write poetry" as early as 1933;[19] in 1934, she wrote, to Morton Zabel:

> I shall produce two or three more [poems], if only to keep my promises to *Poetry* and to you. But thereafter the fountain will be sealed for good, I'm thinking. . . . I can no longer put on the "lofty dissolute air" necessary for poetry's production; I cannot and I will not suffer for it any longer. With detachment and sanity I shall, in the future,

observe; if to fall to the ground with my material makes me a mad-woman, I abjure the trade.[20]

Bogan wrote considerably more than the promised two or three poems after this, including more than half of those that appeared in *The Sleeping Fury* in 1937; but the difficulty of writing poems, which would last the rest of her life, had begun.

As might be expected, *The Sleeping Fury* was, like the earlier books, small: twenty-five poems, all of them new this time, but none of them long, like the two poems in *Dark Summer*. The third book seems not to have been as widely reviewed as the second had been, but it was certainly well received. Although Bogan had written in 1935 that she was "the one poet in America, with a definite note, who is almost unknown,"[21] some of the reviewers of *The Sleeping Fury* seemed not only to know her, but to assume their readers did too; she was, according to John Holmes, "one of the finest poetic reputations of the twentieth century in the United States."[22] If the claims were not quite as extravagant as Van Doren's had been in 1923, or Winters' in 1929, neither were the reviewers examining the work of a new talent: if there were limitations, they were those of an established poet.[23]

Increasingly, Bogan was seen as established in The Tradition. Comparisons with seventeenth-century metaphysical poets were frequent, though the Elizabethans were mentioned at least once, and one reviewer placed her in the "intellectual" as well as the "metaphysical" company of T. S. Eliot.[24]

Most reviewers mentioned craft, the word which had appeared so often in the 1929 reviews, but some began to say what they meant by it, and some, like Tate and Lechlitner in the reviews in this volume, meant those formal elements which had previously been taken for granted. More sure of the talent, the reviewers seemed to have more of substance to say about the poems.

Though several found the poems "concentrated" or "economical," only one or two suggested that they might be obscure. Sometimes reviewers found the words and images clear, even simple.[25] This may well reflect a deliberate change in Bogan's technique. In a 1930 notebook entry, she wrote: "It is necessary to remember and to choose. You must say out to the end what you have long managed to suggest. You must give up symbols. You must be able to see well. To feel clearly and to place every phrase in proportion to the rest."[26] Many of the poems in *The Sleeping Fury*—especially those at the beginning of the volume—are, if not "easier," certainly more direct.

The same poems most directly reflect the difficulties of the 1931–33 period. Like poems near the beginning of Bogan's first two books, several of them may be read as aesthetic statements; one difference is that, in the inevitable opposition between art and life, even the poetry seems wanting: the "Homunculus" is "a slight thing" that "lacks but life," and it is not from powerful music, as in earlier poems, but from "shallow speech alone" that joy must come, in "Henceforth, from the Mind." Certainly the several critics who found bitterness in the book were responding to a strong note.

Not so much noticed was the book's subsequent movement, which Bogan herself described in a 1936 letter: "It rises and falls, from despair, to exaltation, and back again," she wrote, and then outlined the pattern of its four sections: from the "1930–33 period—despair, neurosis and alcoholism," through "further despair" and "the spiritual side," to a final "note of calm."[27] To compare the title poem with the earlier "Medusa" (as two reviewers did), or to follow the progression of "Putting to Sea" to its final joyful line, is to experience something very different from the bitterness of "Henceforth, from the Mind" or "Exhortation."

Although no one described this progression, two critics did notice the resolving "note of calm"; the question was, what to make of it? Walton and Rexroth, in the reviews included here, both referred to the newfound wisdom and maturity of *The Sleeping Fury*; both, too, mentioned the important play of contraries in Bogan's work—emotion and intellect, flesh and spirit—and their resolution in the new book. What differed were their responses: for Walton, this most mature work was also the most "distinguished"; for Rexroth, the resolution and maturity occasioned some regret.

Behind Rexroth's response, which may be seen as the first explicitly feminist reading of Bogan, lay the political background—as well as the changing literary taste—of the period. Not even those with strong political convictions, like Walton, dismissed Bogan's poems on ideological grounds; but political awareness is implicit in Lechlitner's reading of "Putting to Sea" and her placement of Bogan in the school of Being rather than Becoming, and it is central to Zabel's piece, which is more a defense of Bogan's poetry than a review of it. Zabel's review suggests another possible reason, at this stage of Bogan's career at least, for her limited number of readers. By 1937, the question of audience had itself become political.

The poet's own sense of her audience, as well as her sensitivity toward the political climate, was apparent in her answers to the *Partisan Review* questionnaire which the magazine sent to a number of American writers in 1939. As her answers suggest, and her letters and reviews confirm, Bogan's "political" position was easier to define than it was to label, especially as it related to the question of audience. If poetry had a limited audience, it was certainly not defined by class; if poetry should not attempt to speak to "the public" at large, it was partly because, in doing so, it would be used as much Victorian poetry had been, "to back up middle-class social ideals as well as certain philosophical ideals concerning human perfectibility."[28]

If Bogan did not expect to win "the public," one can still detect some resentment of it, even in the *Partisan Review* piece. Expressed as early as 1935, Bogan's disappointment at being "unknown" continued to sound in the years between *The Sleeping Fury* and her first collected poems, which appeared in 1941. When the idea of the book was first broached, only a year after *The Sleeping Fury*, Bogan wrote to Theodore Roethke: "Poor Scribner's is making another feeble attempt to impress me upon an unwilling public."[29] She signed a contract in 1939, but was still hesitating two years later, when she wrote to her editor: "I am so out of the general line, now; and I really have been so battered about that I don't care any more."[30]

But *Poems and New Poems* came out, late in 1941, with sixteen new poems in it. The book employed, for the first time, the basic scheme of all the late volumes: the first three sections corresponded, with minor rearrangement and six deletions, to the poems of the first three books; the fourth section, with only five poems, and the fifth, with eleven in 1941, were new. If one recalls the previous books, sixteen poems in four years seems typical for Bogan; but most of these were written by 1938, and several reviewers questioned whether some of them—the two translations, the entire fourth section[31]—were worthy of inclusion. Reviewers also began to criticize the poet for writing too little throughout her career, several asking for more spontaneity, or simply more. And beyond numbers was the question of whether Bogan had actually progressed in the new work. The complaints in the generally laudatory reviews of Cowley, Deutsch, and Kunitz were voiced elsewhere as well; and while some, like Cowley and Kunitz, were hopeful that the poet was discovering new and less narrow directions, others began to define in more certain terms what they began to call her limitations. Those critics who least liked the book found the poems at once too disciplined or formal, too private or personal, and perhaps too intellectual as well.[32] New standards were being erected, in this post-Marxist era; for some critics, Bogan was indeed "out of the general line."

But more traditional values were being asserted, too, and this first collection of poems was an occasion for several poets to make some strong and important statements about the practice of poetry itself. Auden's review, which Bogan herself admired, was the most impressive of these; cognizant of the possible objections other reviewers did indeed voice, Auden took the opportunity to make what remains an eloquent statement about poetic development and integrity in the modern world. Other reviews reprinted here made brief note of much the same thing: a rejection of self-deception (Marianne Moore), a "capacity for self-disdain" (Kunitz). Bogan, it seemed, was herself becoming a standard of integrity for other poets.

If these same poets could and did talk about craft (Marianne Moore paid more detailed attention to technique than anyone had yet done), it was never in opposition to content: Auden made the book an occasion for discussing the dialectic of life and art; Moore's discussion of craft was fused with an enumeration of Bogan's "thoughts" on various subjects; Kunitz found, in Bogan's best, a fusion of "surface" and "substance"; and Cowley went so far as to find the poet's subject—poetry itself—in the craft. All four were responding to one of Bogan's most remarkable qualities.

The poems were still obscure for Deutsch but not, apparently, for anyone else. The word "right" occurred often in these reviews, echoing comments about the previous two books, and the earlier mention of economy or concentration was developed by Moore and mentioned by others.[33] Finally, Kunitz voiced a new idea which, though he didn't say so, might begin to explain what Deutsch and earlier readers had found difficult about the poems: however clearly the things of the world were drawn in Bogan's work, the poems might indeed be difficult to interpret if, as Kunitz suggested, the things of the underground world of the unconscious were Bogan's truest concerns.

These were significant statements—Auden's, Moore's, Kunitz's; but there were not a great many of them, and Bogan's sense of being "unknown" may have been confirmed simply by the number of 1941 reviews. Certainly the book was reviewed in the usual distinguished places; it was smaller periodicals that seemed to recognize the poet less and less, after *Dark Summer*.

Whether this had anything to do with the decline in Bogan's output is impossible to say; certainly there were more important reasons, voiced in the thirties and echoed now, but Louise Bogan did not write any poems at all for at least five years in the forties. In 1946, she wrote to Rolfe Humphries: "No creative work in five years! 'No wonder you are calm,' as you said to me once, '. . . the daemon has been silenced, and whatever silenced it is sitting pretty.'"[34] Humphries' statement is poignant in light of the last poem in the 1941 collection, in which, in response to the poet's "Must I tell again . . . ?" "The Daemon" of the title says "*Why not?*" and "*Once more.*" Though active in this 1938 poem, the daemon is surely related to the fury who, in the title poem of the 1937 book, is sleeping—and who is surely herself a version of the Medusa, that terrifying but inspiring figure behind so much of Bogan's work: a figure, ultimately, of the muse, of the mother, of the mother-as-muse embedded in the unconscious. A modern name for the muse might be the unconscious,[35] Bogan suggested in a lecture in 1954, two years before she reaffirmed her 1935 refusal to compromise the peace, the calm, the sleeping of the fury: "If it comes again," she wrote, "with a strength which I cannot withstand, and a *benevolence* . . . I can recognize: good! But if not, not.—As I said to you the other night . . . With a great price bought I this freedom."[36]

In the meantime, Bogan continued to write criticism, which may also have contributed to her failure to write poems: "Criticism, when practiced over years, makes the creative side rather timid," she wrote in 1948.[37] Whether the criticism weakened the poetic impulse or not, Bogan certainly continued to be both productive and recognized as a critic during the years when she was writing and publishing little or no poetry. From 1931 until 1969, she was poetry reviewer for the *New Yorker*. In the early fifties, when poems were still infrequent, two books of criticism appeared: *Achievement in American Poetry, 1900–1950*, and *Selected Criticism*.

The first of these was one of six volumes in the Henry Regnery Twentieth Century American Literature series. As Bogan's papers show, she wrote criticism with as much care and hard labor as many poets write poems; there are often several drafts of even short reviews, and *Achievement in American Poetry* had behind it a number of drafts, as well as research and notes. Still, it was written with what for Bogan was unusual speed: begun in August 1950, it was published in 1951. It was short, only 111 pages of text, and most of the reviews told more about the book and its particular requirements of space and period than they did about the author. Reviews appeared in the usual places, where Bogan was known, as well as others, where the poems would not have been noticed: *American Literature*, where Robert E. Spiller carefully distinguished this "personal essay" from academic work, and *Newsweek*, which, from the other side, called Bogan a "poet of distinction in her own right . . . who contributes to The New Yorker Magazine almost the only sustained criticism of modern poetry that the general reader can follow."[38]

That Bogan was not an academic critic was also mentioned in several reviews of *Selected Criticism*, a collection of seventy essays and reviews—many of them originally written for the *New Yorker*—which Bogan published in 1955. The American reviews were few, but intelligent and often illuminating, and when the book was issued in Britain in 1958, lengthy and appreciative reviews appeared in both the *Times Literary Supplement* and the *New Statesman*.[39] Marianne Moore's review[40] was as detailed and discriminating as her 1941 review of the poems had been, though it tended—as reviews of this sort almost inevitably do—to quote and cite more than it described and judged. Other reviews did much the same, but a number of recurrent notes were sounded. Several reviewers, including Moore, commented on the terseness, conciseness, or compactness of Bogan's reviews—some noting that this was an effect of the genre, but the comment is interesting in light of similar comments about the poems. Several reviewers also commented on Bogan's wit, a quality not much noted in the early reviews of the poems, and at least two mentioned her ability to share other writers' experiences—one seeing this as an expression of "the urge of the female

Eros toward relatedness," another as an "expression of vital rapport with the profound experience of another poet like herself."[41]

That these reviews so often described Bogan as a poet writing criticism is a significant reminder that the poet's reputation was, if not wide, deep enough to outlast a period of near silence: in the years between *Poems and New Poems*, in 1941, and *Collected Poems, 1923–53*, Bogan published almost no poems. Only three new poems were added to the new book, all of them appearing at the end of the fifth section—though two of them were unquestionably major, and Bogan herself was delighted when the first, "Song for the Last Act," was finally completed in 1949. Begun in 1947, it was finished with the help of Rolfe Humphries, to whom Bogan wrote in 1949: "so at least one more poetic work will be published, proving that *women* can carry on to some slight degree, *in* their 50's!"[42] The other important new poem in the book was "After the Persian."

Since no book had appeared for thirteen years, it is not surprising that Richard Eberhart, in the *New York Times* review reprinted in this volume, should have seemed to be coming upon one of Bogan's books for the first time. Nor is it surprising, given so little to go on, that other reviewers should have failed to distinguish new poems from old; John Ciardi, in the review appearing here, was unique in doing so, and his response was to additions of 1941 as well as 1954.

What perhaps is surprising is that Bogan was so well known, after so long a silence. Praise was high: "one of America's very best poets," said Kenneth Rexroth, reviewing her for the second time.[43] Once again, many critics approached Bogan as a woman poet; books by Millay and Léonie Adams appeared the same year, and she was often reviewed with one or both of them, rarely compared to male poets.

A notable exception was Reed Whittemore. Reviewing her with Yvor Winters, whose *Collected Poems* had also just appeared, Whittemore cited earlier reviews, emphasizing what had certainly been common, the comparison of Bogan with pre-nineteenth-century poets. Quoting Cowley's statement that Bogan's subject "was always poetry itself," as well as more numerous statements by and about Winters' "principles," Whittemore condemned both poets for "an obsessive interest in Style." "Their passion is rhetoric itself," he said, and "their poems' most noteworthy element is style rather than substance."[44] Whittemore's equation of the two poets mistook the intention of Bogan, for whom emotion, not style, was the starting point and center of all art. But his review, with its repeated reference to the critics' placement of the two poets in the "16th or 17th (or was it 18th?) century," verbalized an irritation which he may have shared with other readers who chose to remain silent.

Silence or brief notice did greet Bogan in a few places where she had previously been discussed at length; but the *Collected Poems* also occasioned serious discussion, including some views of the book as oeuvre. Léonie Adams, in the review included here, saw the book as an occasion not to revise but to "repeat and labor" an essentially unchanging estimate of Bogan; Elder Olson seized on both Bogan's and Adams's books as an opportunity for "considering the larger aspects of their art." His essay, reprinted here, was the first sustained treatment of Bogan's work, though others were soon to follow.

Like Adams, Olson echoed earlier discussions of Bogan, but his sustained and careful analysis elucidated and resolved what had often seemed unclear or in dispute. The earliest reviews had noted that love was Bogan's primary subject; Olson went on to observe the centrality of "the conflict between self-hood and love." Olson saw as reticence what earlier reviewers had called obscurity; he shared with others a sense of the importance of the poems' imagery, but defined with unusual clarity the way Bogan's images actually worked. Ultimately, though no doubt inadvertently, Olson may be seen as reconciling what had seemed to be disagreement among earlier critics, about whether obscurity or clarity most characterized Bogan's poems.

Other points of Olson's review were echoed by other reviewers. Several mentioned style, particularly diction, though no one but Whittemore found it central: the primary focus seemed to be on the tone, the mood, even the content of the poems—which several reviewers, once again, found dark, bitter, tragic.[45] But if readers were disturbed by this vision, most found the poems convincingly sincere ("She means what she says," wrote Rexroth).

Another fourteen years would pass before Bogan's next and last book of poems appeared, but two illuminating pieces about her appeared in the meantime: Harold Bloom's jacket notes for the poet's Yale Series recording in 1958, and Theodore Roethke's essay, which was originally delivered as a Hopwood lecture at the University of Michigan in 1960, and which remains the most widely published, known, and quoted piece on Bogan. Both essays appear in this volume.

Bloom was and is unique in placing Bogan in the romantic tradition, and nearly unique in focusing on the important role of contraries in the poems (Diane Middlebrook's essay, in this volume, shares this focus). Roethke, who had learned a great deal from Bogan,[46] wrote not as a critic but rather as a fellow poet; as he noted, his essay borrowed Marianne Moore's technique of "pointing out," and its strength, like Moore's, lay primarily in its keen and often illuminating comments on individual poems. Some of Roethke's more general points echoed those made by Olson: exactness of diction was one of Bogan's distinguishing characteristics, "obliquity" her customary mode. More originally, Roethke emphasized the importance of time in the poems, compared Bogan to Emily Dickinson and Marianne Moore, and referred, several times, to the unconscious. For him, as for Bloom, there was some progression in

Bogan's work: for the critic, toward at least acceptance of otherwise "unresolved contraries"; for the poet, toward resignation and "the grandeur of generality."

Bogan shared with Bloom and Roethke an interest in poetic development, and probably would have approved their descriptions of her own progression toward resolution and even resignation. As early as 1939, in a review of Millay, she was asking "what a woman poet should concern herself with as she grows older," and suggesting that "wisdom" and "peace" might be relevant to an answer.[47] A question was whether—for Bogan at least—more wisdom and peace might mean less poetry: as the thirties letters suggest, and the 1954 letter quoted above reaffirms, she herself was not willing to sacrifice peace—or freedom—for poems. Nor would she sacrifice integrity. In 1955, she described Emily Dickinson's development as "apprenticeship, a period of full flowering, and a gradual decline in creative energy—the usual progress of a lyric poet who does not force or falsify his gifts."[48]

Not that Bogan didn't continue to hope for a return of that energy. In 1954, the year of the *Collected Poems*, she referred at least twice to the "long prose thing" eventually published as her journals as a means of getting back to "pure writing,"[49] and she did in fact write some remarkably fine poems in the late fifties and sixties. But her late production continued, like Dickinson's, to be small: when her last collection, *The Blue Estuaries: Poems, 1923–1968* appeared, there were only twelve new poems, and three of them ("The Sorcerer's Daughter," "March Twilight," and "Masked Woman's Song") were actuallly written much earlier. These twelve comprised the sixth and final section of the book, which otherwise followed the format of the 1954 volume.

The critical response to *The Blue Estuaries* was not, for the most part, immediate. In March 1969, Bogan wrote: "My poems seem to have fallen down that deep, dark well. Not a review!"[50] This, curiously, ignored William Meredith's October 1968 *New York Times* review, which appears here; but for the most part Bogan was right. The book was not reviewed immediately; it was ignored in places like the *Nation*, the *New Republic*, and the *Saturday Review*, where the previous books had been discussed; and where it eventually was noticed, the reviews tended to be short.

Even in their brevity, most were remarkably respectful, even superlative: the formula of Meredith's "one of the best women poets alive" was repeated, without the qualification of gender, by Hayden Carruth ("one of our finest poets"), the *Virginia Quarterly* reviewer ("one of our most accomplished poets"), and Donald Stanford ("one of America's most distinguished living poets").[51] "No one today is a better craftsman than Miss Bogan nor worthier of careful study by our younger poets," Stanford concluded, echoing a similar statement at the end of Roethke's essay.

Almost all the reviewers cited Roethke, who was quoted at length on the book jacket; several clearly knew his essay, and referred to the "woman" question he raised as well as to the quoted passages. An interesting but unanswerable question is how much Roethke, who had died a well-known poet in 1963, may have had to do with keeping Bogan's reputation alive during this second long period in which no book had appeared.

Whatever the source, and however brief the acknowledgment, several reviewers did have their own very individual sense of both the accomplishment and the significance of Bogan's poetry. Several, like Roethke, focused on craft, and it is worth remembering that formal poetry was a considerably less dominant strain in 1968 than it had been in 1954. The comments of several reviewers reflect this; the surprising thing is that only one repeated the complaint made by Whittemore in 1954. "We are given the completed poem," said Roberts W. French, "but the sense of significant human experience has been lost"; Bogan, relying on style, was apparently reluctant to "descend into the abyss where everyone else is."[52]

Against this judgment were the reviewers who looked for and found not only the human experience that French missed, but also a relevance that made the poetry seem important: Heyen's essay, in this volume, perhaps said as much about why Bogan's poetry mattered as anyone yet had, and Ralph J. Mills, Jr., located a similar relevance in the form itself: citing Rilke, he found in Bogan "a beauty of form which seems to gaze back at us and say: 'You must change your life.' "[53]

Heyen and Meredith, as well as the *Virginia Quarterly* reviewer, were careful to cite new poems, but for the most part reviewers took the subtitle of *The Blue Estuaries* to heart and dealt with the book as *Poems, 1923–1968*, summing up, noting the consistency of vision and technique. This was and is appropriate, but it is perhaps worth noting that there is a summing-up quality in the new poems themselves, a further movement toward resolution, resignation, acceptance. The dark note sounded throughout Bogan's career and heard by reviewers is strong in the new work, and even commented on, in poetic terms: there are symbols of "dis-hope" ("July Dawn") and "loss" ("The Meeting"), and there are "marks of luck changing / From better to worse" ("The Sorcerer's Daughter"). The dark, haunting world of the unconscious, whose earlier presence had been noted by Kunitz, Ciardi, and Roethke, appears here in "The Meeting" and the last "Three Songs," but there is an abundance, too, of careful and often delighted observation of the physical world: the outward-looking voice of "Summer Wish" seems to find its most unfettered expression in these late poems. Nor is it merely a question of outward vision triumphing over inward, or of life overtaking art: though Bogan can speak, in "The Young Mage," of "the vine's triumph over marble," in contrast to the frequent triumph of the marble of art in earlier poems, she can speak in the same poem of "the leaves' silver" and "the flowers' gold." Two late poems end with imperatives which reconcile, with what one can surely see as wisdom and peace, the observed world and the feeling self: "O remember / In your narrowing dark hours / That more things move / Than blood in the heart," says the speaker in "Night," and "Psychiatrist's Song" ends with what is very nearly a prayer: "Vision of earth / Heal and receive me."

Two years after *The Blue Estuaries* appeared, Louise Bogan died. Her death occasioned a number of tributes, several of them delivered at the memorial service held at the American Academy of Arts and Letters, to which she had been elected in 1969. Many of those tributes were cited in William Jay Smith's *Louise Bogan: A Woman's Words*, originally published, with a bibliography, as a Library of Congress pamphlet, and reprinted here. Smith's essay spoke of Bogan with both admiration and affection, offering—along with comments about the poetry and influences on the poet—what almost no one else has given since:[54] a personal reminiscence of the poet.

The Academy was also the occasion for a more formal eulogy by W. H. Auden, who, beyond "technical excellence," spoke admiringly of Bogan's "determination never to surrender to self-pity, but to wrest beauty and joy out of dark places."[55] Similarly, John Ciardi, in a lengthy obituary in the *Saturday Review*, spoke of "the creative joy" that "is always snatched from mortal sadness."[56] The poet's hard-won triumph over difficulty continued to be recognized after her death.

Beyond these tributes, Bogan's death did not generate a flurry of critical activity. One rather comprehensive essay was published in 1970, by Paul Ramsey; the third such discussion, after Olson's and Roethke's, it is reprinted here. Like Roethke, Ramsey used a "pointing out" technique, directing his finger primarily at single poems. Aside from the highly laudatory tone of the essay, its interest lies in its attempts to perform what are still difficult and uncompleted tasks: explications of the poems, and analyses of their metrics.

The same year, 1970, Bogan's first posthumous book appeared. Planned by the poet before her death, and arranged alphabetically by subject, *The Poet's Alphabet* replaced and updated the out-of-print *Selected Criticism*. Reviews of the book were few, but the one significant piece both commented on and followed Ramsey's model. Noting that Bogan "is a poet who generates affectionate approval," Harry Morris said: "On the face of it, Mr. Ramsey would seem to have gone too far, and I believe he has; but I am willing to make the same mistake about [Bogan's] reviews and criticism."[57] Morris was almost alone, though, in reviewing the book at length.

The same cannot be said of the second posthumous book. Appearing in 1973, *What the Woman Lived: Selected Letters of Louise Bogan, 1920–1970* was reviewed on the front page of the *New York Times Book Review*, and at considerable length in *Ms.*, the *New Leader*, and the

Atlantic Monthly.[58] These four reviews were all by women, and two of them reflected the concerns of the growing women's movement. Nancy Milford, in the *Times*, spoke of Bogan in the context of her own personal search "for signals that women wrote and wrote well"; Barbara Grizzuti Harrison, in *Ms.*, found Bogan similarly compelling while she at the same time suggested that the poet "grasped incompletely the irony of woman's situation." Against such minor criticism, there was high praise for the letters: Pearl K. Bell, who in the *New Leader* commented more generally on Bogan's lack of political commitment, compared her letters to those of Keats, Henry James, and Rilke. The reviews were understandably more informative than analytic, but as such they performed two important functions. As Milford remarked, good letters "provide a sort of informal biography," and *What the Woman Lived* was the first extended view of the woman behind the poems. For some readers, like Milford herself, the letters were also an invitation—an entrance—into the poems.

The influence of the women's movement was also apparent in 1977, when Ecco Press reprinted *The Blue Estuaries*. The jacket copy for the book, by Adrienne Rich, presented both a feminist strategy for reading the poems and an eloquent defense of their relevance. Reading Bogan "against the remarkable tradition of female poetry in America," said Rich,

> the problems, crises, and strategies of her apparently lucid, classic poems reveal themselves: the sense of mask, of code, of body-mind division, of the "sleeping fury" beneath the praised, severe, lyrical mode. Her work, like that of Bradstreet, Dickinson, and H. D., is a graph of the struggle to commit a female sensibility, in all its aspects, to language. We who inherit that struggle have much to learn from her.

Speaking from a tradition Bogan herself recognized,[59] Rich both echoed and expanded the significance of Roethke's closing statement: Bogan could be a model for women, as well as for "the young."

Though the search for a women's tradition continued to point feminist critics in the direction of poets like Bogan, Rich's lead was not immediately followed. On the one hand, the women's movement itself made attention to Bogan suspect: Clara Claiborne Park, perhaps more impatient than earlier reviewers had been with the obscurity she found in the poems, wondered whether the reissue of *The Blue Estuaries* might have "less to do with a new admiration for the traditional lyric than with the new clout of Women's Studies."[60] On the other hand, women writing out of that new discipline were sometimes inclined to regard Bogan with a different kind of suspicion. When anthologies of women poets began to appear, Bogan was sometimes included, sometimes not. A notable inclusion was by Cora Kaplan, who referred to Bogan as "perhaps the most talented" of the "remarkable generation of American women poets born in the 1880's and the 1890's." Citing Bogan and H. D. as among the first "to use the concept of the female unconscious in poetry," Kaplan also noted—much as the thirties reviewers had done—that Bogan's concerns were more personal than political.[61]

As the women's movement began to recognize that the personal often *was* political, comments began to come from another direction. Gloria Bowles and Jaqueline Ridgeway, in essays in a single issue of *Women's Studies*,[62] both recognized and approved the importance of personal experience in the poems; but both were concerned, too, that Bogan had not been able to depict that experience more directly, or to deal more fully with what Bowles called the poet's "unique experience as a woman." Ridgeway's central concern was form, which she saw as a psychological as well as a literary "necessity" for Bogan; but some of the early feminist mistrust of form as unduly "masculine" seems to lie behind her generally appreciative essay.[63] In passing, Ridgeway and Bowles, like Kaplan, regretted that Bogan had not reprinted more poems. There are traces here of old complaints: Whittemore's objection to style was essentially an objection to form, and the more common statements about obscurity were less focused versions of the feminist cry for directness and relevance. The cry for "more" was not, of course, new.

However difficult Bogan herself proved as a model for feminist critics and poets, there is no doubt that the women's movement helped to revive interest in the poems, and at the same time to provide tools for understanding and appreciating the very difficulties some readers found in them. The tracing of influence was one such tool. Elizabeth Frank, in the 1977 essay reprinted here, dealt at length with the influence of Millay on Bogan; less thoroughly, another article discussed Bogan in relation to Sara Teasdale.[64] Though neither essay was presented from an explicitly feminist perspective, both tacitly acknowledged a women's tradition.

A more important tool, the need for which was implicit in Bowles' and Ridgeway's discussions, was biography. Of interest for its own sake, as feminist critics explored the question of what it meant to be a woman artist, biographical information began to prove particularly useful for explaining Bogan's difficult poems. The 1980 entry in *Notable American Women*, also by Elizabeth Frank, included the most complete and accurate biography that had yet appeared.[65] The final result of Frank's research is the forthcoming critical biography that, by Frank's own description, "examines the relationship between Louise Bogan's life and work, and draws for information upon a good deal of unpublished and uncollected sources. . . . It also examines the development and the waning of her ambition as a poet, and what can only be called her spiritual growth through personal difficulties."[66]

The latest of Bogan's posthumous books has also provided biographical information. *Journey Around My Room: The Autobiography of Louise Bogan*, edited and published by Ruth Limmer in 1980, includes the "long prose thing" Bogan worked on in the fifties and sixties, subsequently published as the "Journals of a Poet";[67] several short stories from the thirties; scattered notebook entries, also primarily from the thirties; published and unpublished poems; and a long unpublished lecture on women writers. The most impressive writing in the book is no doubt the journals, which give the reader a new appreciation of both the person and the prose stylist Louise Bogan was;[68] but the lecture is useful for exploring the complex question of what Bogan thought of other women writers.

This volume itself testifies to the interest the women's movement has continued to generate, directly or indirectly, in Bogan's poetry. All five of its original essays were written by women; and while only Diane Middlebrook's uses an explicitly feminist approach, Deborah Pope's and Ruth Limmer's essays are centrally informed by a consciousness of what it means to be a woman artist. Pope's essay develops at length the idea first touched on by Jones in 1923, and defined by Olson in 1954 as a conflict between selfhood and love. Pope traces the careful arrangement of the first book; Middlebrook, defining a similar conflict in more general and more clearly dualistic terms, also focuses on early poems. Limmer, on the other hand, addresses the question at least implied in many reviews of the late work: why did Bogan write so little—and, as she grew older, so much less? Limmer's answer, informed by her acquaintance with both the poet and her letters and manuscripts, indirectly touches, once again, on the obscurity of the poems.

If that obscurity has contributed to Bogan's relative lack of popularity among some readers, for whom the current interest in women poets' lives and works may provide some help, it is worth remembering other readers—including Limmer—for whom obscurity was never an obstacle. In recent years, as in the thirties, these readers have tended to be poets, many of whom have—against what was sometimes the mainstream of free verse—maintained a respect for formal poetry. Yvor Winters, who had first reviewed Bogan in 1929, included her among a small number of modern poets in his 1967 *Forms of Discovery*; and while his late assessment may seem unnecessarily cantankerous ("Miss Bogan does not think, or thinks as little as possible," he wrote),[69] it is worth mentioning that Winters continued, like Roethke, to teach Bogan with enthusiasm. I was one of Winters' students; Robert Pinsky, who included a discussion of "Simple Autumnal" in *The Situation of Modern Poetry*, was another.[70] Traditional though the Wintersian source may have been, it is interesting that Pinsky cited Bogan as an example of a distinctly modern technique; another example of such treatment is Charles O. Hartman's sensitive and illuminating use of "The Cupola" in his recent

Free Verse.[71] Pinsky and Hartman are poets; so is Carol Moldaw, whose original essay in this volume focuses on the important relation between form and emotion in Bogan's poems. Moldaw's detailed explication and analysis of individual poems, accomplished without reference to biography, may stand as representative of the formalist approach through which many poets have continued to learn from and teach Bogan.

That "nature" appears in Moldaw's title in conjunction with form and emotion, rather than in opposition, as in Pope's essay, is partly the result of her emphasis on later poems. That emphasis is shared by Sandra Cookson, in the last essay in this volume. Recognizing, like Pope and others, that autobiography lies beneath even the most oblique of Bogan's poems, Cookson locates the ultimate source of the poetry in the unconscious, which itself transforms image to symbol. Cookson also discovers several literary sources and echoes, and briefly suggests some imagistic connections between early and late poems.

All these recent essays, but particularly Cookson's, suggest some critical directions that others might follow. As this volume itself suggests, more attention might be paid to late poems: readers, reviewers, and anthologists have tended to return to early favorites like "Medusa," ignoring such poems as "After the Persian" and "Song for the Last Act." Through careful attention to the poems themselves, sometimes aided by biography, many readers are beginning to get through the difficulty once experienced even by some of Bogan's strongest admirers. But biography is not enough, I think, and approaches that provide vantage points for seeing how the poems work—how to approach them, what to look for—will be useful. In this era of psychoanalytic interest and criticism, more readings like Cookson's are likely to appear; both Freud and Jung, whom Bogan read, may prove useful.

Overviews of the work may help, too, particularly those which show how images, words, or perspectives function throughout the work: Pope's and Cookson's discussion of landscape is an example, and attention to other images, words, and motifs—fire and water, houses, birds; sight, memory, music—might be instructive. The technical virtuosities poets have admired and learned from have not been thoroughly explained, either: how images work—from within, from without, as description, as symbol; how sound, including prosody, often conveys the subtle sense.

More detailed attention to literary influence—beyond the mere mention of period or poet—may place Bogan more exactly and usefully in relation to other poets, male and female,[72] and the noting of verbal echoes, however distant, may—as in Cookson's example—help to explain some of the richness of the poems. Manuscripts, most of which are in the Amherst College Library,[73] may help in other ways. Though Ruth Limmer has published most of the notebook and journal entries that seem worthy of print, reading notes, drafts of poems and prose, plans for books, lecture notes and letters may be useful to readers interested in knowing how Bogan worked. The published and unpublished short stories may be worthy of further attention, too.

Finally, though, the work that will be most useful will be the kind that suggests not only what has made Bogan so much admired by poets and others, but also how to experience that pleasure. Pleasure is Bogan's word: "The Pleasures of Formal Poetry" is deservedly one of her best known essays, and late in her life she said, "Enjoy, enjoy. That's what poetry's for, is to enjoy."[74] In a 1936 letter criticizing a translation she didn't like, Bogan cited examples of Baudelaire's virtues, using the word "embedded": an image is "right in, embedded in, the idea of the clock's sound;" all the poet's "effects are embedded and not detachable in any way."[75] Useful though explications of Bogan's difficult poems are, and enlightening as analyses of prosody, image, and other "effects" may be, the ultimate pleasure of reading any poet—but particularly, I think, of reading a poet like Bogan—is to be found in the thorough fusion of intellectual, emotional, and aural attention. The critics in this volume have, for the most part, done such reading; their work, like that of any good criticism that is interested in the poem itself, is to say Look, Listen, Enjoy.

MARTHA COLLINS

Notes

1. *Journey Around My Room: The Autobiography of Louise Bogan*, ed. Ruth Limmer (New York: Viking, 1980), p. 50.

2. See also A. Donald Douglas, "Body of This Death," *New Republic*, 5 December 1923, pp. 20–21.

3. Letter to Edmund Wilson, 1 March 1924, in *What the Woman Lived: Selected Letters of Louise Bogan, 1920–1970*, ed. Ruth Limmer (New York: Harcourt, 1973), p. 5.

4. *Dial*, 76 (March 1924), 289.

5. Robert L. Wolf, "Impassioned Austerity," *Poetry*, 23 (March 1924), 336–37.

6. See, for instance, Gloria Bowles, "Louise Bogan: To Be (or Not to Be?) Woman Poet," *Women's Studies*, 5 (1977), 134.

7. Reprinted in Louise Bogan, *A Poet's Alphabet: Reflections on the Literary Art and Vocation* (New York: McGraw-Hill, 1970), pp. 219–20.

8. See unpublished lecture, "Is the Modern Poet Audible?" 9 April 1959, in the Louise Bogan Papers, Amherst College, box 15, folder 10; and reading, Library of Congress, 18 November 1968, Library of Congress Recorded Sound Division, Tape LWO 5504.

9. Letter to John Hall Wheelock, 7 December 1928, in *Letters*, p. 40.

10. There are copies of reviews from 1929 on—many supplied by a clipping service—in the Bogan Papers, box 18, folders 13–23. Copies of earlier reviews may have perished in the 1929 fire which destroyed most of Bogan's papers and books.

11. William James Price, *Interludes: A Magazine of Poetry and Prose*, May 1930, p. 23; John T. Frederick, *The Midland*, 16 (March–April 1930), 127; Parker Tyler, "Five Contemporary Poets," *New World Monthly*, February 1930, p. 159.

12. Horace Gregory, *New York Evening Post*, 23 November 1929, p. 12m; Louis Untermeyer, "In a Gold Stain," *Saturday Review*, 1 February 1930, p. 692.

13. Herbert Gorman, *Century*, 120 (Winter 1930), 158. Bogan cited the French poets in her answer to the 1939 *Partisan Review* questionnaire, which appears in this volume.

14. Lee Wilson Dodd, *Yale Review*, 19 (December 1929), 390. In response to a question at a Library of Congress reading, 18 November 1968, Bogan herself cited Housman. See Library of Congress Recorded Sound Division, Tape LWO 5504.

15. *New York Sun*, 14 December 1929 (clipping in Bogan Papers, no page number available). It is interesting to compare this review with Deutsch's 1941 evaluation, reprinted in this volume, and her later discussion in *Poetry in Our Time* (1952; rpt. New York: Doubleday, 1963), pp. 265–67.

16. In a lecture in the sixties, Bogan said that "a writer's power is based not upon his intellect so much as upon his intuition and his emotions. All art, in spite of the struggles of some critics to prove otherwise, is based on emotion and projects emotion" (*Journey*, p. 120).

17. Quoted in *Letters*, p. 8, and *Journey*, p. 60.

18. Other stories had appeared in *The American Caravan: A Yearbook of American Literature*, ed. Van Wyck Brooks et al. (New York: Macaulay, 1927, 1928). Bogan's first review appeared in the *New Republic* in 1924.

19. *Journey*, p. 74.

20. 27 July 1934, in *Letters*, p. 79.

21. Letter to John Hall Wheelock, [June] 1936, in *Letters*, p. 132.

22. *Boston Evening Transcript Book Review Section*, 17 April 1937, p. 5.

23. The one exception was an extremely negative review by J. G. E. H[opkins], in *Spirit*, 4 (May 1937), 63. In striking contrast to the authors of other reviews, Hopkins said: "Words are used, not because they are inevitable . . . but seemingly because they look and are odd in their context. The images . . . do not appear to arise out of the thought; they are produced first and the thought or emotion seems tagged on or worked in. . . ."

24. Lodwick Hartley, *Raleigh [N. C.] Observer*, 6 June 1937 (clipping in Bogan Papers).

25. See Zabel, in this volume, and a very brief review in *Springfield Republican*, 18 April 1937, p. 7e.

26. Bogan Papers, box 20, folder 2.

27. Letter to Morton D. Zabel, 8 December 1936, in *Letters*, p. 145.

28. "The Pleasures of Formal Poetry" (1953), in *Poet's Alphabet*, p. 150. See also, in the same volume, Bogan's 1946 review of Robert Graves and Norman Rosten, pp. 202–04.

29. *Letters*, p. 182.

30. Letter to John Hall Wheelock, 24 February 1941, in *Letters*, p. 215.

31. There was apparently some debate about whether the "light verse" that eventually became the fourth section should be included. See letter to Morton D. Zabel, 2 June 1941, in *Letters*, p. 218.

32. The most critical of these were J[ohn] G[illand] B[runini], *Spirit*, 9 (July 1942), 92–93, and Mary M. Colum, *New York Times Book Review*, 30 November

1941, p. 20. More respectful ("The limitation has its limitation in turn"), but making similar criticisms, was W. R. Moses, *Accent*, 2 (Winter 1942), 120–21. William Rose Benét also used the word "limitations" in *Saturday Review*, 25 April 1942, pp. 22–23.

33. See especially Earl Daniels, *Voices*, 108 (Winter 1942), 54–55. Daniels' review is extremely laudatory: "Miss Bogan is our most civilized poet. I would go further, and say that no poet—man or woman—writing in America today, is more essentially poet, producing work which is poetry on a level so uniformly high."

34. 7 October 1946, in *Letters*, p. 255.

35. Lecture notes dated 27 November 1956, Bogan Papers, box 14, folder 36.

36. Letter to May Sarton, 28 January 1954, in *Letters*, p. 283.

37. Letter to Katharine S. White, 14 October 1948, in *Letters*, p. 262.

38. *American Literature*, 25 (March 1953), 117–18; *Newsweek*, 3 December 1951, pp. 96–97.

39. "The Exact Impression," *Times Literary Supplement*, 16 May 1958, p. 268; Richard Mayne, "Far but not wee," *New Statesman*, 22 March 1958, pp. 383–84.

40. *Poetry London-New York*, 1 (March–April 1956), 36–39; reprinted in *A Marianne Moore Reader* (New York: Viking, 1961), pp. 229–32.

41. Jean Starr Untermeyer, "A Seasoning of Wit," *Saturday Review*, 24 December 1955, p. 24; Kenneth Rexroth, *New York Herald Tribune*, 5 February 1958 (clipping in Bogan Papers).

42. *Letters*, p. 267.

43. *New York Herald Tribune Book Review*, 4 July 1954, p. 5.

44. "The Principles of Louise Bogan and Yvor Winters," *Sewanee Review*, 63 (Winter 1955), 161–68.

45. See, as well as the reviews reprinted here, Rexroth, cited above, and Josephine Jacobsen, *Baltimore Sun*, 9 July 1954 (clipping in Bogan Papers).

46. See Bogan's letters to Roethke, in *Letters*, and Roethke's to and about Bogan, in *Selected Letters of Theodore Roethke*, ed. Ralph J. Mills, Jr. (Seattle: Univ. of Washington Press, 1968). For a striking parallel, compare Roethke's "Interlude" (*The Open House*, 1941), with Bogan's "Old Countryside" (*Dark Summer*, 1929).

47. Reprinted in *Poet's Alphabet*, p. 299.

48. Reprinted in *Poet's Alphabet*, p. 93. It is interesting to compare this statement with an earlier (1945) description of Dickinson's "clear line of development": "a classic line, rising through early sentiment and experiment to a middle ground of technical and spiritual control. Beyond this middle period the 'great' expression begins" (*Poet's Alphabet*, p. 90).

49. See journal entry for 12 January 1954, in *Journey*, p. 161; and letter to May Sarton, 28 January 1954, *Letters*, p. 283.

50. Letter to Ruth Limmer, 26 March 1969, in *Letters*, p. 378.

51. Hayden Carruth, "A Balance Exactly Struck," *Poetry*, 114 (August 1969), p. 330; *Virginia Quarterly Review*, 45 (Winter 1969), xviii; D[onald] E. S[tanford], *Southern Review*, 5 (April 1969), xvi–xvii.

52. *Concerning Poetry*, 2 (Spring 1969), 96–99.

53. *Chicago Sun-Times Book Week*, 29 September 1968 (clipping in Bogan Papers).

54. An exception is May Sarton, "Louise Bogan," *A World of Light: Portraits and Celebrations* (New York: W. W. Norton, 1976), pp. 215–34.

55. "Louise Bogan, 1897–1970," *Proceedings of American Academy of Arts and Letters/National Institute of Arts and Letters*, 2nd. ser., No. 21 (1970), p. 66.

56. *Saturday Review*, 21 February 1970, p. 20.

57. "Poets and Critics, Critics and Poets," *Sewanee Review*, 80 (October–December 1972), 627.

58. Nancy Milford, *New York Times Book Review*, 16 December 1973, pp. 1–2; Barbara Grizutti Harrison, "A Troubled Peace," *Ms.*, November 1974, pp. 40, 46, 93–94, 96; Pearl K. Bell, "A Woman of Letters," *New Leader*, 4 February 1974, pp. 23–24; Katie Louchheim, "A True Inheritor," *Atlantic Monthly*, 1 February 1974, pp. 90–92.

59. See especially Bogan, *Achievement in American Poetry, 1900–1950* (Chicago: Regnery, 1951), pp. 22–27.

60. "Poetry, Penetrable and Impenetrable," *Nation*, 3 September 1977, p. 185.

61. Cora Kaplan, *Salt and Bitter and Good: Three Centuries of English and American Women Poets* (New York: Paddington, 1975), pp. 273–74.

62. Gloria Bowles, "Louise Bogan: To Be (or Not to Be?) Woman Poet," and Jaqueline Ridgeway, "The Necessity of Form to the Poetry of Louise Bogan," *Women's Studies*, 5 (1977), 131–35, 137–49.

63. An extreme version of this kind of objection—to obliquity as well as to form—is central to Patrick Moore, "Symbol, Mask, and Meter in the Poetry of Louise Bogan," in *Gender and Literary Voice, Women and Literature*, N. S. 1, ed. Janet Todd (New York: Homes and Meier, 1980), 67–80. Moore's bias results in what is at best an idiosyncratic reading of Bogan's poetry.

64. Russell Anne Swafford and Paul Ramsey, "The Influence of Sara Teasdale on Louise Bogan," *CEA Critic*, 41 (May 1979), 7–12.

65. Elizabeth Perlmutter [Frank], "Bogan, Louise," *Notable American Women: The Modern Period*, IV (Cambridge Mass: Harvard Univ. Press, 1980), 88–90. An entry on Bogan, by Theodora R. Graham, also appeared in *American Women Writers*, I (New York: Frederick Ungar, 1979), 183–86.

66. Letter received from Elizabeth Frank, 1 December 1981.

67. "From the Journals of a Poet," *New Yorker*, 30 January 1978, pp. 39–70.

68. For an appreciative and widely read review of the book, which also deals with biography and letters, and compares Bogan with Roethke, see Mary Kinzie, "Books: Two Lives," *American Poetry Review*, 10 (March–April 1981), 20–21.

69. *Forms of Discovery: Critical and Historical Essays on the Forms of the Short Poem in English* (N. p.: Alan Swallow, 1967), pp. 278–83.

70. *The Situation of American Poetry: Contemporary Poetry and Its Traditions* (Princeton: Princeton Univ. Press, 1976), pp. 97–103.

71. *Free Verse: An Essay on Prosody* (Princeton: Princeton Univ. Press, 1980), pp. 61–63.

72. Gloria Bowles is currently working on this subject.

73. The primary exceptions are letters, large numbers of which are in the Newberry Library in Chicago and the libraries of Princeton University, the University of Washington, and the University of Michigan. Bogan's working library resides in the King Library at Miami University, and tapes of her reading, as well as various manuscripts, are available in the Library of Congress.

74. Reading, Library of Congress, 18 November 1968, Library of Congress Recorded Sound Division, Tape LWO 5504.

75. Letter to Morton D. Zabel, 15 April 1936, in *Letters*, p. 130.

REVIEWS AND ESSAYS

[Louise Bogan] Llewellyn Jones*

The poetry of Louise Bogan is probably already known to many people through her appearances in the New Republic and in a number of the magazines of poetry. Her first volume, "Body of This Death," is a small one but one of concentrated poetry. As the title implies, it is the poetry of struggle against—shall we say, circumstance? Not circumstance in the gross sense of the word, but against all that stifles, diverts, and disarms life in its original intention; against the pettiness that haunts the footsteps of love, especially against the limitations, imposed and self-imposed, on women; and, at the same time a cry for something positive, for something compelling:

> Notes on the tuned frame of strings
> Plucked or silenced under the hand
> Whimper lightly to the ear,
> Delicate or involute,
> Like the mockery in a shell.
> Lest the brain forget the thunder
> The roused heart once made it hear—
> Rising as that clamor fell—
> Let there sound from music's root
> One note rage can understand,
> A fine noise of riven things.
> Build there some thick chord of wonder:
> Then, for every passion's sake,
> Beat upon it till it break,

the poet sings in "Sub Contra," and "Women"—women in general—she indicts for their failure to live flamingly and courageously:

> Women have no wilderness in them,
> They are provident instead,

*Reprinted, with the permission of George W. Jones, from *First Impressions: Essays on Poetry, Criticism and Prose* (New York: Knopf, 1925), pp. 118–22.

> Content in the tight hot cell of their hearts
> To eat dusty bread. . . .
>
> They hear in every whisper that speaks to them
> A shout and a cry.
> As like as not, when they take life over their door-sills
> They should let it go by.

It will be seen that for this mood of protest and of assertion of an austere and uncompromising scale of values Miss Bogan has an appropriately austere style, both of diction and of rhythm. Rhythmically she has learned something from Edwin Arlington Robinson, and from the later Yeats, but, like Yeats especially, she has not sacrificed beauty to this austerity—her rhythms have a very individual and moving quality. And she is not afraid to deck her beauty in imagery, natural or classical, as the following lines bear witness:

STANZA

> No longer burn the hands that seized
> Small wreaths from branches scarcely green.
> Wearily sleeps the hardy, lean
> Hunger that would not be appeased.
> The eyes that opened to white day
> Watch cloud that men may look upon:
> Leda forgets the wings of the swan;
> Danaë has swept the gold away,

in which the last two lines are an extraordinarily effective clinching of the matter—so effective, indeed, that the poem ought not to have been adduced as an example of beauty decked in imagery, because it is really an example of incarnation rather than of ornament. Better examples of sheer decorative resourcefulness could be taken from "A Letter," in which the author describes a visit, as a convalescent, to the country, late in autumn, when:

> The thickets not yet stark but quivering
> With tiny colors, like some brush strokes in
> The manner of the pointillists; small yellows
> Dart shaped, little reds in different pattern,
> Clicks and notches of color on threaded bushes,
> A cracked and fluent heaven, and a brown earth.

And here is the description of the countryside:

> This is a countryside of roofless houses,—
> Taverns to rain,—doorsteps of millstones, lintels
> Leaning and delicate, foundations sprung to lilacs.
> Orchards where boughs like roots strike into the sky.
> Here I could well devise the journey to nothing,
> At night getting down from the wagon by the black barns,

The zenith a point of darkness, breaking to bits,
Showering motionless stars over the houses.
Scenes relentless—the black and white grooves of a woodcut.

There is extraordinary resourcefulness in description there, and it is matched by Miss Bogan's sheer power when she writes poetry without any resources. What, for instance, could be more free from any poetic apparatus than this "Song":

Love me because I am lost;
Love me that I am undone.
That is brave,—no man has wished it,
Not one.

Be strong, to look on my heart
As others look on my face.
Love me,—I tell you that it is a ravaged
Terrible place.

The reader may find that some of Miss Bogan's poems are recondite. This is because she has written some of her poems of inner experience in a natural symbolism instead of directly; in a sort of dream imagery. "A Tale," the first poem in the book, though this particular poem is in the third person, is written in this manner. It must be read rather for the emotional drama which the imagery symbolizes than for any explicit story with a physical locale. "Medusa" is, on the other hand, not in the least recondite or obscure; it is simply the record in very beautiful imagery of a sort of nightmare state in which we seem "held up" in time and space. And where one or two other poems may seem obscure, the reader must make allowances for what, after all, is a natural reticence in a poet who is giving us subjective poetry distilled from what is evidently intense experience, and who must not be expected to tell us always the outer occasion as well as the inner response.

Louise Bogan   Mark Van Doren*

It is impossible to say what these twenty-seven poems are, and it would be difficult to say what they are like. The temptation is to speak of them only in images, for they are not susceptible to paraphrase; they take effect directly upon the imagination. One thing about them, however, seems plainly, prosaically sure. The thirty pages which they cover are packed as tightly with pure poetry as any thirty pages have been for a generation. The poet would be rare at any time who could achieve

*A review of *Body of This Death*. Reprinted, with permission, from the *Nation*, 31 October 1923, p. 494.

so much concentration and so unquestionably sustain it. Practically every one of these bare, stricken lines is suggestive of riches; the words dig deep, bringing up odors of earth and life that will live a long time in the memory. There is no rhetoric—hardly a phrase could be reduced by a word—but there is the sheer eloquence of passion; there is no tunefulness, but there is music "from music's root," "a fine noise of riven things."

Under a diversity of forms Miss Bogan has expressed herself with an almost awful singleness. Again, however, it is impossible to say what it is she has said; again one must resort to an image—or to her images. One can be certain that experience of some ultimate sort is behind this writing, that something has been gone through with entirely and intensely, leaving the desolation of a field swept once for all by fire. But the desolation is not vacancy or lassitude. The charred grass is brilliantly black, and the scarred ground is fascinating in its deformity. There still is life, hidden and bitterly urgent.

> I burned my life, that I might find
> A passion wholly of the mind,
> Thought divorced from eye and bone,
> Ecstasy come to breath alone.
> I broke my life, to seek relief
> From the flawed light of love and grief.
>
> With mounting beat the utter fire
> Charred existence and desire.
> It died low, ceased its sudden thresh.
> I had found unmysterious flesh—
> Not the mind's avid substance—still
> Passionate beyond the will.

This poem alone would establish Miss Bogan's excellence in her art. There are twenty-six others, all of which ought to be read. There is A Tale, for instance, which says all that can be said on the subject of mutability, and says it in strains of music at once ancient and weirdly new. There is Medusa, with its perfect rendering of a world suddenly frozen:

> This is a dead scene forever now.
> Nothing will ever stir.
> The end will never brighten it more than this,
> Nor the rain blur.
>
> The water will always fall, and will not fall,
> And the tipped bell make no sound.
> The grass will always be growing for hay
> Deep on the ground.
>
> And I shall stand here like a shadow
> Under the great balanced day,

My eyes on the yellow dust, that was lifting in the wind,
And does not drift away.

And there is Fifteenth Farewell, one portion of which pierces with quick genius exactly to the center of an important idea:

I erred, when I thought loneliness the wide
Scent of mown grass over forsaken fields,
Or any shadow isolation yields.
Loneliness was the heart within your side.
Your thought, beyond my touch, was tilted air
Ringed with as many borders as the wind.
How could I judge you gentle or unkind
When all bright flying space was in your care?

Miss Bogan has spoken always with intensity and intelligent skill; she has not always spoken clearly. Now and then her poetry comes too immediately from a personal source to mean very much to others. Nevertheless, this first volume places her near the lead of those poets today—Anna Wickham, Charlotte Mew, Genevieve Taggard, and others— who are passionately exploring the endless, narrow paths of woman's (and man's) experience. It is absolutely individual, yet it reaches toward the race. It may be a classic.

The Poetry of Louise Bogan   Yvor Winters*

This, Miss Bogan's second volume, includes the best poems from her first, so that a reading of it offers a complete view of her talent to the present time. The chief stylistic influence discernible is that of E. A. Robinson, and that only here and there. Two of the early poems reprinted in this book—"Portrait" and "The Romantic"—close on a typically Robinsonian epigram; and there are a good many similar passages in her first book, "Body of This Death." She has either escaped or absorbed this influence in her later work, progressing toward a more purely lyrical mode that culminates in "The Mark," "Come break with time," and "Simple Autumnal": poems that demand—and will bear— comparison with the best songs of the sixteenth and seventeenth centuries, whether one select examples from Campion, Jonson, or Dryden. One might quote, as examples of her style at its purest and most intense, this quatrain from "Simple Autumnal":

The measured blood beats out the year's delay.
The tearless eyes and heart, forbidden grief,

---

*A review of *Dark Summer*. Reprinted, with the permission of Janet Lewis Winters, from the *New Republic*, 16 October 1929, pp. 247–48.

> Watch the burned, restless, but abiding leaf,
> The brighter branches arming the bright day.

Or the final stanza from "The Mark":

> The diagram of whirling shade,
> The visible, that thinks to spin
> Forever webs that time has made
> Though momently time wears them thin
> And all at length are gathered in.

But these fragments are parts of closely organized wholes and it is really unjust to tear them off in this fashion.

She has certain technical limitations. She apparently has little or no understanding of free verse, and her more regular unrhymed verse (one hesitates to call it blank verse), though extremely interesting from a purely metrical standpoint, divulges an inability to treat the long line and the long poem as such—she treats them rather as series of stylistic and perceptive incidents that would probably have gone into short rhymed lines had they been able to gather about themselves a little more symbolic value. They almost drop from the limb that bears them into separate identity, but never quite; neither, most of the time, are they quite organically necessary to that limb. And the movement of the long unit is hopelessly impeded by—one is tempted to say, made up of—minor, decorative digressions. This, from any standpoint, is an incorrect technique for a long poem, whether narrative or philosophical. One sometimes sees the opposite phenomenon in the lyrics of a novelist, those of Mr. Joyce, for example: the novelist is accustomed to use these minor felicities occasionally and with discretion in prose, but is unable, if he is simply a novelist, to give them poetic intensity when he rhymes them. The result is minute, if sometimes charming, lyrics. But either way there is a failure to comprehend the essential nature of the form.

The intricacy of some of the best of Miss Bogan's poems is, I imagine, an intricacy of feeling, and hence of style, rather than of idea. The basic ideas of her work do not appear to be particularly complex. The writer of our period finds himself tempted, on one side, by the roads to rhythmic salvation offered by the various sects of tree-climbing mystics, and on another by the faint moribund murmurs of transatlantic, Middle-Western, and middle-aged Whitmanism: these, and related manifestations of our democratic era and of its Pragmatic Providence, our educational system, have to be avoided. Miss Bogan, one suspects, has avoided them as a cat avoids water rather than as a philosopher avoids nonsense—and the result is a kind of instinctive distrust of certain ranges of experience that either might or might not involve some kind of spiritual looseness. She plays safe and allows no implications to enter a poem that are not defined in its subject-matter: she thus achieves the irreproachable mastery of her best poems, but she also causes each poem

to be a sort of insulated unit, even pu   ˡlv, as
in "Old Countryside," to a certain dr
twelve-line lyric on the passage of ti   ..uive the
tragedy and the wisdom of the whole   .-uxperience; there is a
kind of emotional current passing into the form from the formless recol-
lections of the man; the gesture, the cadence, the pauses, indicate a
richness of wisdom and experience not defined in the meaning of the
words. In Miss Bogan's poems, as in those of Jonson or Landor, this
is the case, if at all, to a very limited degree. The poem is a sharply
defined segment of experience, raised to something very near to major
power by the sheer brilliance of the craftsmanship. But if the poem deals
with the message of time, it deals with that and nothing more, in its
effect on an isolated entity as such. To see what I mean, one may compare "In Time of 'The Breaking of Nations,'" "During Wind and Rain,"
or "Afterwards," to "The Mark" or "Simple Autumnal." Neither poet
will suffer particularly by the comparison: the integrity of each is perfect
and the execution superb. But the underlying wisdom, the experiential
reach, of Hardy's poetry is the greater.

The poet of the present age, in order to free himself from the
handicap of the philosophical misconceptions of the age, has, I believe,
to turn metaphysician in a profound and serious way if he is not to be
victimized by false emotions, as most of our contemporaries in at least
a measure are; or, if he is not to be, as Miss Bogan in some degree is,
limited rather more than some of his more fortunate forefathers. Very
few contemporary poets seem aware of the difficulty or seem willing to
make the effort. I am thoroughly convinced that the effort need not be,
as Mr. Allen Tate seems certain that it is, fruitless. The least—and the
most—that one can demand of it is that it clear the air once and for all
of a great deal of nonsensical doctrine and belief, along with the
attendant feelings, and that it justify, and make it possible to assume
with a measure of ease, a normal and more or less classical dignity of
attitude toward human destiny and human experience, an attitude that
at least *seems* natural to Hardy but that is achieved by only a few
contemporaries (Miss Bogan among them) and by most of them (Miss
Bogan included) only with a good deal of effort, suspicion, and trembling. The means to this end may strike the innocent bystander as
unjustifiably complicated, but it is still the only means that will accomplish the end in a thoroughly satisfactory fashion. The short cuts
invariably end in bogs, and the avoidance of the labor ends either in
bogs or in insecurity.

But Miss Bogan's subject-matter, or rather attitude, if it seems
limited in the way I have indicated, is as central, as fundamental, as any
attitude so limited could be. It would take only a turn, a flicker, to
transform her into a major poet; it is conceivable that the flicker may be
taking place as I write, that it may even have occurred in her book,

à mon insu. The least that the most defamatory of critics can say in her praise is that she suffers no diminution by comparison with the best of the English lyricists, that she is certainly as good in every respect as a great many of the best, and that she is beyond any doubt one of the principal ornaments of contemporary American poetry.

The Flower of the Mind   Morton Dauwen Zabel*

Richness of intellectual and emotional experience is present in every detail of Miss Bogan's poetry. *Dark Summer*, like *Body of This Death*, is the product of strict selection and rigid discipline in the practice of her art. Where each page yields its memorable phrase and where every stanza is slowly turned to the final perfection of statement and sugges- tion, any suspicion of meagre inspiration may be dismissed immediately. With a creative patience rivaled by that of few other living poets, she has brought her verse to a state of ripe completeness; it does not seek its reward through stylistic variety or the diversity of its ideas and pictures, but rather in the fine unity of purpose and craftsmanship it achieves. Probably no English-writing poet of the moment could be found who has taken so enthusiastically to heart the precept of Gautier:

> . . . L'oeuvre sort plus belle
> D'une forme au travail
> Rebelle.

Since her artistry insists always upon a fine intensity of statement and upon as complete a reduction of poetic content as possible, the two longer poems in this book—the analytical narrative called *The Flume* and the dialogue *Summer Wish*—do not present her best work. To draw out to the length of full analysis an experience or problem requires a greater control of externals, of the real events which surround and con- dition the activities of the mind. Miss Bogan lacks Lola Ridge's lively understanding of the reality of action. Drama—except of the allegorical or suggestive kind she employed in her earlier poems, *A Tale* and *Fif- teenth Farewell*—is outside her range. Insight produced by a quick sympathy and interest is present, but not in sufficient quantity to stir into life the people with whom she is concerned. Her finest poems grow as ideas which seek their embodiment in nearby symbols. The discrim- inating reader would not for a moment think of doing without *The Flume* and *Summer Wish*; their exquisite imagery and the skill whereby they snare elusive meanings make them far too valuable for that.

*Reprinted, with the permission of Mrs. Alta M. Sutton and the editor, from *Poetry*, 35 (December 1929), 158–62. Copyright 1929 by the Modern Poetry Association.

But their presence in this book, surrounded by the sharp austerity of the lyrics and sonnets, is enough to reveal limitations of which Miss Bogan herself is aware. She usually restricts herself to a kind of lyric poetry in which her mastery remains sure and undisputed.

Signs of this mastery are abundant in *Dark Summer*. The delicate use of imagery is probably first among them. Instead of employing irrelevant pictorial devices or garnishing a poem with elaborate ornaments and decorations, she carves the image out of the concept with scrupulous care. The poem finds its substance in the mind and its shape grows around the symbol which the mind selects from experience. This process has produced *The Cupola, The Drum, The Mark*, and this *Song for a Slight Voice*:

> If ever I render back your heart,
> So long to me delight and plunder,
> It will be bound with the firm strings
> That men have built the viol under.
>
> Your stubborn piteous heart, that bent
> To be the place where music stood,
> Upon some shaken instrument
> Stained with the dark of resinous blood,
>
> Will find its place, beyond denial,
> Will hear the dance, oh be most sure,
> Laid on the curved wood of the viol
> Or on the struck tambour.

Aloof as this may seem from any desire to write in easy popular phrases or to appeal to a careless reader, it shows at the same time Miss Bogan's keen human feeling and her unwillingness to deny the natural impulses of a woman. In *The Romantic*, one of several fine poems she has reprinted from her first book, she outlines with memorable skill the tragedy of a life frustrated by discipline and authority, and the exquisite *Chanson un peu naïve* gives expression to the same problem in terms of a haunting melancholy. In *The Crossed Apple* a rich humorous balladry is suggested, while *Old Countryside* and *Simple Autumnal* reveal a subtle interest in homely realism.

In *Old Countryside* this is especially memorable:

> Beyond the hour we counted rain that fell
> On the slant shutter, all has come to proof.
> The summer thunder, like a wooden bell,
> Rang in the storm above the mansard roof,
>
> And mirrors cast the cloudy day along
> The attic floor; wind made the clapboards creak.
> You braced against the wall to make it strong,
> A shell against your cheek.

Long since, we pulled brown oak-leaves to the ground
In a winter of dry trees; we heard the cock
Shout its unplaceable cry, the axe's sound
Delay a moment after the axe's stroke.

Far back we saw, in the stillest of the year,
The scrawled vine shudder, and the rose-branch show
Red to the thorns, and, sharp as sight can bear,
The thin hound's body arched against the snow.

Fiend's Weather and *I Saw Eternity*, by their clear eloquent phrases, and *Tears in Sleep* and *Sonnet*, by their poignancy, go further in showing that this collection, which at first glance seems marked by severe austerity and formality, has a real range of feeling and expression. Miss Bogan may be trusted to explore that range further, but never to produce a weak or careless line. By her fine craftsmanship and sure judgment, she has made herself a master of her art, and given us, in her second book as in her first, a rare and beautiful group of poems.

[Review of *Dark Summer*]   Louis Untermeyer*

Louise Bogan's "Dark Summer" is as exquisite in content as it is in format—and it would be difficult to find higher praise. The lines seem fashioned for these chastely composed pages with sparse but all the more effective ornament. It is not a large book—thirty-six poems in all, of which eleven are reprinted from "Body of This Death"—but its quality lifts it high above the merely adequate writing published in such quantities by women in these so literate states. Here is no attitudinizing, no self-pity listening to its own self-affecting music, no "pretty tunes of coddled ills." Rather are these songs of the spirit, a spirit at once individual and impersonal. By that is meant an ability to fix the shifting scene with details and gestures wholly her own, yet a refusal to capitalize either the scene or the treatment of it. Miss Bogan is never arbitrary in dealing with her properties; her figures are living, her landscapes real to the smallest forsythia's dripping branch and the last "scrawled vine" and "the axe's sound delaying a moment after the axe's stroke"; but she pierces "reality" to the secret behind appearance. Again and again, she lets flash before us the vision that sees "through, not with the eye"—especially in poems like "Simple Autumnal," "Medusa," "The Alchemist," "Come, Break with Time," and the one long painful narrative, "The Flume," a story told entirely by suggestion and undertone. The

*Reprinted, with permission, from "In a Gold Stain," a review of Bogan and Léonie Adams, in *Saturday Review*, 1 February 1930, p. 692.

smallest of these compositions preserves her accurate quality. For example:

CASSANDRA

To me, one silly task is like another.
I bare the shambling tricks of lust and pride.
This flesh will never give a child its mother,—
Song, like a wing, tears through my breast, my side,
And madness chooses out my voice again,
Again. I am the chosen no hand saves:
The shrieking heaven lifted over men,
Not the dumb earth, wherein they set their graves.

Miss Bogan's is an unusually exact economy—unusual even in these days when lush emotion is suspect and *démodé*—and her reconstructions are unequivocally authentic. Sometimes her spare definiteness brings her close to dessication and the slow pace of her measures is too consciously thickened with "the dark of resinous blood"; but for the greater part mood and measure join to sharpen thought and build a poetry almost perfect of its kind.

Verse Delicate and Mature   Eda Lou Walton*

We have had no book from Louise Bogan since her small and exquisite first volume "Body of This Death." Those poems were as delicate as bone, but they reflected like a crystal an intense and bitter mind intent upon the analysis of its betraying heart, punishing itself in a kind of proud confessional. A spiritual pride and a heart wiser than its desires were there written down in flawless perfection of language. No other poet in America has a more inevitable sense of the exact word to be employed than has Miss Bogan. In "Dark Summer" the same immaculate spirit and restless heart continue their discourse in language which shows no flagging of the poet's critical employment of her tool. The tool is the same and the creator the same; only the season has changed. For in "Body of This Death" a young woman examined the warfare of mind and heart and found brief respite in passionate interludes, whereas in "Dark Summer" a mature woman examining the same warfare finds it deathless.

Here is an immortality unique with Miss Bogan: no harvest fills the bins while the cycle of years spins by so rapidly that images of spring and summer must be forever in the mind's eye. Memory will not give us

---

*A review of *Dark Summer*. Reprinted, with permission, from the *Nation*, 4 December 1929, pp. 682, 684.

pause even in autumn. The heart must bleed and the mind be unaccepting even while the flesh chills. Therefore these unquiet lives. In the long narrative poem The Flume a woman protected by love cannot be convinced of love in any way save by betrayal. In the dialogue Summer Wish the first voice must protest against the violence of memory which makes Spring a repetition, while the second voice argues for an acceptance of promised beauty. Inescapable beauty must destroy the shell-like spirit and yet the voice be proud to speak:

> Within the mind the live blood shouts aloud;
> Under the breast the willing blood is burned,
> Shut with the fire passed and the fire returned.
> But speak, you proud!

The intensity of "Dark Summer" is the intensity of fear always alive in the mind though the heart be at home with love:

> The willing mouth, kissed never to its own beauty
> Because it strained for terror through a kiss,
> Never quite shaped over the lover's name
> Because the name might go.

Miss Bogan's poetic creed may be said to be in her lines:

> Speak out the wish like music, that has within it
> The horn, the string, the drum pitched deep as grief.
> Speak it like laughter, outward. O brave, O generous
> Laughter that pours from the well of the body and draws
> The bane that cheats the heart: aconite, nightshade,
> Hellebore, hyssop, rue—symbols and poisons
> We drink, in fervor, thinking to gain thereby
> Some difference, some distinction.
> Speak it, as that man said, *as though the earth spoke*,
> By the body of rock, shafts of heaved strata, separate,
> Together.
>   Though it be but for sleep at night,
> Speak out the wish.
> The vine we pitied is in leaf; the wild
> Honeysuckle blows by the granite.

At the time when so much of poetry is merely energetic echoing or forced attempt at individuality, we have among us those few, and among them Louise Bogan, who are not only excellent technicians but true poets in that they have an extremely sensitive approach to their physical world and a definite poetic outlook concerning it.

"Henceforth from the Mind"   Eda Lou Walton*

This is Louise Bogan's first book of lyrics since the publication in 1929 of "Dark Summer," and it is unmistakably the poet's most mature and distinguished volume. Miss Bogan's admirable precision of language and expert craftsmanship remain unchanged, but the conflict between emotional intensity and an intellectual analysis almost equally violent—so characteristic of all her work—is in these poems resolved.

Betrayal has long been Miss Bogan's theme. At first it was the betrayal inevitable in love. Now this poet sees betrayal as common to all, as a betrayal by life itself. It is life itself which so changes body and spirit that they become their opposites. This is the ultimate, bitter truth. And whatever of personal bitterness there was in Miss Bogan's earlier lyrics becomes in these later poems either a deep impersonal hatred of human fate or an austere acceptance of that fate. In the long title poem, built upon a magnificent image, the Fury who has tortured the poet is faced at last and seen:

> Beautiful now as a child whose hair, wet with rage and tears
> Clings to its face. And now I may look upon you,
> Having once met your eyes. You lie asleep and forget me.
> Alone and strong in my peace, I look upon you in yours.

Or, again, we find the main theme of the book in such a stanza as this:

> Henceforth, from the mind,
> For your whole joy, must spring
> Such joy as you may find
> In any earthly thing,
> And every time and place
> Will take your thought for grace.

Distinguished is the word one always thinks of in connection with Louise Bogan's poetry. Whatever form she tries, her art is sure, economical, and self-definitive. There is never in her poems a wasted adjective or phrase but always perfect clarity and a consistent mood precisely set down. She can write the completely artless lyric or the very subtle poem worked out through complex imagery. Sensuousness is here but it is always reined in by the strict mind. Poems like "Italian Morning" express perfectly the atmosphere of the old carved rooms and the sense of timelessness in contrast with personal time and loss. The sheer passion to create in words is behind much of this poetry and is the theme of one of the loveliest lyrics in the book "Roman Fountain." This passion, the poet believes, persists despite defeat in life. Another poem in Swiftian mood denounces Swift as a rare hypocrite in his letters to Stella. Miss

*A review of *The Sleeping Fury*. Reprinted, with permission, from the *Nation*, 24 April 1937, p. 488.

Bogan is a good hater, but never allows hatred to become mere emotionalism:

> With so much hatred still so close behind
> The sterile shores before us must be faced;
> Again, against the body and the mind,
> The hate that bruises, though the heart is braced.

And so, in the end, one is impressed by a kind of wisdom in these poems, the wisdom of profound intuition and of a rapier analysis turned inward rather than outward.

[Review of *The Sleeping Fury*]   Kenneth Rexroth[*]

From the publication of her first book, Louise Bogan established a special province of the "modern temper" as peculiarly her own. Her poetry, at its most characteristic, concerned itself with the conflicts arising from a sort of basic erotic dissatisfaction; the old war of flesh and spirit, translated into a critical disillusion with what might be called post-suffragism. Militant femininity, once it had actually gained the objectives of Ellen Key or Inez Milholland, after Hedda Gabler had left home and entered upon her New Freedom, found that it had gained and given, as Miss Bogan has said in her best known poem, "the staff without the banner." Disabilities and exploitations still existed in the relations of men and women, even in literary circles, even in the world of Mabel Dodge and Muriel Draper, where the linen was so tastefully embroidered with mottoes like Liberty, Equality and Fraternity.

Of course, a male may not speak with unquestioned authority, but it is probable that the fruits of so doubtful a conquest were pretty bitter eating. It was the ability to express this bitterness, to do what our Marxist friends, in other contexts, call, "raising the revolution to a new plane of struggle," that gave Miss Bogan's poetry a penetrating and profoundly disturbing quality, a force of acid insinuation rather than impact. Her dry, critical hysteria was a precious virtue in a period in American poetry largely devoid of any concern for explicit values. She was able to integrate this attitude with an expression that mirrored perfectly the conflicts and probings of her personality. Her best poems were each intense gnomic dramas, phrased in a metric that was as full of surprises and distortions as a movie serial.

The title of this book is indicative of what has happened. This Fury has found the time to rest, the conflict has been at least partially ac-

[*]Reprinted, with the permission of the author, from the *San Francisco Chronicle*, 25 July 1937, p. 4D.

cepted. "Strangers lie in your arms . . . As I lie now" (With an ambiguity in the word "lie.") "That in me you are matched, and that it is silence that comes from us," "Years back I saw the stubble burn Under darker sheaves," and of Venus, "Serve us in your own way, Brief planet, shining without burning."

Supposedly this is what is called mellowing, this is matured wisdom, and Miss Bogan's style has mellowed with it. The irregular metric, the eccentric imagination, have made their adjustments, too. Doubtless this is in many ways a better book, but something very valuable is going from Miss Bogan's talent, and nothing new but "wisdom" is coming to replace it. Men and women still speak of Freedom and exploit one another; we haven't yet, and won't likely soon, find that idyllic Dance of Life around some corner. But perhaps we are just a little more aware of why not than we once were, and perhaps, after Miss Bogan's Fury has rested a while, she will arise and again "carry the revolt to a new plane of struggle." Possibly one of the most remarkable poems she has written, "Hypocrite Swift" in this volume, is a presage of that awakening.

[Review of *The Sleeping Fury*]   Allen Tate*

Miss Louise Bogan has published three books, and with each book she has been getting a little better, until now, in the three or four best poems of *The Sleeping Fury*, she has no superior within her purpose and range: among the women poets of our time she has a single peer, Miss Léonie Adams. Neither Miss Bogan nor Miss Adams will ever have the popular following of Miss Millay or even of the late Elinor Wylie. I do not mean to detract from these latter poets; they are technically proficient, they are serious, and they deserve their reputations. Miss Bogan and Miss Adams deserve still greater reputations, but they will not get them in our time because they are "purer" poets than Miss Millay and Mrs. Wylie. They are purer because their work is less involved in the moral and stylistic fashions of the age, and they efface themselves; whereas Miss Millay never lets us forget her "advanced" point of view nor Mrs. Wylie her interesting personality.

This refusal to take advantage of the traditional privilege of her sex must in part explain Miss Bogan's small production and the concentrated attention that she gives to the detail of her work. Women, I suppose, are fastidious, but many women poets are fastidious in their verse

*Reprinted, with the permission of Louisiana State University Press, from "R. P. Blackmur and Others," a review of nine books of poetry, in *Southern Review*, 3 (Summer 1937), 190–92.

only as a way of being finical about themselves. But Miss Bogan is a craftsman in the masculine mode.

In addition to distinguished diction and a fine ear for the phrase-rhythm she has mastered a prosody that permits her to get the greatest effect out of the slightest variation of stress.

> In the cold heart, as on a page,
> Spell out the gentle syllable
> That puts short limit to your rage
> And curdles the straight fire of hell,
> Compassing all, so all is well.

There is nothing flashy about it; it is finely modulated; and I think one needs only to contrast Miss Bogan's control of her imagery in this stanza, the toning down of the metaphor to the simple last line, with the metaphorical juggernaut to which Miss Field's[1] muse has tied herself, to see the fundamental difference between mastery of an artistic medium and mere undisciplined talent. Miss Bogan reaches the height of her talent in "Henceforth, from the Mind," surely one of the finest lyrics of our time. The "idea" of the poem is the gradual fading away of earthly joy upon the approach of age—one of the stock themes of English poetry; and Miss Bogan presents it with all the freshness of an Elizabethan lyricist. I quote the two last stanzas:

> Henceforward, from the shell,
> Wherein you heard, and wondered
> At oceans like a bell
> So far from ocean sundered—
> A smothered sound that sleeps
> Long lost within lost deeps,
>
> Will chime you change and hours,
> The shadow of increase,
> Will sound you flowers
> Born under troubled peace—
> Henceforth, henceforth
> Will echo sea and earth.

This poem represents the best phase of Miss Bogan's work: it goes back to an early piece that has been neglected by readers and reviewers alike—"The Mark"—and these two poems would alone entitle Miss Bogan to the consideration of the coming age.

But there is an unsatisfactory side to Miss Bogan's verse, and it may be briefly indicated by pointing out that the peculiar merits of "The Mark" and "Henceforth, from the Mind" seem to lie in a strict observance of certain limitations: in these poems and of course in others, Miss Bogan is impersonal and dramatic. In "The Sleeping Fury" she is philosophical and divinatory; in "Hypocrite Swift" she merely adumbrates an obscure dramatic situation in a half lyrical, half eighteenth-century, satirical style. Neither of these poems is successful, and the failure can be traced to all levels of the performances; for example, to the prosody, which has little relation to the development of the matter and which merely offers us a few clever local effects.

Notes

1. Sara Bard Field, whose *Darkling Plain* is discussed earlier in Tate's essay (editor's note).

[Review of *The Sleeping Fury*]   Ruth Lechlitner*

Since the publication of her distinguished first book, "Dark Summer," Louise Bogan has achieved a mastery of form rare in the realm of modern poetry. There is creative architecture in even the slightest of her lyrics. Miss Bogan works not as a landscape painter (while her visual imagery is exact, it does not depend on color alone), nor yet as a musician—although in many of her poems the auditory imagery is superior to the visual: the ear listens, even as the eye sees. Her art is that of a sculptor: to fix in the "heroic mould" the texture and motion of flesh and spirit; to capture the terrible (but corruptible) vitality and beauty of the living in deathless marble.

The sculptor's hand is evident—consciously so—in the powerful figures and symbols of "The Sleeping Fury" poems. "This marble herb, and this stone flame," "Their strong hair molded to their foreheads," "The big magnolia, like a hand, repeats our flesh"—to choose out of context only a few. In one of the most flawlessly formed and motivated sonnets that has come from any poet writing in our day, this exquisite building with words is readily seen: the matchless, concentrated use of "weighted" vowels, the careful assonance, the release and recapitulation of rhythmic phrasing:

> Now, you great stanza, you heroic mould,
> Bend to my will, for I must give you love:
> The weight in the heart that breathes, but cannot move,
> Which to endure flesh only makes so bold.
>
> Take up, take up, as it were lead or gold,
> The burden; test the dreadful mass thereof.
> No stone, slate, metal under or above
> Earth, is so ponderous, so dull, so cold.

*Reprinted, with the permission of the author, from the *New York Herald Tribune Books*, 30 May 1937, p. 2.

Too long as ocean bed bears up the ocean,
As earth's core bears the earth, have I borne this;
Too long have lovers, bending for their kiss,
Felt bitter force cohering without motion.

Staunch meter, great song, it is yours, at length,
To prove how stronger you are than my strength.

That Miss Bogan is indebted to those excellent form-masters, the metaphysical poets—Herbert, Donne, Vaughan—is obvious. In three of the most significant poems in the present collection it will be seen to what extent she has progressed from an earlier assimilation of the metaphysical concepts. "Baroque Comment" interestingly parallels Wallace Stevens's "Ideas of Order," in that it is concerned with the "ornaments" of death in civilization; in other words, with the symbols of romantic decadence that are "coincident with the lie, anger, lust, oppression, and death in many forms."

"The Sleeping Fury," the title poem, recalls Miss Bogan's earlier "Medusa." This legendary Gorgon head of hissing serpents, the sight of which turned the unwary beholder to stone, naturally attracts as symbol a sculptor-poet. But what Miss Bogan says here is important if one would understand her beliefs: that the masses of humanity, "huddled like sheep for sacrifice," are scourged by the Gorgon's whips; those likewise who seek comfort in each other's possessive arms feel the hissing adders of her hair. Only he who looks upon Medusa in her sleep, seeing her in another guise, will dare confront the waking, horrible image, and conquer and appease her. The demanding ego must be subjugated: but to what?

"Putting to Sea" has also significant points of interest. Because of its symbolic images and theme, one thinks of D. H. Lawrence's poems in "The Ship of Death." But there are dissimilarities to be noted here. Both poets write of the "voyage" of the individual and of humanity through the sea of years. In her poem, Miss Bogan sets forth with exquisite irony the argument of a "utopia" dreamer:

"O, but you should rejoice! The course we steer
Points to a beach bright to the rocks with love,
Where, in hot calms, blades clatter on the ear;

And spiny fruits up through the earth are fed
With fire; the palm trees clatter; the wave leaps.
Fleeing a shore where heart-loathed love lies dead
We point lands where love fountains from its deeps."

To which her answer is:

With so much hatred still so close behind
The sterile shores before us must be faced;

> Again, against the body and the mind,
> The hate that bruises, though the heart is braced.

She expresses, further, the fear that the creative imagination, afoot in some "utopia" of regimented ease and plenty, may have "too much light," not enough to struggle against: hence it may perish.

As Aldous Huxley has remarked in his discerning essay on Lawrence, there are two schools of poets: one that bases its ideas on the concept of Being; the other on the concept of Becoming. One school hopes to find something "permanent" beyond Change—a core or center, to which the individual can attach himself. The other does not recognize the importance of the individual as a fixed entity, but sees him, with all humankind, in a state of constant flux or change. To the former group belong most of the metaphysicians—and the poetry, for instance, of James Joyce, of Wallace Stevens, of Louise Bogan. To the latter belong (of the moderns) D. H. Lawrence, W. H. Auden and his associates, and certain of the younger "social" poets in this country. Miss Bogan has stated her beliefs with the sharp discipline of the sure artist; in contrast, Lawrence—even Auden—seldom approach her perfection of form. Perhaps Lawrence found the answer which Miss Bogan is still seeking. However, since "we know what we are, but not what we may become," and since the higher activities of all genuine poets (like those of nature) are largely unpredictable, we can do no less than honor Louise Bogan for her superb technical contribution to the poetic art of our time.

The Flame in Stone   Ford Madox Ford*

There is one word singularly useful that will one day no doubt be worn out. But that day I hope is not yet. It is the word "authentic." It expresses the feeling that one has at seeing something intimately sympathetic and satisfactory. I had the feeling acutely the other day when slipping along the east side of the Horseshoe Bend, in the long broad valley that runs down to Philadelphia. I saw sunlight, and almost in the same moment a snake fence wriggling its black spikedness over the shoulder of what in England we should call a down, and then the familiar overhanging roof of a Pennsylvania Dutch barn. It would take too long and it would perhaps be impolite to the regions in which these words will be printed to say exactly why I felt so much emotion at seeing those objects. Let it go at the fact that I felt as if, having traveled

*A review of *The Sleeping Fury*. Reprinted, with the permission of Janice Biala and the editor, from *Poetry*, 50 (June 1937), 158–61. Copyright 1937 by the Modern Poetry Association.

for a very long time amongst misty objects that conveyed almost nothing to my inner self—nothing, that is to say, in the way of association or remembrance—I had suddenly come upon something that was an integral part of my past. I had once gone heavily over just such fields, stopping to fix a rail or so on just such a fence, and then around the corner of just such a barn onto a wet dirt road where I would find, hitched up, the couple of nearly thoroughbred roans who should spiritedly draw over sand and boulders my buck-board to the post office at the cross-roads. I had come, that is to say, on something that had been the real part of my real life when I was strong, and the blood went more swiftly to my veins, and the keen air more deeply into my lungs. In a world that has become too fluid, they were something authentic.

I had precisely the same sense and wanted to use that same word when I opened Miss Bogan's book and read the three or four first words. They ran:

> Henceforth, from the mind,
> For your whole joy . . .

Nothing more.

I am not any kind of a critic of verse poetry. I don't understand the claims that verse poets make to be (compared with us prosateurs) beings set apart and mystically revered. Indeed if one could explain that, one could define what has never been defined by either poet or pedestrian: one could define what poetry is.

But one can't. No one ever has. No one ever will be able to. You might almost think that the real poet, whether he write in prose or verse, taking up his pen, causes with the scratching on the paper such a vibration that that same vibration continues through the stages of being typed, set up in print, printed in magazine, and then in a book—that that same vibration continues right through the series of processes till it communicates itself at last to the reader and makes him say as I said when I read those words of Miss Bogan's: "This is authentic." I have read Miss Bogan for a number of years now, and always with a feeling that I can't exactly define. More than anything, it was, as it were, a sort of polite something more than interest. Perhaps it was really expectation. But the moment I read those words I felt perfectly sure that what would follow would be something stable, restrained, never harrowing, never what the French call chargé—those being attributes of what one most avoids reading. And that was what followed—a series of words, of cadences, thought and disciplined expression that brought to the mental eye and ear, in a kind of television, the image of Miss Bogan writing at the other end of all those processes all the words that go to make up this book.

There are bitter words. But they are not harassingly bitter:

> And you will see your lifetime yet
> Come to their terms, your plans unmade—
> And be belied, and be betrayed.

There are parallel series of antithetical thoughts, but the antithesis is never exaggerated:

> Bend to the chart, in the extinguished night
> Mariners! Make way slowly; stay from sleep;
> That we may have short respite from such light.

> And learn, with joy, the gulf, the vast, the deep.

There are passages that are just beautiful words rendering objects of beauty:

> . . . The hour wags
> Deliberate and great arches bend

> In long perspective past our eye.

> Mutable body, and brief name,
> Confront, against an early sky,
> This marble herb, and this stone flame.

And there are passages of thought as static and as tranquil as a solitary candle-shaped-flame of the black yew tree that you see against Italian heavens:

> Beautiful now as a child whose hair, wet with rage and tears
> Clings to its face. And now I may look upon you,
> Having once met your eyes. You lie in sleep and forget me.
> Alone and strong in my peace, I look upon you in yours.

There is, in fact, everything that goes to the making of one of those more pensive seventeenth century, usually ecclesiastical English poets who are the real glory of our twofold lyre. Miss Bogan may—and probably will—stand somewhere in a quiet landscape that contains George Herbert, and Donne and Vaughan, and why not even Herrick? This is not to be taken as appraisement. It is neither the time nor the place to say that Miss Bogan ranks with Marvell. But it is a statement of gratification—and a statement that from now on, when we think of poetry, we must think of Miss Bogan as occupying a definite niche in the great stony façade of the temple to our Muse. She may well shine in her place and be content.

Lyric Authority   Morton Dauwen Zabel*

Lyric poetry often falls from grace, and usually for reasons of its own making. It does not require much acuteness to see what excesses brought the personal and amatory verse of the past fifteen years into disrepute and directed writers once more toward impersonal ideas, humanitarian causes, a more external and critical kind of poetry. When a poet arrives at an impasse of self-consciousness or becomes disgusted with the self-advertising vulgarity into which lyrists descend who lack vigor for a really profound search into the heart or character, a turn toward human and social purposes may come not merely as a corrective but as a means of salvation. This does not mean that the poet himself is necessarily saved. The art of public and proletarian purposes offers its own delusions if, by remaining ungrounded in personal sincerity, it uses moral and hortatory arguments to disguise a poverty in more fundamental spiritual forces. It is likely then to produce an eloquence as false, a rhetoric as inflated, and a sentiment as spurious as anything the conventional lyric versifier is guilty of. And its fault is likely to seem more serious, since it leads to the enervation not only of personal integrity but of an urgent human faith. In such straits the example of the lyric discipline becomes imperative and indispensable.

Louise Bogan's earlier books, "Body of This Death" in 1923 and "Dark Summer" in 1929, won their fame for sufficient reasons. Their rigor of form and emotion was an immediate reproach to the lyric slovenliness around them. They showed a poetry that said nothing that did not come from the deepest sources of personal and poetic sincerity, and that allowed no word or phrase to remain untested by an extreme pressure of creative necessity. Her new book is as spare and severely compiled as its predecessors, and in a new decade it points a similar distinction and moral. Whether it will be greeted by the same high respect is beside the point. Fashions in poetry may change but not the accent and austerity of poetic truth, a phrase that has its meaning refreshed by the finest entries in this volume—the title poem, "Italian Morning," "To My Brother," "Roman Fountain," "Kept," "Man Alone," the first and final songs. Here there is nothing to disguise, prop or confuse the thing said: no front of "beliefs," no leaning on borrowed arguments or literary and political allusion, and none of that fretting preciosity which has become a recent lyric fashion. The word, phrase and stanza have their simplest construction (Miss Bogan is still at her best away from free verse or experimental forms); the imagery is simple and final; the symbol stamps the mind with an indelible impression and shows the poignance of meanings extracted from a depth of mind and consciousness

*A review of *The Sleeping Fury*. Reprinted, with the permission of Mrs. Alta M. Sutton, from the *New Republic*, 5 May 1937, pp. 391–92.

that alone ensures a compelling form of truth. It is because they show so firmly what this depth can yield that these poems bring the finest vitality of the lyric tradition to bear on the confusions that threaten the poets who, by satire or prophecy, indignation or reform, have reacted against that tradition and cast it into contempt. Poets like Yeats and Rilke met this crisis of sincerity in their careers, and comparison loses its odium when Miss Bogan's finest lyrics are set in the company of theirs. She has kept to the hardest line of integrity a poet can follow and has sacrificed the easier victories of many of her contemporaries. Her work, instinctive with self-criticism and emotional severity, speaks with one voice only; her rewards and those of her readers have a common source in the discipline to which the clarity of her music and her unsophistic craftsmanship are a testimony. It should be a model for poets in any decade or of any ambition.

The Situation in American Writing:
Seven Questions   Louise Bogan*

1. *Are you conscious, in your own writing, of the existence of a "usable past"? Is this mostly American? What figures would you designate as elements in it? Would you say, for example, that Henry James's work is more relevant to the present and future of American writing than Walt Whitman's?*

Because what education I received came from New England schools, before 1916, my usable past has more of a classic basis than it would have today, even in the same background. The courses in English Literature which I encountered during my secondary education and one year of college were not very nutritious. But my "classical" education was severe, and I read Latin prose and poetry and Xenophon and the Iliad, during my adolescence. Arthur Symons' The Symbolist Movement, and the French poets read at its suggestion, were strong influences experienced before I was twenty. The English metaphysicals (disinterred after 1912 and a literary fashion during my twenties) provided another literary pattern, and Yeats influenced my writing from 1916, when I first read Responsibilities.— The American writers to whom I return are Poe (the Tales), Thoreau, E. Dickinson and Henry James. Whitman, read at sixteen, with much enthusiasm, I do not return to, and I never drew any refreshment from his "thought." Henry James I discovered late, and I read him for the

*Reprinted, with the permission of Ruth Limmer, from *Partisan Review*, 6 (Fall 1939), 103, 105–08. From a series of replies to a questionnaire submitted to a number of American writers.

first time with the usual prejudices against him, absorbed from the inadequate criticism he has generally received. It was not until I had developed some independent critical judgment that I recognized him as a great and subtle artist. If civilization and great art mean complexity rather than simplification, and if the humane can be defined as the well understood because the well-explored, James' work is certainly more relevant to American writing, present and future, than the naive vigor and sentimental "thinking" of Whitman.

2. *Do you think of yourself as writing for a definite audience? If so, how would you describe this audience? Would you say that the audience for serious American writing has grown or contracted in the last ten years?*

I have seldom thought about a definite "audience" for my poetry, and I certainly have never believed that the wider the audience, the better the poetry. Poetry had a fairly wide audience during what was roughly known as the "American poetic renaissance." It has been borne in upon me, in the last ten years, that there are only a few people capable of the aesthetic experience, and that, in this group, some persons who are able to appreciate "form" in the graphic arts, cannot recognize it in writing, just as there are writers who cannot "hear" music, or "see" painting. This small element in the population remains, it seems to me, more or less constant, and penetrates class distinctions. People may be led up to the threshold of the aesthetic experience, and taught its elements and its value, but I have never seen a person in whom the gift was not native actually experience the "shock of recognition" which a poem (or any work of art) gives its appreciator. And it is individuals to whom the aesthetic experience is closed, or those who know what it is, but wish to load it with a misplaced weight of "meaning" (and it seems incredible that such people as the last named exist; it is one of the horrors of life that they do)— it is such people who think that this experience can be "used."— Certainly the audience for the disinterested and the gratuitous in writing was never very large, in America. The layer of American "culture" has always been extremely thin. And it has not deepened in itself, but has been subject to fashions hastily imposed upon it. And the American "cultural" background is thick with ideas of "success" and "morality." So a piece of writing which is worth nothing, and means nothing (but itself) is, to readers at large, silly and somewhat immoral. "Serious writing" has come to mean, to the public, the pompous or thinly documentary. The truly serious piece of work, where a situation is explored at all levels, disinterestedly, for its own sake, is outlawed.

3. *Do you place much value on the criticism your work has received?*
Would you agree that the corruption of the literary supplements by
advertising—in the case of the newspapers—and political pressures—
in the case of the liberal weeklies—has made serious literary criticism
an isolated cult?

No.—The corruption of the literary supplements is nearly complete, but who would expect it to be otherwise, when publishers
admit that they are selling packaged goods, for the most part: that
their products, on the whole, stand on the same level as cigarettes
and whiskey, as sedatives and pain-killers?—I have written criticism
for liberal weeklies and can testify that in the case of one of them,
no pressure of any kind has ever been put upon me. I have also
been left perfectly free by a magazine which makes no claim to be
anything but amusing. . . . Serious criticism is, now in America,
seriously hampered by the extraordinarily silly, but really (on the sentimental public at large), amazingly effective under-cover methods of
certain pressure groups. But if there is no one who has the good sense
to see the difference between warmed-over party tracts and actual
analysis—if the public swallows such stuff whole—perhaps that is
what the public deserves. Perhaps there is a biological bourgeoisie,
thick headed and without sensibilities, thrown up into every generation, as well as an economic one. I discovered, long ago, that there
are human attributes the gods themselves, as some one has said,
cannot war against, and some of them are stupidity, greed, vanity,
and arrogance.

4. *Have you found it possible to make a living by writing the sort of*
thing you want to, and without the aid of such crutches as teaching
and editorial work? Do you think there is any place in our present
economic system for literature as a profession?

I have never been able to make a living by writing poetry and it
has never entered my mind that I could do so. I think the place in our
present American set-up for the honest and detached professional
writer is both small and cold. (But then, it was both small and cold
for Flaubert, in 19th century France.)

5. *Do you find, in retrospect, that your writing reveals any allegiance*
to any group, class, organization, region, religion, or system of thought,
or do you conceive of it as mainly the expression of yourself as an
individual?

My writing reveals some "allegiances" (if this term means certain
marks made upon it by circumstance). I was brought up in the Roman

Catholic Church, and was exposed to real liturgy, instead of the dreary "services" and the dreadful hymnody of the Protestant churches. There was a Celtic gift for language, and talent in the form of a remarkable excess of energy, on the maternal side of my family. And I was handed out, as I have said, a thorough secondary classical education, from the age of twelve through the age of seventeen, in the public schools of Boston. I did not know I was a member of a class until I was twenty-one; but I knew I was a member of a racial and religious minority, from an early age. One of the great shocks of my life came when I discovered that bigotry existed not only among the Catholics, but among the Protestants, whom I had thought would be tolerant and civilized (since their pretentions were always in that direction). It was borne in upon me, all during my adolescence, that I was a "Mick," no matter what my other faults or virtues might be. It took me a long time to take this fact easily, and to understand the situation which gave rise to the minor persecutions I endured at the hands of supposedly educated and humane people.—I came from the white-collar class and it was difficult to erase the dangerous tendencies—the impulse to "rise" and respect "nice people"—of this class. These tendencies I have wrung out of my spiritual constitution with a great deal of success, I am proud to say.—Beyond these basic influences, I think of my writing as the expression of my own development as an individual.

6. *How would you describe the political tendency of American writing as a whole since 1930? How do you feel about it yourself? Are you sympathetic to the current tendency towards what may be called "literary nationalism"—a renewed emphasis, largely uncritical, on the specifically "American" elements in our culture?*

The political tendency of American writing since 1930 is, I believe, more symptomatic of a spiritual *malaise* than is generally supposed. Granted that the economic crisis became grave; it is nevertheless peculiar and highly symptomatic that intellectuals having discovered that "freedom" is not enough, and does not automatically lead to depth of insight and peace of mind, threw over *every scrap of their former enthusiasms,* as though there were something sinful in them. The economic crisis occurred when that generation of young people was entering the thirties; and, instead of fighting out the personal ills attendant upon the transition from youth to middle age, they took refuge in closed systems of belief, and automatically (many of them) committed creative suicide. . . . "Literary nationalism" has valuable elements in it; it opened the eyes of writers, superficially at least, to conditions which had surrounded them from childhood, but which they had spent much effort "escaping." But when this nationalism took a fixed form (when it became more fashionable to examine the situation of the share-cropper, for example, than the situation of slum-dwellers in Chelsea, Massachusetts, or Newark, New Jersey) its value dwindled. And the closing of one foreign culture after another, to the critical and appreciative examination of students, is one deplorable result of thinking in purely political terms. Any purely chauvinistic enthusiasm is, of course, always ridiculous.

This is the place, perhaps, to state my belief that the true sincerity and compassion which humane detachment alone can give, are necessary before the writer can pass judgment upon the ills of his time. To sink oneself into a party is fatal, no matter how noble the tenets of that party may be. For all tenets tend to harden into dogma, and all dogma breeds hatred and bigotry, and is therefore stultifying. And the condescension of the political party toward the artist is always clear, however well disguised. The artist will be "given" his freedom; as though it were not the artist who "gives" freedom to the world, and not only "gives" it, but is the only person capable of enduring it, or of understanding what it costs. The artists who remain exemplars have often, it is true, become entangled in politics, but it is not their political work which we remember. Nonsense concerning the function of the arts has been tossed about for centuries. Art has been asked, again, as the wind changed, to be "romantic," "filled with sensibility," "classic," "useful," "uplifting" and whatnot. The true artist will instinctively reject "burning questions" and all "crude oppositions" which can cloud his vision or block his ability to deal with his world. All this has been fought through before now: Turgenev showed up the pretentions of the political critic Belinsky; Flaubert fought the battle against "usefulness" all his life; Yeats wrote the most superb anti-political poetry ever written. Flaubert wrote, in the midst of one bad political period: "Let us [as writers] remain the river and turn the mill."

7. *Have you considered the question of your attitude towards the possible entry of the United States into the next world war? What do you think the responsibilities of writers in general are when and if war comes?*

In the event of another war, I plan to oppose it with every means in my power. The responsibilities of writers in general, I should think, lie in such active opposition.

The Rewards of Patience   W. H. Auden*

"Genius has only an immanent teleology, it develops itself, and while developing itself this self-development projects itself as its work. Genius is therefor in no sense inactive, and works within itself perhaps harder than ten business men, but none of its achievements have any exterior telos. This is at once the humanity and the pride of genius; the humanity lies in the fact that it does not define itself teleologically in relation to other men, as though there were any one who needed it; its pride lies in the fact that it immanently relates itself to itself. It is modest of the nightingale not to require anyone to listen to it; but it is also proud of the nightingale not to care whether anyone listens to it or not. . . . The honored public, the domineering masses, wish genius to express that it exists for their sake; they only see one side of the dialectic of genius, take offence at its pride, and do not see that the same thing is also modesty and humility."

So wrote Kierkegaard in 1847; he did not foresee that by 1942 the masses would have acquired such buying power that genius itself would, in many cases, be thinking of its self-development as a process of learning how to sell itself competitively to the public, that the poet whose true song, unlike that of the nightingale, continually changes because he himself changes, would be tempted to dissociate his song from his nature altogether, until the changes in the latter come to be conditioned, not by changes in himself, but by the shifting of public taste—that he would become, in other words, a journalist.

A public is a disintegrated community. A community is a society of rational beings united by a common tie in virtue of the things that they all love; a public is a crowd of lost beings united only negatively in virtue of the things that they severally fear, among which one of the greatest is the fear of being responsible as a rational being for one's individual self-development. Hence, wherever there is a public, there arises the paradox of a tremendous demand for art in the abstract, but an almost complete repudiation of art in the concrete. A demand because works of art can indeed help people along the road of self-development, and the public feels more helpless than ever; a repudiation because art can only help those who help themselves. It can suggest directions in which people may look if they will; it cannot give them eyes or wills, but it is just these eyes and wills that the public demand, and hope to buy with money and applause.

Subjectively, the situation of the poet is no less difficult. In ages when there was such a thing as a community, the self-development of which his works are the manifestation, arose, in part at least, out of his life as a

*A review of *Poems and New Poems*. Reprinted, with permission, from *Partisan Review*, 9 (July–August 1942), 336–40. Copyright 1942, © 1970 by *Partisan Review*.

member, assenting or dissenting, of and within that community; in an age when there is only a public, his self-development receives no such extraneous help, so that, unless he replaces it by taking over the task of directing his life by his own deliberate intention, his growth and hence his poetry is at the mercy of personal accidents, love-affairs, illnesses, bereavements, and so forth.

Again it was in the community that he formerly found a source of value outside himself, and unless he now can replace this vanished source by another, or at least search for it, his only standard for appreciating experience is The Interesting, which in practice means his childhood and his sex-life, so that he escapes being a journalist who fawns on the public only to become a journalist who fawns on his own ego; the selection and treatment of experience is still conditioned by its news value. In the case of much 'advanced' poetry, the public is therefore, though quite unjustifiably, quite right in repudiating it; not because, as the public thinks, it is too difficult, but because, once one has learned the idiom, it is too easy; one can translate it immediately and without loss of meaning into the language of the Daily Press. Far from being what it claims to be, and is rejected by the public for being,

> The shrieking heaven lifted over men

it is, what the public demands but finds elsewhere in much better brands,

> The dumb earth wherein they set their graves

A volume of good poetry, like this collection of Miss Louise Bogan's, represents today therefore a double victory, over the Collective Self and over the Private Self. As her epigraph she uses a quotation from Rilke—

> Wie ist das klein womit wir ringen,
> was mit uns ringt, wie ist das gross

And the poems that follow are the fruit of such a belief, held and practised over years, that Self-development is a process of self-surrender, for it is the Self that demands the exclusive attention of all experiences, but offers none in return.

> The playthings of the young
> Get broken in the play,
> Get broken, as they should.

In the early sections Miss Bogan employs her gift in the way in which, as a rule, it should at first be employed, to understand her weakness to which it is dialectically related, for wherever there is a gift, of whatever kind, there is also a guilty secret, a thorn in the flesh and the first successful poems of young poets are usually a catharsis of resentment.

> Cry, song, cry
> And hear your crying lost

Poems at this stage are usually short, made up of magical lyric phrases which seem to rise involuntarily to the consciousness, and their composition is attended by great excitement, a feeling of being inspired.

Some excellent poets, like Housman and Emily Dickinson, never get beyond this stage, because the more successful the catharsis, the more dread there must be of any change either in one's life or one's art, for a change in the former threatens the source of the latter which is one's only consolation, and the latter can only change by ceasing to console. Miss Bogan, however, recognised this temptation and resisted it.

> My mouth, perhaps, may learn one thing too well,
> My body hear no echo save its own,
> Yet will the desperate mind, maddened and proud,
> Seek out the storm, escape the bitter spell.

But the price and privilege of growth is that the temptation resisted is replaced by a worse one. No sooner does the mind seek to escape the bitter spell than the lying Tempter whispers—

> The intellect of man is forced to choose
> Perfection of the life or of the work

The poet who escapes from the error of believing that the relation of his life to his work is a direct one, that the second is the mirror image of the first, now falls into the error of denying that there need be any relation at all, into believing that the poetry can develop autonomously, provided that the poet can find it a convenient Myth. For the Myth is a set of values and ideas which are impersonal and so break the one-one relationship of poetry to experience by providing other standards of importance than the personally interesting, while at the same time it is not a religion, that is to say, it does not have to be believed in real life, with all the effort and suffering which that implies.

Thus we find modern poets asking of a general idea, not Is It True?, but Is It Exciting? Is It Poetically useful?, and whether they are attracted to Byzantium and The Phases of the Moon, like Yeats, or to the Id or Miss History like his younger and less-talented colleagues, the motive and its motions are the same.

But the escape from the Self without the surrender of the Self is, of course, an illusion, for it is the Self that still chooses the particular avenue of escape. Thus Yeats, the romantic rebel against the Darwinian Myth of his childhood with its belief in The Machine and Automatic Progress, adopts as poetic 'organisers' woozy doctrines like The Aristocratic Mask and the Cyclical Theory of Time while remaining personally, as Eliot rather slyly remarks, 'a very sane man'; others fashion an image out of the opposites of puritanical parents or upper class education. And still the personal note appears, only now in the form of its denial, in a certain phoney dramatisation, a 'camp' of impersonality. Further the adoption of a belief which one does not really hold as a means of integrating experience poetically, while it may produce fine poems, limits their meaning to the immediate context; it creates Occasional poems lacking any resonance beyond their frame. (Cf., for example Yeats' *Second Coming* with Eliot's *East Coker*).

To have developed to the point where this temptation is real, and then to resist it, is to realise that the relation of Life to Work is dialectical, a change in the one presupposes and demands a change in the other, and that belief and behaviour have a similar relation, that is to say, that beliefs are religious or nothing, and a religion cannot be got out of books or by a sudden vision, but can only be realised by living it. And to see this is to see that one's poetic development must be restrained from rushing ahead of oneself while at the same time one's self-development must not be allowed to fall behind.

Reading through Miss Bogan's book, one realizes what is the price and the reward for such a discipline.

The hasty reader hardly notices any development; the subject matter and form show no spectacular change: he thinks—"Miss Bogan. O yes, a nice writer of lyrics, but all these women poets, you know, slight. Only one string to their bow." It is only by reading and rereading that one comes to appreciate the steady growth of wisdom and technical mastery, the persistent elimination of the consolations of stoicism and every other kind of poetic theatre, the achievement of an objectivity about personal experience which is sought by many but found only by the few who dare face the Furies.

> You who know what we love, but drive us to know it;
> You with your whips and shrieks, bearer of truth and of solitude;
> You who give, unlike men, to expiation your mercy.
>
> Dropping the scourge when at last the scourged advances to meet it,
> You, when the hunted turns, no longer remain the hunter
> But stand silent and wait, at last returning his gaze.
>
> Beautiful now as a child whose hair, wet with rage and tears
> Clings to its face. And now I may look upon you,
> Having once met your eyes. You lie in sleep and forget me.
> Alone and strong in my peace, I look upon you in yours.

In the last two sections, in poems like *Animal, Vegetable and Mineral* and *Evening in the Sanitarium* Miss Bogan turns to impersonal subjects, and here again the hasty will say: "too slight. I prefer her earlier work," because he cannot understand the integrity of an artist who will not rush her sensibility, knowing that no difficulty can be cheated without incurring punishment.

But the difficulty of being an artist in an age when one has to live everything for oneself, has its compensations. It is, for the strong, a joy to know that now there are no longer any places of refuge in which one can lie down in comfort, that one must go on or go under, live danger-ously or not at all.

It is therefor impossible today to predict the future of any poet because the future is never the consequence of a single decision but is continually created by a process of choice in which temptation and op-portunity are perpetually presented, ever fresh and ever unforseen. All one can say is that Miss Bogan is a poet in whom, because she is so clearly aware of this, one has complete faith as to her instinct for direc-tion and her endurance, and that, anyway, what she has already written is of permanent value. Future generations will, of course, be as foolish as ours, but their follies like our own and those of every generation will mainly effect their judgment of their present which is always so much more 'interesting' than the silly old past.

Miss Bogan, I fancy, is then going to be paid the respect she deserves when many, including myself, I fear, of those who now have a certain news value, are going to catch it.

[Review of *Poems and New Poems*]   Malcolm Cowley*

Critics writing about Louise Bogan have usually discussed her tech-nique, and there is good reason for this emphasis. What seemed to be the subject matter of her first two volumes was not at all striking—love that is all-powerful but fleeting, chastity that is a lie, tears shed alone at night; in general the themes that were being treated by dozens of women poets during the 1920's. But her real subject, implicit in her manner of writing, was always poetry itself. She was saying by her example that the duty of the poet is to crowd all possible meaning into a few short lines; to find the exact word, the one right image, the rhythm just awkward enough to vary the pattern without breaking it entirely. She was saying that such poetry is terrifyingly difficult to write, but worth all the years and pains one devotes to it. And she was saying that art is fearful as well as beautiful; it is the Gorgon's head that can forever fix an evanescent landscape:

> The water will always fall, and will not fall,
> And the tipped bell make no sound.
> The grass will always be growing for hay
> Deep on the ground.

*Reprinted, with the permission of the author, from "Three Poets," *New Republic*, 10 November 1941, p. 625.

With such a theory of art, it is difficult or impossible to write a great deal. "Poems and New Poems" is not a big volume, but it contains everything that Miss Bogan thinks is worth saving from her work of the last twenty years. There are seventy-two poems, mostly short lyrics, taken from her three earlier books; and sixteen others written in various manners since "The Sleeping Fury" appeared in 1937. Other poets publish more in a single season. Even quantitatively, however, Miss Bogan has done something that has been achieved by very few of her contemporaries: she has added a dozen or more to our small stock of memorable lyrics. She has added nothing whatever to our inexhaustible store of trash.

Nevertheless, I hope she now decides to make some change in her theory and practice of the poet's art. Together they have been confining her to a somewhat narrow range of expression. Her new poems—meditative, witty and sometimes really wise—suggest that she has more to say than can be crowded into any group of lyrics; and that perhaps she should give herself more space and less time. Most American poets write too much and too easily; Miss Bogan ought to write more, and more quickly, and even more carelessly. There are poems, sometimes very good ones, that have to be jotted down quickly or lost forever.

[Review of *Poems and New Poems*]   Babette Deutsch*

In the four years that have elapsed since her last volume was published, Miss Bogan, working with her accustomed scrupulousness, has produced comparatively little. As the title of the present collection suggests, most of the lyrics it contains will prove familiar to her public. One may regret that, for the sake of a thin sheaf of new poems, one must make room on one's shelves for "Dark Summer" and "The Sleeping Fury" all over again in a different binding, and even more that Miss Bogan has found it necessary to pad this collection with two translations of no great merit and several entertaining but unimpressive original pieces. But so profound and intimate is the emotion that beats in most of these lines, so deliberate the art controlling it, that one ends by greeting the old lyrics and welcoming the new with almost unqualified delight.

There are two strains in Miss Bogan's poetry that contend with and support one another as in counterpoint. One is the influence of the Metaphysicals—indeed, "I Saw Eternity" is the work of a twentieth-century Traherne; the other is the expression of a modern woman, self-

*Reprinted, with the permission of the author, from the *New York Herald Tribune Books*, 28 December 1941, p. 8.

probing, passionate and ironic. One has heard these voices before, notably in the performance of Elinor Wylie, of which not a few of Miss Bogan's lyrics are reminiscent. One has heard them, more thinly and more purely, in the exquisite verse of Léonie Adams. One hears them sound again from these pages, with renewed resonance. If Miss Bogan, like the English poets of the seventeenth century, compresses subtle speculations in a little space, it is not surprising that, like them, she should sometimes be obscure. And if, with a feminine pathos which the male poet not seldom exhibits, she confides matters of purely private import to her verse, it is natural that she should not always find the objective correlative that will give the poem a more general validity. For the most part, however, Miss Bogan sustains her performance at a level to which the fewest of her contemporaries can rise, matching an uncommonly responsive and penetrating sensibility with an equally rare technical felicity.

Whether her verse follows strictly a conventional pattern or is regulated solely by the poet's impeccable ear, cadence and verbal texture are always right, and the fustian of a line like "Shall I be made a panderer to death?" is so extraordinary as to suggest the intrusion of another hand. It is indicative of Miss Bogan's sensitiveness to the weight and color of her syllables that so many of her poems should be about music or written to be sung. Thus, one finds "Juan's Song," "Chanson un Peu Naïve," "Girl's Song," "Song for a Slight Voice," "Spirit's Song," "Song for a Lyre," "To Be Sung on the Water," not to mention simply "Song" and "Second Song." It is noteworthy that in no case does Miss Bogan offer the verse equivalent of songs without words: however clear and fluent her melody, there is always a given base of thought or feeling, distinguishable from the song yet related to it.

So careful a craftsman would, of course, be scornful of poetic fashions, and the character of Miss Bogan's work has not altered noticeably in nearly twenty years. It is therefore odd to find her including a piece originally published with the subtitle "Imitated from Auden" and honoring neither the model nor the copyist. She is wittier when she imitates nobody but herself. The more memorable poems from her previous book, "The Sleeping Fury," the title-poem, "Single Sonnet," "Baroque Comment," among others, differ from her earlier work only in showing greater depth and power. They are not exceeded, nor, indeed, equaled by any of her more recent poems. The present collection is as a whole distinguished by the testimony it bears to the integrity of so accomplished a poet.

Compactness Compacted   Marianne Moore*

Women are not noted for terseness, but Louise Bogan's art is compactness compacted. Emotion with her, as she has said of certain fiction, is "itself form, the kernel which builds outward form from inward intensity." She uses a kind of forged rhetoric that nevertheless seems inevitable. It is almost formula with her to omit the instinctive comma of self-defensive explanation, for example, "Our lives through we have trod the ground." Her titles are right poetically, with no subserviences for torpid minds to catch at; the lines entitled "Knowledge," for instance, being really about love. And there is fire in the brazier—the thinker in the poet. "Fifteenth Farewall" says:

> I erred, when I thought loneliness the wide
> Scent of mown grass over forsaken fields,
> Or any shadow isolation yields.
> Loneliness was the heart within your side.

One is struck by her restraint—an unusual courtesy in this day of bombast. The triumph of what purports to be surrender, in the "Poem in Prose," should be studied entire.

Miss Bogan is a workman, in prose or in verse. Anodynes are intolerable to her. She refuses to be deceived or self-deceived. Her work is not mannered. There are in it thoughts about the disunities of "the single mirrored against the single," about the devouring gorgon romantic love, toward which, as toward wine, unfaith is renewal; thoughts about the solace and futilities of being brave; about the mind as a refuge—"crafty knight" that is itself "Prey to an end not evident to craft"; about grudges; about no longer treating memory "as rich stuff . . . in a cedarn dark, . . . as eggs under the wings," but as

> Rubble in gardens, it and stones alike,
> That any spade may strike.

We read of "The hate that bruises, though the heart is braced"; of "one note rage can understand"; of "chastity's futility" and "pain's effrontery"; of "memory's false measure." No Uncle Remus phase of nature, this about the crows and the woman whose prototype is the briar patch: "She is a stem long hardened. / A weed that no scythe mows." Could the uninsisted-on surgery of exposition be stricter than in the term "red" for winter grass, or evoke the contorted furor of flame better than by saying the fire ceased its "thresh"? We have "The lilac like a heart"

*Reprinted, with the permission of Viking Penguin Inc., from *Predilections*, by Marianne Moore (New York: Viking, 1955), pp. 130–33. Copyright 1941, © renewed 1969 by Marianne Moore. This essay, a review of *Poems and New Poems*, first appeared in the *Nation* in 1941.

(preceded by the word "leaves"); "See now the stretched hawk fly"; "Horses in half-ploughed fields / Make earth they walk upon a changing color." Most delicate of all,

> . . . we heard the cock
> Shout its unplaceable cry, the axe's sound
> Delay a moment after the axe's stroke.

Music here is not someone's idol, but experience. There are real rhymes, the rhyme with vowel cognates, and consonant resonances so perfect one is not inclined to wonder whether the sound is a vowel or a consonant—as in "The Crossed Apple":

> . . . this side is red without a dapple,
> And this side's hue
> Is clear and snowy. It's a lovely apple.
> It is for you.

In "fed with fire" we have expert use of the enhancing exception to the end-stopped line:

> And spiny fruits up through the earth are fed
> With fire;

Best of all is the embodied climax with unforced subsiding cadence, as in the song about

> The stone—the deaf, the blind—
> That sees the birds in flock
> Steer narrowed to the wind.

When a tune plagues the ear, the best way to be rid of it is to let it forth unhindered. This Miss Bogan has done with a W. H. Auden progression, "Evening in the Sanitarium"; with G. M. Hopkins in "Feuer-Nacht"; Ezra Pound in "The Sleeping Fury"; W. B. Yeats in "Betrothed"; W. C. Williams in "Zone." All through, there is a certain residual, securely equated seventeenth-century firmness, as in the spectacular competence of Animal, Vegetable, and Mineral.

What of the implications? For mortal rage and immortal injury, are there or are there not medicines? Job and Hamlet insisted that we dare not let ourselves be snared into hating hatefulness; to do this would be to take our own lives. Harmed, let us say, through our generosity— if we consent to have pity on our illusions and others' absence of illusion, to condone the fact that "no fine body ever can be meat and drink to anyone"—is it true that pain will exchange its role and become servant instead of master? Or is it merely a conveniently unexpunged superstition?

Those who have seemed to know most about eternity feel that this side of eternity is a small part of life. We are told, if we do wrong that grace may abound, it does not abound. We need not be told that life is never going to be free from trouble and that there are no substitutes for the dead; but it is a fact as well as a mystery that weakness is power, that handicap is proficiency, that the scar is a credential, that indignation is no adversary for gratitude, or heroism for joy. There are medicines.

Land of Dust and Flame   Stanley Kunitz*

On the jacket of this omnibus volume of Louise Bogan's work, containing in all some ninety poems, Allen Tate is quoted in praise of Miss Bogan as "the most accomplished woman poet of our time." The praise, to my mind, is justified; but I suspect that to be perennially classified and reviewed as a "woman poet" must prove discomfiting, at the least, to a poet of Miss Bogan's superlative gifts and power. It is true that she is a woman and a poet and that her motivations and themes, like those of her sister poets, relate essentially to her special experiences in a man-world—and why not?—but the virtue of her work is not a quality of gender. Stephen Spender recently made the somewhat rash generalization that when men write poetry they have their eyes fixed on several things at once—the form of the poem, the effect of the poem on the reader, their own personalities—whereas women lose themselves in the subject-matter, the experience behind the poetry, and are careless of words themselves and the rhythmic pattern. This indictment cannot even be applied to Miss Bogan's earliest poems, of which the following, with its conspicuously familiar theme, is an example:

> Men loved wholly beyond wisdom
> Have the staff without the banner.
> Like a fire in a dry thicket
> Rising within women's eyes
> Is the love men must return.
> Heart, so subtle now, and trembling,
> What a marvel to be wise,
> To love never in this manner!
> To be quiet in the fern
> Like a thing gone dead and still,
> Listening to the prisoned cricket
> Shake its terrible, dissembling
> Music in the granite hill.

Miss Bogan's work is occasionally pretty, with a deliberately wrought elegance of lyric style; it is never, or almost never, girlishly arch

*Reprinted, with the permission of the author, from *A Kind of Order, A Kind of Folly* (Boston: Little, Brown, 1975), pp. 194–97. This essay, a review of *Poems and New Poems*, first appeared in *Poetry* in 1942.

or matronly sticky. She is exempted from sentimentality by her respect for her art; by her discipline in self-seeing; by that nervous capacity for self-disdain without which the romantic poet, in an age of non-romantic values, no longer can endure.

Miss Bogan understands form: she writes a poem from beginning to end disdaining the use of filler. Her ear is good: she is sensitive to verbal quantity and quality. When she succeeds—and she succeeds remarkably often—the surface of her poem is only the other side of its substance, without holes to fall through. In the poem already quoted I doubt that there is a word that could be changed without impairing the whole structure. The distillation of her talent is in a deceptively simple quatrain, so just in style, so mature and witty in sensibility, that a long life can safely be predicted for it:[1]

> Slipping in blood, by his own hand, through pride,
> Hamlet, Othello, Coriolanus fall.
> Upon his bed, however, Shakespeare died,
> Having endured them all.

Aside from this quatrain and two other pieces, "The Dream" and "The Daemon," her new poems seem to me less consummately organized than before. (I am not discussing the silly section of *New Yorker*ish verses, which might well have been omitted.) In the new poems there are indications that Miss Bogan is experimenting in an effort to release her poetic energies more fully and to extend her range. Her long-held ideal of geometric perfection, her creative illusion of "cool nights, when laurel builds up, without haste, / its precise flower, like a pentagon," has undoubtedly, in some respects, fettered her talent, so that one feels at times that she has reworked her materials to excess, at the expense of associative spontaneity. I should like to see further manifestations of the mood of savage irony that produced "Hypocrite Swift"; and I find in "Kept," with its cold abnegating pity—"the playthings of the young / get broken in the play, / get broken, as they should"—a kind of writing that no one else can do half as well.

But I am persuaded that the true world of Miss Bogan's imagination, of which she has up to now given us only fragmentary impressions, is "the sunk land of dust and flame," where an unknown terror is king, presiding over the fable of a life, in the deep night swarming with images of reproach and desire. Out of that underworld she has emerged with her three greatest poems, spaced years between, of which the latest is "The Dream":

> O God, in the dream the terrible horse began
> To paw at the air, and make for me with his blows.
> Fear kept for thirty-five years poured through his mane,
> And retribution equally old, or nearly, breathed through his nose.

Coward complete, I lay and wept on the ground
When some strong creature appeared, and leapt for the rein.
Another woman, as I lay half in a swound,
Leapt in the air, and clutched at the leather and chain.

Give him, she said, something of yours as a charm.
Throw him, she said, some poor thing you alone claim.
No, no, I cried, he hates me; he's out for harm,
And whether I yield or not, it is all the same.

But, like a lion in a legend, when I flung the glove
Pulled from my sweating, my cold right hand,
The terrible beast, that no one may understand,
Came to my side, and put down his head in love.

In the body of Miss Bogan's work "The Dream" stands with "Medusa" and "The Sleeping Fury" in violence of statement, in depth of evocation. They give off the taste of pomegranates: Persephone might have written them.

Notes

1. It is gratifying to see a prophecy confirmed. The posthumous publication of the first draft of this quatrain in *What the Woman Lived: Selected Letters of Louise Bogan, 1920–1970*, p. 82, provides a valuable insight into the poet's working habits, as well as a lesson in the art of revision. Her extemporaneous lines, as they appeared in a letter to Edmund Wilson, dated October 16, 1934, read:

For every great soul who died in his house and his wisdom
Several did otherwise.
God, keep me from the fat heart that looks vaingloriously toward peace and maturity;
Protect me not from lies.
In Thy infinite certitude, tenderness and mercy
Allow me to be sick and well,
So that I may never tread with swollen foot the calm and obscene intentions
That pave hell.
Shakespeare, Milton, Matthew Arnold died in their beds,
Dante above the stranger's stair.
They were not absolved from either the courage or the cowardice
With which they bore what they had to bear.
Swift died blind, deaf and mad;
Socrates died in his cell;
Baudelaire died in his drool;
Proving no rule.

[Review of *Collected Poems, 1923–53*]

John Ciardi*

Louise Bogan's poetry has much in common with [Léonie] Adams's. Here are the opening lines of three of Miss Bogan's early poems:

> In fear of the rich mouth
> I kissed the thin,—

and

> I make the old sign.
> I invoke you,
> Chastity.

and

> Now that I know
> How passion warms little.

At that point at least—and down to the Puritan marrow of Miss Wylie's bones—Miss Adams and Miss Bogan were surely sisters in the same aesthetic convent; and while I must confess that I have often wondered why that sisterhood insisted on wearing its chastity belts on the outside, poetry nevertheless remains wherever the spirit finds it. If that starting illusion was necessary to the poem, what matters is that the poems came—clean, hard, rigorously disciplined, and reaching to the nerve. Miss Bogan's capture in such an early piece as "Medusa" is enough to justify a whole burial ground of Puritan marrows.

But—speaking as one reader—if I admire objectively the poems of the first three (the earlier) sections of Miss Bogan's collection, with the poems of section four, I find myself forgetting the thee and me of it. I am no longer being objective about the excellences of a poet who leaves me shrugging down to the Neapolitan marrow of my bones. I am immediately engaged. Miss Bogan began in beauty, but she has aged to magnificence, and I find myself thinking that the patina outshines the gold stain. One has only to compare "The Dream" on page 109 with the poems whose openings I have already cited to see how much more truly Miss Bogan sees into herself in the late poems—and not only into herself, but deeply enough into herself to find within her that jungle—call it the Jungian unconscious if you must—that everyone has in himself. "The Dream" is not only Miss Bogan's; it is everyone's.

Beginning with the poems of section four, that is, Miss Bogan leaves the convent. She comes out of timelessness into time. Nor is this a

---

*Reprinted, with the permission of the author and the publisher, from "Two Nuns and a Strolling Player," a review of Léonie Adams, Bogan, and Edna St. Vincent Millay, in the *Nation*, 22 May 1954, pp. 445–46.

matter of topical reference. No such thing. It is, rather, that the kind of inward perception that marks the later poems speaks not only an enduring motion of the human spirit but an enduring motion that is *toward* the timeless *from* the times. The more difficult demon has been wrestled with.

[Review of *Collected Poems, 1923–53*]

Richard Eberhart*

Louise Bogan's poems adhere to the center of English with a dark lyrical force. What she has to say is important. How she says it is pleasing. She is a compulsive poet first, a stylist second. When compulsion and style meet we have a strong, inimitable Bogan poem.

There is relatively little technical innovation in her poems. She writes mainly in traditional verse forms, handled with adroitness and economy. The originality is in the forceful emotion and how this becomes caught in elegant tensions of perfected forms. She has delved in antique mysteries and brought up universal charms from deep sources, from a knowledge of suffering and from full understanding of the lot of man.

Some of her short lyrics have been known for a long time. To these she adds an arsenal of profound and beautiful poems. Her struggle is to throw off the nonessential, to confront naked realities at their source. Her poems are rich in passionate realizations, expressing in turn irony, bitterness, love and joy.

Her attitudes come down to a deep sincerity, the result of her strongly searching quality. A profundity of psychological knowledge works in the poems. One feels that truths of life, death and love have been confronted and uncompromising answers given.

Miss Bogan writes portrait poems like "The Romantic" and satirical poems like "At a Party." There is a small body of sententia, as "To an Artist, to Take Heart." She has a group of story or parable poems, such as "The Crossed Apple," "Medusa," "Cartography" and "Evening in the Sanitarium." I made a list of what I call her universal poems. This was quite long, including "My Voice Not Being Proud," "The Alchemist," "Men Loved Wholly Beyond Wisdom," "Memory" and "Cassandra."

This is a rich vein. I also made a list I called pure lyrics, a long list including "Song for a Slight Voice," "I Saw Eternity," "Old Countryside," "Exhortation," "Man Alone," "To My Brother," "Spirit's Song," "Heard by a Girl" and "The Dream." Her finest work is also in this vein.

*Reprinted from the *New York Times Book Review*, 30 May 1954, p. 6. Copyright 1954 by the New York Times Company. Reprinted by permission.

Miss Bogan, who reviews poetry for The New Yorker, has year to year devoted careful thought to other poets, presenting their work in review with precise commentaries. She has developed these to a fine point of critical interest and sagacity. One had the notion that she wrote sparingly herself. This book is most welcome in giving the reader for the first time the full dimension of her poetic talent. The feeling is of somber strength, of a strong nature controlling powerful emotions by highly conscious art. There is marked skill in her restraint. Her best poems read as if time would not be likely to break them down.

There are many poems one would like to quote. Here is the last part of one, "Sub Contra."

Let there sound from music's root
One note rage can understand,
A fine noise of riven things.
Build there some thick chord of wonder;
Then, for every passion's sake,
Beat upon it till it break.

Perhaps that will indicate Miss Bogan's depth.

"All Has Been Translated into Treasure"

Léonie Adams[*]

The immediate significance of this book is twofold. It provides, in an admirable arrangement and with some fine additions, work whose excellence had been recognized, but which had been for some years out of print, and it provides occasion for calling it to the attention of the wider audience it deserves.

Self-possessed, from the beginning intact, Miss Bogan's talent has never been in dispute, nor had the unhappy, often questionable merit of "eluding" definition. Since the brilliant and early beginning of Body of This Death, she has not stood still, nor advanced by fits and starts. After the poems in The Sleeping Fury, though still to bring forth those true fruits which always surprise, she could hardly exceed herself in her characteristic mode. With the publication of Poems and New Poems, the distinguished quality of her work had been asserted and as far as possible perhaps discriminated by some of those most competent to do this. The present reviewer feels no need for revision of their essential estimate. Indeed an old jacket reminds one that things were said of her

[*]A review of Collected Poems: 1923–53. Reprinted, with the permission of the author and the editor, from Poetry, 85 (December 1954), 165–69. Copyright 1954 by the Modern Poetry Association.

poems in 1923 which are still, in effect, being said with perfect soundness in 1954.

What there is need of, and opportunity for, is to repeat and labor
a little the estimate alluded to. The virtues of her writing which have
been most often spoken of are, I should suppose, firmness of outline,
prosodic accomplishment, chiefly in traditional metrics, purity of diction
and tone, concision of phrase, and, what results in craft from all these,
and at bottom from a way of seizing experience, concentrated singleness
of effect.

The description might well delimit the classic form of the short lyric,
any time, any place, abstractly, and so hold for any example, and none.
Actually its elements have seldom, and never for long periods, been
held in English verse in any serenity of balance, and this poet's particular management of them remains to be discussed.

Louise Bogan has not written a large body of work, nor addressed
herself—though this will seem less true by concentrating on the later
sections of the book—to peculiarly modern preoccupations. Just as a
certain inner rhythm can be found—and some other effects of sound
patterning cannot—only within freely absorbed metrical forms, a certain
lyric reduction can perhaps be reached only for recurrent norms of
experience, a little beneath and apart from immediate phenomena.
The evidence of the poems is that this poet has rarely written except
when impelled by the strong experience of the private person. Though
adhering more closely to traditional forms than many poets find will
meet their case, the language of the poems is as well of now as not,
their temper of mind and presuppositions perfectly so.

A large part of their moral force derives from the refusal to be
deluded, or to be overborne. The learning of the unwanted lesson, the
admission of the harsh fact, a kind of exhilaration of rejection, whether
of the scorned or the merely implausible, the theme appears in the
earliest work, and reaches maximum power in Section III. To mention
some of the well known pieces there, *The Sleeping Fury*, like *The
Dream*, finds an image for such admission within the self; *At a Party*
situates its scene; the finely sustained *Putting to Sea* encompasses both
these, the elegiac tone of innocence, and the deeper one of some inclusive mystery of survival. *Henceforth from the Mind* is the theme's more
abstracted song.

Yet despite this theme's prevalence, though there are pieces which
might be classified as small ironic portraits (*The Romantic, The Alchemist, Man Alone*) and even an epigram or so, the true vein of her
work is not ironic in the usual sense, nor satiric, but something at once
simpler and more desperately human. In the best of these poems what
makes possible their strong charging of the formal balance is this: the
explicit matter is unimpeded delineation; its cost, seldom adumbrated,
resounds. Thus in the early *If You Take All Gold* there is some indul-

gence of its tonality; in *Henceforth from the Mind*, surely one of the perfect lyrics of the period, one hears its more fixed and absolute reverberation:

> Henceforward, from the shell,
> Wherein you heard, and wondered
> At oceans like a bell
> So far from ocean sundered—
> A smothered sound that sleeps
> Long lost within lost deeps,
>
> Will chime you change and hours,
> The shadow of increase,
> Will sound you flowers
> Born under troubled peace—
> Henceforth, henceforth
> Will echo sea and earth.

The note is present, compelling by its confinement to overtone, even where the overt scene or mood is so demoniac as in *At a Party*. *Exhortation* perhaps lacks it, and the *wholeness* of the other poems. One is reminded of Mr. Eliot's comment on the musical autonomy of Shakespeare's songs. Here, it might be said, however stringent the discipline of recognition, the sense of "All that is worth grief" remains. And to know this, though glad enough to have it, one does not need the explicit statement of *Summer Wish, Roman Fountain*, or

> Attest, poor body, with what scars you have
> That you left life, to come down to the grave.

Nor should one be surprised to find another balance, of acceptance, in some of the last lyrics in the book.

Yet the temper of being and pressure of experience just discussed is important to much of the work, to its quality of decision of style. Miss Moore has written of Louise Bogan's "compactness compacted." It is not the concentration of density, dazzling or murky, to be found in some modern work, but of rapid elucidation, and its secret is again that of the poise of elements in the poem. A few examples of the early period, in the symbolist-imagist manner, do more to develop the reserves of the image, and the last poem in the book does so magnificently; any number of phrases throughout are witness to "sensibility" for objects. "Listen but once" she oftenest tells that faculty and refuses to freight the poem with more than can be brought incisively to its light. She has always seen the use of the dramatic figure or mask, not for elaboration, but statement of the essence of a situation. (Longer pieces, like *The Sleeping Fury, Summer Wish*, are a progressive unfolding, in the same style.) Her musicianship works for what Hopkins distinguished as "candour, style" (harmony of tone) rather than "margaretting" (pearling with musical effects?). Many of her best poems should be related—for the lyric has other ancestors than the spontaneous cry—to the sort of choric lyric which speaks its comment nearest to the scene.

It is an art of limits, the limit of the inner occasion and of the recognized mode. This is part of its relevance, when writing often reminds us that there is no end to the remarks to be made, the matters to be noted; or, on the other hand, that the literary vegetation abounds less with forms, as in Mr. Stevens' phrase, than with techniques for exploitation.

Ranging only as far as may be from a personal center, this is a civilized poetry. Its *there* of "ordre et beauté, luxe, calme et volupté" is the humane terrain described in *After the Persian*, the "temperate threshold, the strip of corn and vine," where

> All is translucence (the light!)
> Liquidity, and the sound of water.

and

> . . . day stains with what seems to be more than the sun
> What may be more than my flesh.

> All has been translated into treasure.

Her eye is often on its objects, whether "currant on the branch" or "This marble herb, and this stone flame." Her voice is nearly always of it. That it is seen as approached on "mindless earth," from "the lie, anger, lust, oppression and death," and found in fragments, "continents apart," that the crisis of its access is often described in terms of the psyche, is part of the burden here of modernity.

Louise Bogan and Léonie Adams   Elder Olson*

It would be generally conceded, I think, that Louise Bogan and Léonie Adams are among the four or five American women who have produced poetry of high distinction, thus far in this century. Their reputations, solidly established in the twenties, have survived a number of spectacular revolutions in literary taste, theory, and practice; certain of their poems seem to have become permanently imbedded in anthologies of contemporary poetry; in short, their situation is excellent, except for the danger that the greater part of their work may be ignored precisely because a piece or two remains in high favor. I, for one, should be sorry to see all their craft and skill come to be represented merely

*Reprinted, with the permission of the author and the publisher, from the *Chicago Review*, 8 (Fall 1954), 70–87.

by so much as is manifest in a few poems; and I should like to do what I can to prevent this, by considering the larger aspects of their art. Both poets have very recently published volumes which span their careers up to the present;[1] so that such consideration is now possible.

The greater part of Miss Bogan's poems deal with the experiences of love; love, that is, as suffered by a certain individual. Like many other lyric poets, Bogan tends to portray a single character who appears constantly, or nearly so, in her work; whether this character is the poet or a dramatic figment, whether her experiences are real or imagined, it would be impertinent, and indeed pointless, to inquire. What is to the point is that this character is of a certain order, and that her experiences, as suggested by the individual poems, tend to follow a certain pattern. The character is a woman: sensitive, passionate, sensuous, and I should say, strong-willed; intelligent, but emotional rather than intellectual; led against her reason, almost against her will, into love; loving violently and prodigal in her love, but quick to resent any betrayal or any attempt at domination by her lover. For her, love is neither such a merging of two into one as we see in Donne's *The Ecstasy*, nor the ensouling of woman by man, nor of man by woman; it is a conjunction of two distinct persons, the essential condition of which is that, as conjoined, they should remain distinct. It is neither love wholly spiritualized, nor a merely physical attraction. It is likely to be transitory, not because romantic conventions demand that it should be so, but because the difficult conditions of its existence cannot be long maintained. Like romantic love, it has its pleasures and pains, but these are not always alternations of rapture with anguish; they remain pretty much life-size.

For such a woman, the history of love is almost bound to follow a certain course; there are, thus, poems which express intense desire, or bitter resistance to it; delight, not merely with love itself, but with life as transformed by love; resignation, pain, bitterness, or regret as love ends. This course seems to grow out of the conflict between self-hood and love, and special emotions are generated as now one triumphs, now the other; significantly, love is often seen in the poems in terms of war, with its wounds, surrenders, victories, and scars, or of some natural force raging beyond control, or else of some thralldom or bitterly resented enchantment, some "bitter spell" that must be suffered.

This may remind some instantly of Millay; but in fact there is very little, if any, resemblance. In Millay, when the woman is not simply "feminine" in the sense of whimsical, fickle, impulsive, and so on, she is supposedly of divine or heroic mold; and the whole history of love is similarly magnified and exaggerated. The fates are involved, the fortunes of nations hang in the balance, the gods watch or even intervene, the lover is not a man but a god, love makes the woman god-like, too, or at any rate comparable to Danae, Europa, Leda, and others who "had a god for guest." All pain is insupportable agony, all pleasure is transcendent ecstasy. (Lest it be supposed that I exaggerate this, look at Sonnets I, IV, V, VII, XII, XIV, XV, XVI, XXVI, XLII, LII of *Fatal Interview*.) Millay sought to give the love she described something of tragic stature by equating it with the great loves of myth and legend; she failed, I think, because in her poems we are told rather than shown that the love is of so exalted an order. It is one thing to claim that you are suffering as much as Othello or Lear; quite another to be what they are, and suffer such anguish as they do.

Miss Bogan never attempts this tragic or epic strain. She shows us a human being suffering perfectly human, if violent, passions; lovers are brought together or separated, not by the Fates or Cupid or Aphrodite, but by the course of nature; the love depicted is not that of Iseult or Dido, but love as most of us know it; we see the events, not against any romantic background, but in perfectly ordinary, if vivid, settings—chiefly New England countryside; and what happens is important because of the individuals concerned, not because of any greater consequences.

We must beware of reading independent lyric poems as if they made up a novel. Miss Bogan's poems, for instance, are independent lyrics, and they nearly always depict a single moment of passion or thought. But poems which deal with a moment may or may not deal with it as involved in a context of other events. In the case of Herrick's "Whenas in silks my Julia goes," for example, we never dream of asking in what particular circumstances the lover spoke, or of asking what happened before or after; the moment is separated from all circumstance and from any other event. Miss Bogan's poems sometimes deal, similarly, with the isolated moment; more characteristically, however, they imply a context of events; and it is that context which I am attempting to suggest here. Moreover, I should say that she scores special triumphs by selecting, not the moment when affairs themselves are at a crisis, but the moment which makes its context most significant and intelligible. I have a distinction in mind which a single example may make clear. Think of *Porphyria's Lover*; Browning had the choice of depicting a moment of crisis, say the strangulation of Porphyria, or the moment when the whole course of events could best be manifested and contemplated; quite different effects must follow, of course, as one or the other is shown, though in any case the tale must be one of violent emotions. Hardly anyone would doubt, I think, that Browning gets a particular effect by showing the lover, serene and mad, holding his strangled mistress in his arms as if she were still alive, and musing calmly on what has happened. Passions do not rage to the point of murder in Miss Bogan's poems, but she does similarly select the comprehensive rather than the climactic.

I have been speaking of *what* she depicts; the manner in which she depicts it serves to heighten and reinforce the characteristics of her subject. She tends to be reticent as to what is happening or what has happened, while at the same time she sets forth the attendant circumstances in vivid detail. That reticence she manages in various ways; her character speaks with all the assumptions consequent upon shared experience, as in *Old Countryside*, or makes guarded references to what has happened, as in *For a Marriage*, or interprets something as only a person who has suffered devastating passion would interpret it, as in *Feuer-Nacht*, or uses a narrative technique which simply does not tell all it might, as in *The Changed Woman*.

The consequence is that the personages of these poems appear to us as they might by a lightning-flash, or as they might be glimpsed from a swift train; they are caught in attitudes obviously significant, which we cannot interpret, they make gestures passionate but mysterious. In *Porphyria's Lover*, Browning tells us what happened; Bogan hints. But the setting, the whole circumstantial periphery of action, is shown with great vividness, the sharp images compel our imagination and our belief, the reticent and yet pregnant method of representation forces us to wonder and conjecture; and a part of the inexhaustible fascination of these poems surely resides in the fact that no conjecture fully satisfies us. I am blundering here, I know, for I find all this very difficult to say; let me try one last comparison: her poems are like pictures of scenes from some passionate and bitter play which we have not seen; the décor is brilliantly clear, the characters are fixed in poses which betray much, if only we could interpret.

Old Countryside is a perfect example of this method:

> Beyond the hour we counted rain that fell
> On the slant shutter, all has come to proof.
> The summer thunder, like a wooden bell,
> Rang in the storm above the mansard roof,
>
> And mirrors cast the cloudy day along
> The attic floor; wind made the clapboards creak.
> You braced against the wall to make it strong,
> A shell against your cheek.
>
> Long since, we pulled brown oak-leaves to the ground
> In a winter of dry trees; we heard the cock
> Shout its unplaceable cry, the axe's sound
> Delay a moment after the axe's stroke.
>
> Far back, we saw, in the stillest of the year,
> The scrawled vine shudder, and the rose-branch show
> Red to the thorns, and, sharp as sight can bear,
> The thin hound's body arched against the snow.

Here the physical circumstances are as clear as possible; but what is the further history which is hinted at in "all has come to proof"? Perhaps only the growth of love; perhaps more.

A Packet of Letters is less concerned with circumstance, but is charged with bitter mystery:

> In the shut drawer, even now, they rave and grieve—
> To be approached at times with the frightened tear;
> Their cold to be drawn away from, as one, at nightfall,
> Draws the cloak closer against the cold of the marsh.
>
> There, there, the thugs of the heart did murder.
> There, still in murderers' guise, two stand embraced, embalmed.

Again, in one of her best and longest poems, the extraordinary *Summer Wish*:

> . . . the betraying bed
> Is gashed clear, cold on the mind, together with
> Every embrace that agony dreads but sees
> Open as the love of dogs.

Indeed, she can imply a whole history of terror and pain in a line or so:

> Never, for them, the dark turreted house reflects itself
> In the depthless stream.

Her images range over all kinds of feelings. Here are a few samples of her visual imagery; this, from *Statue and Birds*:

> The birds walk by slowly, circling the marble girl,
> The golden quails,
> The pheasants, closed up in their arrowy wings,
> Dragging their sharp tails.

This, from *Winter Swan*:

> Here, to the ripple cut by the cold, drifts this
> Bird, the long throat bent back, and the eyes in hiding.

This, from *Summer Wish*:

> The cloud shadow flies up the bank, but does not
> Blow off like smoke. It stops at the bank's edge.
> In the field by trees two shadows come together.
> The trees and the cloud throw down their shadow upon
> The man who walks there. Dark flows up from his feet
> To his shoulders and throat, then has his face in its mask,
> Then lifts.

And this, from *The Flume*, a remarkable narrative poem which she does not include in her *Collected Poems*:[2]

> At night his calm, closed body lay beside her . . .
> Her hair sweeps over his shoulder, claiming him hers . . .

She is as brilliant in depicting other sensations:

> . . . she gave her kisses
> Beside rough field-stones piled into a wall
> Cold as the wind in every particle.

Here is a tremendous auditory image, from *A Letter*, which I believe she has not reprinted since her first book:

> the scene where that girl
> Lets fall her hair, and the loud chords descend
> As though her hair were metal, clashing along
> Over the tower, and a dumb chord receives it?

These images are striking even in isolation, because of the perceptions which they record. In one way, as I have just said, they are quite various; in another, they are all of a single kind. Images can be classified according as they give us the unmodified perception, or the perception as modified by the state and circumstance of the perceiver.[3] Miss Bogan limits herself, I think almost entirely, to the first kind; she gives the object simply, "as it is"—that is, as any good perceiver, unaffected by emotion or a particular point of view, would see it; and as a consequence she builds up a very real and solid world to serve as the theater of her brief and poignant dramas. Any reader of Defoe knows how circumstantiality produces belief; conviction is even greater when the circumstance is rendered in a vivid image.

Imagery of this order has to be an "accurate" depiction of the object; Miss Bogan is accurate to the point where her images seem to deal with permanent and inalienable aspects of the objects, and to do so definitively; one has the feeling that, whatever else might be said about the objects, these things *must* be said, and that it would be difficult if not impossible to say anything further about them, in this objective fashion. For example, she speaks of

> the pillared harp, sealed to its rest by hands—
> (On the bright strings the hands are almost reflected,
> The strings a mirror and light.)

After that, I submit, it is a little hard to say anything more about harps.

She does not merely choose the salient and "essential" characteristics, however; she chooses those which in addition imply other characteristics, and thus she effects wonders with a few strokes. Look at that winter swan again; it is not merely a swan, but a whole season seen in terms of a swan. Or see how, in two lines of *Hypocrite Swift*, she conveys the silence, the immobility, the spaciousness, the chill and formal elegance, even the eerie loneliness of a scene:

> On the walls at court, long gilded mirrors gaze.
> The parquet shines; outside, the snow falls deep.

Since she deals with experiences which we all have, seen clearly and without exaggeration and distortion, she usually avoids figurative language, and remains perfectly literal; when she does use metaphor, it is with telling force. In the lines just quoted, "gaze" is the only metaphor; but it gives us immediately an impression of fixity, of still brightness untroubled by reflected motion, over a long period of time. "The parquet shines"; and "shines" echoes that notion; we get the impression that the mirrors reflect the parquet, the parquet reflects the mirrors; there is nothing else, except that, dumbly, "outside, the snow falls deep." No presence, no sound, no motion—not so much as a candle's flickering—in the chambers, though our view has ranged from ceilings to floors with the word "long" and along the floors with the word "shines." When we see a place once noisy and crowded, now vacant and silent, an eeriness comes over us; the more spacious it is, the more crowded with tokens of its former busyness, the sharper the feeling; that is why, I think, we feel it so keenly here. In short, late winter night in the eighteenth century, in a palace, complete in all essentials; sixteen words.

Her style is generally plain, terse, bare to the point of austerity, seldom involving uncommon words or constructions; we are not likely to notice this because of the absorbing things she does with it. When we do notice it, we are likely to conclude hastily that hers is simply the style of common speech. This is not quite the case; indeed, she achieves some startling feats by using a common word, literally and apparently in its usual sense, and yet with extraordinary force. A single example must serve here. "Mix" is surely a common enough word; few would suppose, offhand, that it could be used to much poetic effect, let alone for a whole variety of effects. But look what she can do with it:

> A mirror hangs on the wall of the draughty cupola.
> Within the depths of the glass mix the oak and the beech leaf . . . .

> The crafty knight in the game, with its mixed move . . .

> Dream the mixed, fearsome dream.

To sum this up hastily: Bogan is a poet of the violent emotions; she depicts with severe economy, with reticence and by implication; her images are "objective," and her language is plain and natural. In each of these respects, Léonie Adams is her opposite. Miss Adams is a poet of the calm and gentle emotions; life and love and death are here, to be sure, but not as arousing any fierce passion; grief is changed to melancholy, even joy, perhaps, to quiet delight. Bogan deals largely with thoughts and emotions aroused by external events; Adams' poetry is private, in the sense that she is moved not so much by what happens as by what her subtle and exquisite mind makes of it. She depicts, not with economy and implication, but by aggregation and suggestion. Since the starting point of her emotions and reflections is generally a particular imaginative perception, her imagery is seldom objective; and since her poems record the experiences of a mind of extraordinary quality, literal language and the forms of common speech are inadequate for her; she is forced to use many metaphors and other figures, and her diction is elaborate, rich, and artificial.

A mind and a style really unique are impossible to describe; and Miss Adams' art is so delicate that to say it produces an effect of enchantment, that it places one in landscapes of vision or dream, is at once to vulgarize it. It does produce enchantment, and does deal in visions and dreams, however. Her imagination translates her sensations into something rare and strange. Common objects appear as they would under special conditions of light and atmosphere, strangely brightened and enhanced, and somehow made portents and tokens of something still more strange. I have said that Louise Bogan's imagery is solid and substantial because it ranges over all forms of feeling, and gives us objects as they naturally and familiarly appear. Adams' imagery is chiefly visual and auditory; objects seem weightless as they do in dreams, shapes are etherealized, colors are made purer and more luminous, sounds clearer and more delicate. All things appear, whatever sense they appeal to, as they might to one in a drowsy fever, or between sleeping or waking, or fast in a spell.

Chiefly she seems to "outstare substantial stuff," as she herself says:

> The day comes wildly up the east,
> Because the cup of vision broke,
> And those clear silver floods released
> Go ravaging the calm sky of night;
> And all who to that seeing woke
> Look coldly on a common sight,
> As to outstare substantial stuff.
> The substance never is enough
> When lids are drenched apart by light . . . .

Her marvelous imagination, or, if you will, her vision, thus gives her extraordinary things: waters, for instance, so clear

> They will stain drowning a star,
> With the moon they will brim over.

or sky

> . . . in which the boughs were dipped
> More thick with stars than fields with dew

or leaves

> . . . deepening the green ground
> With their green shadows, there as still
> And perfect as leaves stand in air . . .

When she does offer us what I have called "objective" imagery, however, she does so with great effect. Here, for instance, is the very essence of a winter nightfall, more economical and precise than Eliot's first *Prelude*:

> December, mortal season, crusts
> The dark snows shuffled in the street,
> And rims the lamp with sleet.
> The beggar, houseless, chill, and thin,
> Leans to the chestnut vendor's coals,
> The cart creaks off which trails the winter bush,
> And the thick night shuts in.

This is surely very close to the vein of Shakespeare's "When icicles hang by the wall" or Blake's "When silver snow decks Susan's clothes / And cold jewel hangs at th' shepherd's nose."

Like Bogan, she exhibits a single character; herself, quite probably; and we see her chiefly as engaged in the exquisite contemplation of the phantasma of her thought. *Twilight Revelation* is typical of her art:

> This hour was set the time for heaven's descent,
> Come drooping toward us on the heavy air,
> The sky, that's heaven's seat, above us bent,
> Blue faint as violet ash, you near me there
> In nether space, so drenched in goblin blue
> I could touch Hesperus as soon as you.
>
> Now I perceive you, lapped in singling light,
> Washed by that blue which sucks whole planets in,
> And hung like those top jewels of the night,
> A mournful gold too high for love to win.
> And you, poor brief, poor melting star, you seem
> Half to sink, and half to brighten in that stream.
>
> And these rich-bodied hours of our delight
> Show like a mothwing's substance when the fall
> Of confine-loosing, blue, unending night
> Extracts the spirit of this temporal.
> So space can pierce the crevice wide between
> Fast hearts, skies deep-descended intervene.

Here a perception transmuted by imagination generates all; she sees twilight, not as we do, as simple twilight; she sees it as the descent of the heavens, as the actual incursion of outer space into the earth's atmosphere. And thus her lover, near her as he is, seems remote "in nether space"; "so drenched in goblin blue," so "washed by that blue which sucks whole planets in," that he is remote as a star. She feels him, thus, "too high for love to win"; he is, moreover, seen as but a brief and transitory thing among the perduring stars, even as he is momentarily transfigured by the light which he shares with them; and all the time of love, rich as it is, seems suddenly insubstantial as a moth's wing. Thus, she muses, between even the most closely-bound hearts, the skies intervene; and twilight has become a portent both of the brevity of love (for merely by setting it against the eternal, we see that it is not) and of the essential isolation of the human soul; this whatever lovers feel or say.

Notice that all the imagery is of the same order as, and is a consequence of, the very first image; and the moment we imagine the first, we enter into her own thought, strikingly original as it is, and feel as she does, in perfect sympathy with her. Identification and sympathy or empathy are not so general in art as theorists have tended to claim; they result only when the artist has brought us perfectly into the frame of mind of his character and set forth the cause or object of emotion precisely as the character apprehends it. In Miss Bogan's poetry, for instance, the effect depends upon our considering the poetic character as distinct from ourselves; Miss Adams, on the contrary, demands identification. This is one reason why she uses more imagery than Bogan; she must at all times make us see things as she sees them, to carry us with her.

It is a reason, too, why she depends upon suggestion, rather than implication. Implication can operate only when we are familiar with consequences; where interpretations and consequences are very unusual, we cannot infer to any great effect. I doubt, for example, whether many of us—if any of us—would have been able of ourselves to see twilight as "heaven's descent" in the sense in which Miss Adams does, and whether any of us would have been able to intuit from it, as she does so easily and naturally, the transience and loneliness of love, together with the poignant beauty of that transience and loneliness. Suggestion is another matter; our minds can be led along a given course, familiar or unfamiliar, by the evocation of certain ideas in certain conjunctions. When Bogan makes us feel the still brightness of the court, it is by implication, and we can reduce it to syllogism: *if* the mirrors "gaze" and the parquet shines with unbroken tranquillity, *then* the chambers are deserted, and so on. But compare that with the following lines from Adams' *The Rounds and the Garlands Done*:

> Day that cast the lovely looks is sped,
> And from the turf, circled with white dew,
> The lovers and the children are gone;
> Leaving the wreath, the bouquet fresh, looped up with grasses.

> All the golden looks are spent,
> And the time of the rounds and the garlands done.

Here we feel that we are looking upon the earth of the Golden Age, or at least that of some eternal pastoral; the sunlight was surely not ours, but that which shines in the poems of Sappho, in *Daphnis and Chloe*, or in Sidney's *Arcadia*. But the poet has neither said nor implied that it was; she has merely suggested it by a few cunning phrases; and her magic is so subtle and immediate that we must make a special effort to realize that perhaps, after all, she was talking about a scene in a park.

Indeed, her words bring to mind almost constantly the customs, beliefs, arts, and sciences of an older day; they cast, thus, a veil which half brightens, half obscures the immediate reality. These excerpts call to mind old customs, for example:

> Then, tatter you and rend,
> Oak heart, to your profession mourning . . .

> "Of my father's father I got a proud steed,
> And a barb of my father I took" . . . .

> The lost was twenty jewels worth . . .

These, surely, recall an old cosmogony:

> Cast on the turning wastes of wind
> Are cords that none can touch or see . . . .

>   . . . older than the golden sun
> And his measure trod with night.

The following, again, recall Renaissance sculpture and pre-Renaissance painting:

> There marble boys are leant from the light throat,
> Thick locks that hang with dew and eyes dewlashed,
> Dazzled with morning, angels of the wind,
> With ear a-point for the enchanted note.

>   . . . so at the innocent lady's feet
> The blond, the young, delicate ones of heaven,
> Stare at the pretty painted skies.

If her thought is in an older key, her language shows the same deliberate archaism. It has been called Elizabethan; as a matter of fact, it is not; yet there is this much truth in calling it so, that she reminds one more of the Elizabethans and of certain metaphysical poets—Traherne and Marvell especially, I should say—than of anyone else, even such astute imitators of the Elizabethan and Jacobean as Darley and Beddoes. It would be absurd to condemn her on this account, and I do not suppose that any sensible person ever would; perhaps nine-tenths of the greatest glories of English poetry are written in some sort of artificial language. The real question is whether her diction is effective or not; and her successes are so overwhelming that there is no point to the question.

All this archaism has the same function: to remove any sense of immediacy which might produce violent emotion, and to address the gentler instead; that is, to soften and transform emotion much as time itself does. The wilder emotions are produced by immediacy, the gentler by remoteness; the *Iliad* sets us in the very midst of its events, ancient and half-mythical as they were, and excites emotions of one kind; the *Eve of St. Agnes* places its events far back, and evokes emotions of the other.

But there is this point, too, as far as the archaism of her ideas is concerned: that ideas function very differently in poetry from the manner in which they do in science or philosophy. In the latter they have value as they are adequate or true, and as they have logical consequences of some value; in poetry they have value as they affect imagination and emotion. For ideas have an imaginative and emotional dimension as well as an intellectual one; Dante's notion of Hell is a sublime and terrifying one, whether it be true or false, and poets of our own day (Millay, for one) have continued to use the idea of the planetary atom, discarded though it is by science, because of the sheer magnificence of the notion that our universe could thus consist of an infinity of worlds within worlds, a thought, as Emerson says, "to dwindle our astronomy into a toy." Donne and Milton similarly used outworn conceptions of science purely for their emotional effect. The question of when philosophic or scientific thought becomes poetic material—a question often raised since the early nineteenth century—seems to me to have a very obvious and certain answer; it does so whenever the emotional qualities of thought can be actualized.

In an age of startling poetic innovations, neither Miss Bogan nor Miss Adams has been thought of as an innovator. I think they have not quite had their rights in this matter. In the matter of versification alone, each made important advances. Bogan broke up the "tight" and regular stanza-forms with some very original variations, while retaining the general effect of strictness and regularity, and she also contrived, in *Summer Wish*, for example, a distinctly modern development of blank verse, highly plastic and serviceable. Adams' innovations in versification are too numerous and too subtle to discuss here; I shall bluntly say, at whatever risk of exciting indignation, that no poet of our day, not even Yeats, can be said to have a finer and more delicate ear.

The question of how much of the work of these poets will last is a natural and unavoidable one; it is also rather a futile one. The only guarantee an artist can have against fortune lies in the integrity, soundness, and discipline manifest in his art. That Miss Bogan and Miss Adams possess this guarantee is, I should say, beyond question.

Notes

1. *Collected Poems: 1923–53*, by Louise Bogan, The Noonday Press (New York, 1954); *Poems: A Selection*, by Léonie Adams, Funk and Wagnalls Company (New York, 1954).

2. Both Miss Bogan and Miss Adams have omitted excellent and characteristic poems from their volumes, to my very great regret. I have nevertheless considered their work as a whole in this essay; I hope that they do not mind.

Miss Adams' volume contains many drastic revisions, particularly of the poems in her second volume, *High Falcon*. In every instance they seem to me very much for the worse, even where a point of grammar was involved (e.g., in *Winter Solstice* she had originally written "gamester's shop," on the mistaken notion that a gamester dispensed game; I should rather have that than "steamy shop," where the idea of steam contradicts the feeling of intense cold given by the rest of the passage). I have, however, followed her latest text in every quotation; perhaps my reactions to her revisions are merely the consequence of having carried around *High Falcon* until I wore it out.

3. Perhaps these points should be developed, in case anyone is interested in them. The terms *image, symbol, description*, and *metaphor* are often used interchangeably. I think this usage blurs important distinctions; at any rate, for the purposes of this essay I should like to distinguish them as follows.

An image is any verbal expression immediately activating the imagination, whether a phantasm of some sensory impression is formed (as when a sight, sound, taste, and so on are imagined) or some other "feeling" (such as of pressure, motion, weight, heat, cold, vertigo, lassitude, energy, or the bodily conditions attending particular emotions). A description is an account which addresses the intellect rather than the imagination, dealing with ideas rather than with imaginative syntheses; if the imagination is thus activated, it is through the mediation of an idea. When I say the ice was one hundred twenty feet high, I describe it; the reader who wishes to imagine it does so of his own accord, and he must do so by first visualizing an object which he knows to be of similar height, say, a water-tower. When I say the ice was mast-high, the reader immediately forms a picture of a berg in relation to a ship.

A metaphor is a transposition of names or terms, on the ground of similarity. Mr. Charles Feidelson, Jr., argues to the contrary (*Symbolism and American Literature* [The University of Chicago Press, 1953], pp. 58 ff.). I can only say here that I can accept none of his arguments. Metaphor may be present without image, image without metaphor: Marvell's "My love is of a birth as rare," etc., in *The Definition of Love* involves metaphor without image, even though the metaphor of birth is insisted upon; conversely, there is no metaphor in "Ice mast-high came floating by / As green as emerald"; but there is certainly an image.

A symbol, as I have argued elsewhere (*Critics and Criticism, Ancient and Modern*, ed. R. S. Crane [The University of Chicago Press, 1952], pp. 567–594) results from an identification of one concept with another; when an image is linked to a symbolic concept, the image is itself symbolic; but it is neither the case that all images are symbols, nor that all symbols are images.

Taking the term *image* as thus distinguished, we may, for literary purposes, differentiate three kinds: 1) images which present an unmodified perception, so that we feel we have received an "objective" account; 2) those which seem modified by the character or condition of the perceiver, and in this group we may distinguish between images in which (a) we primarily conceive the object to be possessed of certain qualities, or (b) we primarily interpret the perception as significant of the condition of the perceiver. Thus Miss Bogan's images give the effect of accurate perceptions; Miss Adams', as I shall try to show later, give the effect of imaginative interpretations of perceptions and feelings; while the speaker in Tennyson's *Maud*, saying of the "dreadful hollow" that "Its lips in the field above are dabbled with blood-red heath, / The red-ribbed ledges drip with a silent horror of blood" is actually telling us less about the hollow than about his own condition. I intend this not as a distinction of images as good or bad but as differing in kind and as having different effects. Nor do I mean to imply that images of the first class involve no poetic imagination; on the contrary, I assume that the poetic imagination is at work, though diversely, in all of them.

All these kinds of images permit of various modes of construction, which seem to cause the imagination of the reader to operate in different ways. It may be worthwhile to note a few of these: 1) images based on comparison, in which we are forced to imagine one thing as a standard for another, as in "ice mast-high"; 2) those based on mental transit from cause to effect, whenever the cause is in some way remarkably potent for good or evil, or remarkable simply, as in Bogan's "Like fire in a dry thicket / Rising within women's eyes"; 3) those based on transit from effect to cause, under the same conditions, as in Keats' "And the long carpets rose along the gusty floor"; 4) those based on startling contrast, as in Wallace Stevens' "rouged fruits in snow"; 5) those based on dynamic interrelation, as in "And the owls have awakened the crowing cock." There are many more which cannot be discussed here.

All of these have varying effectiveness in varying contexts; hence we can, in these terms, reach judgments as to a poet's art in handling them. To offer a single example here: nothing is more trite than the comparison of passion to a flame, and the imagination will not respond to it; Bogan's "Like fire in a dry thicket" is another matter entirely.

Louise Bogan   Harold Bloom*

Louise Bogan is usually categorized as a poet in the metaphysical tradition or meditative mode, following Donne, Emily Dickinson, and older contemporaries like Eliot and Ransom. Yet, like so many modern poets, she is a Romantic in her rhetoric and attitudes, and her procedure at least tends towards the visionary mode, in the tradition of Blake and Yeats. Her best and most characteristic poems establish their structure by a conflict of contraries, akin to Blake's clashes of Reason and Energy and Yeats' dialogues between Self and Soul. As in Blake and Yeats, there is no transcendence of this strife in Miss Bogan's poems; it is not resolved in the traditional consolations of religious belief, or in the expectation of

*Reprinted, with the permission of the author, from jacket notes, *Louise Bogan Reads from Her Own Works*, Yale Series of Recorded Poets, Decca Records, DL 9132. Copyright 1958 by Harold Bloom.

any permanent abiding place for the human spirit. The frequent fierce-
ness of Miss Bogan's rhetoric proceeds from a bitterness born of the
unresolved contraries, the demands of reason and energy, of limiting
form and the exuberance of desire, for Miss Bogan is purely a lyrical
poet, and lacks the support of the personal systems of Blake and Yeats,
by which those poets were able more serenely to contemplate division
in the psyche. Miss Bogan is neither a personal myth-maker in the
full Romantic tradition, like her near-contemporary Hart Crane, nor an
ironist in the manner of Tate, to cite another poet of her generation.
The honesty and passion of her best work has about it, in consequence,
a vulnerable directness.

The poems on this recording largely follow the sequence of Miss
Bogan's *Collected Poems*, for that sequence hints at a kind of ordering,
in which the unresolved contraries of the poet's world move towards a
delicate and tentative balance. *Medusa* makes an effective introduction
to the landscape of Miss Bogan's poetry. What is conveyed here is a
sense of unreality pervading a desolation. The scene has a frozen-fast
quality pointing towards the inner significance of the Medusa myth.
The poem is altogether oblique in its presentation. What is offered is
an image of the memory itself turned to stone, a hint of the theme of
the rejection of nostalgia to be developed in the later poems.

Men Loved Wholly Beyond Wisdom is a gnomic parable, with overtones of the Blake of *Ah Sunflower!* and the Yeats of "Never give all the
heart." The poem is a miniature dialectic, with the contrary statement
rising from the sixth line onwards. The final figure of the cricket is a
striking emblem akin to those of Blake's state of Experience. Lighter
and still more laconic is the subtle lyric, *The Crossed Apple*, with its
flavor of New England speech. Here, in a poem "about" the co-existent
contraries of the freedom and necessity of choice one can observe re-
minders of the archetypal apple-tasting in Eden, but we recognize a
humanistic emphasis:

> This apple's from a tree yet unbeholden,
> Where two kinds meet,—

The preceding poems are preparations for Miss Bogan's most am-
bitious poem, *Summer Wish*, which marks the crisis and mid-point of
her work. Here the influence of Yeats is explicit and acknowledged, with
the poem's epigraph being the opening of the pastoral lament for
Robert Gregory, *Shepherd and Goatherd*. Two voices speak in alternation in *Summer Wish*, with the passionate soul expressing its longings,
and the observent self describing the phenomena of its mutable world
moving slowly towards summer, the season desired by the soul. The
two voices fail consistently to heed the other, in an extended ironic
vision of the divided psyche.

The first voice begins by crying out for full rebirth, rejecting the spring as a false hope. The second voice counters by calmly describing the very end of winter, the first touches of spring. The first voice reminds itself that experience denies the reality of its full, earlier yearning forwards, and categorizes love as fantasy. The second voice moves on to detail the early growth of the signs of renewal. The first voice, reproving itself yet more harshly, rejects the saving grace of memory. The second voice describes early April, and the movement towards summer. The first voice increases in bitterness, expounding the contraries of passion. The second voice, as if almost in response, describes the meeting of two figures with a gradual revelation of the man of the pair. Half in response, the first voice rejects the self-comfort to be found by the pride of one's own solitariness. The second voice now ceases to be as purely neutral in its descriptiveness, and emphasizes the sensuous beauty still to be found in the fading of the day. The first voice, again turning from refuges, rejects the mind as comfort. The second voice describes the spring planting, with a new note of purposefulness. The first voice, in its final outcry, acknowledges that earth's year begins, and responds to it, defying itself and the past with wish and laughter, and finding in rock a symbol of ultimate desperation and yet a mode of heroic consolation. The second voice completes the poem with the Yeatsian figure of the hawk's flight as an image both of acceptance and of the effort to hold oneself open to experience:

> See now
> Open above the field, stilled in wing-stiffened flight,
> The stretched hawk fly.

Summer Wish is Miss Bogan's *Resolution and Independence*. Her later poems either celebrate the consequences of having cast out remorse, or return to a fiercer, more impatient preoccupation with the self.

Henceforth From the Mind is an exultant Romantic lyric, chanting in Yeatsian accents the greater sweetness that has flowed into the remorseless breast, and yet acknowledging with regret (as in the second stanza) the necessity for resignation to some permanent sense of loss. The Wordsworthian image of the sea-shell betokens a darker music of mature imagination, similar to the "sober-coloring" of the close of the *Intimations* ode.

The Sleeping Fury renews the Medusa image in an address to the self as the soul's dark double, "my scourge, my sister," and ends in the deliverance of a fuller awareness of both self and soul. *Putting to Sea* praises the enterprise of entering the abyss of the self, the dangerous exploration of our darkness. *The Dream* is Miss Bogan's most dramatic and convincing portrayal of the split in the self, with its renewal of the ancient myth of the appeased fury. *Song for the Last Act* is a graceful parting poem, being both a love song and a ritual of acceptance. Read at the end, it serves to round off the record of a life of humanistic craftsmanship.

The Poetry of Louise Bogan   Theodore Roethke*

Two of the charges most frequently levelled against poetry by women are lack of range—in subject matter, in emotional tone—and lack of a sense of humor. And one could, in individual instances among writers of real talent, add other aesthetic and moral shortcomings: the spinning-out; the embroidering of trivial themes; a concern with the mere surfaces of life—that special province of the feminine talent in prose—hiding from the real agonies of the spirit; refusing to face up to what existence is; lyric or religious posturing; running between the boudoir and the altar, stamping a tiny foot against God; or lapsing into a sententiousness that implies the author has re-invented integrity; carrying on excessively about Fate, about time; lamenting the lot of the woman; caterwauling; writing the same poem about fifty times, and so on.

But Louise Bogan is something else. True, a very few of her earliest poems bear the mark of fashion, but for the most part she writes out of the severest lyrical tradition in English. Her real spiritual ancestors are Campion, Jonson, the anonymous Elizabethan song writers. The word order is usually direct, the plunge straight into the subject, the music rich and subtle (she has one of the best ears of our time), and the subject invariably given its due and no more. As a result, her poems, even the less consequential, have a finality, a comprehensiveness, the sense of being all of a piece, that we demand from the short poem at its best.

The body of her complete poetic work is not great, but the "range," both emotional and geographical, is much wider than might be expected from a lyric poet. There is the brilliant (and exact) imagery of her New England childhood; there is also the highly formal world of Swift's Ireland; the rich and baroque background of Italy called up in the evocative "Italian Morning." And, of course, her beloved Austria. Her best lyrics, unlike so much American work, have the sense of a civilization behind them—and this without the deliberate piling up of exotic details, or the taking over of a special, say Grecian, vocabulary.

Invariably these effects are produced with great economy, with

*Reprinted, with the permission of the publisher, from *On the Poet and His Craft: Selected Prose of Theodore Roethke*, ed. Ralph J. Mills, Jr. (Seattle: University of Washington Press, 1965), pp. 133–48. This essay first appeared in *Critical Quarterly* in 1961.

the exact sense of diction that is one of the special marks of her style. Even out of context, their power, I believe, is evident. Thus, in "Hypocrite Swift," a curious tour de force which incorporates many actual phrases from Swift's Journal to Stella, there suddenly occurs the stanza:

> On walls at court, long gilded mirrors gaze.
> The parquet shines; outside the snow falls deep.
> Venus, the Muses stare above the maze.
> Now sleep.

For one terrifying instant we are within Swift's mind, in eighteenth-century Ireland, sharing the glitter, the horror and glory of his madness. Again, from the poem "Italian Morning," the lines:

> The big magnolia, like a hand,
> Repeats our flesh. (O bred to love,
> Gathered to silence!) In a land
> Thus garnished, there is time enough
>
> To pace the rooms where painted swags
> Of fruit and flower in pride depend,
> Stayed as we are not.

The "garnished" and the "painted swags" are triumphs of exactitude in language; they suggest the elaborate background without recourse to merely baroque diction.

This is only one, and by no means the best, of Miss Bogan's poems on time, on change, on the cessation of time. Even in her earliest work, she seems to be seeking a moment when things are caught, fixed, frozen, seen, for an instant, under the eye of eternity.

A very early piece, "Decoration," printed in her first book, *Body of This Death*, but not in the Collected, is, I believe, a beginning, a groping toward this central theme:

> A macaw preens upon a branch outspread
> With jewelry of seed. He's deaf and mute.
> The sky behind him splits like gorgeous fruit
> And claw-like leaves clutch light till it has bled.
> The raw diagonal bounty of his wings
> Scrapes on the eye color too chafed. He beats
> A flattered tail out against gauzy heats;
> He has the frustrate look of cheated kings.
> And all the simple evening passes by:
> A gillyflower spans its little height
> And lovers with their mouths press out their grief.
> The bird fans wide his striped regality
> Prismatic, while against a sky breath-white
> A crystal tree lets fall a crystal leaf.

This is a vulnerable poem in spite of certain felicities (the fine "and all the simple evening passes by," for instance). But the uncharitable might say hardly beyond magazine verse. And even though Miss Bogan disarms us with her title, the poem remains too static, not very interesting syntactically, and the final line plays upon one of the clichés of the twenties: "A crystal tree lets fall a crystal leaf." Still, the scene is looked at steadily and closely: the poem is what it is.

Another early piece, "Statue and Birds," is already a much better poem on essentially the same theme. However, the "Medusa," printed on the page opposite "Decoration" in the first book, is a breakthrough to great poetry, the whole piece welling up from the unconscious, dictated as it were:

> I had come to the house, in a cave of trees,
> Facing a sheer sky.
> Everything moved,—a bell rung ready to strike,
> Sun and reflection wheeled by.
>
> When the bare eyes were before me
> And the hissing hair,
> Held up at a window, seen through a door.
> The stiff bald eyes, the serpents on the forehead
> Formed in the air.
>
> This is a dead scene forever now.
> Nothing will ever stir.
> The end will never brighten it more than this,
> Nor the rain blur.
>
> The water will always fall, and will not fall,
> And the tipped bell make no sound.
> The grass will always be growing for hay
> Deep on the ground.
>
> And I shall stand here like a shadow
> Under the great balanced day,
> My eyes on the yellow dust, that was lifting in the wind,
> And does not drift away.

Now, what does this poem mean?—in final terms? It could be regarded, simply, as a poem of hallucination—a rare enough thing—that maintains its hold on the reader from the very opening lines to the end. But we are told some other things, with the repetitiousness of obsession: "I had come to the house, in a cave of trees": the house itself is in a cave, a womb within a womb, as it were. But notice: "facing a sheer sky"—obviously the "scene" is being played against a backdrop of heaven, of eternity, with everything moving yet not moving—"the bell hung ready to strike."

Then the terrifying moment: "the bare eyes," "the hissing hair," of the anima, the Medusa, the man-in-the-woman, mother—her mother, possibly—again "held up at the window," "seen through a door": certainly feminine symbols. And notice, "the stiff bald eyes, the serpents on the forehead formed in the air"—in erectus, in other words.

The last three stanzas bring us the self-revelation, the terrible finality of the ultimately traumatic experience. I shan't labor the interpretation further, except—why "yellow dust"? To me, it suggests the sulphurous fires of hell, here under the sheer sky of eternity.

I suggest that this is a great lyric and in an area of experience where most writers are afraid to go—or are incapable of going.

Miss Bogan is a contender, an opponent, an adversary, whether it be the devouring or overpowering mother, or time itself. And she can quarrel with her daemon, her other self, as in "Come, Break With Time." Here she manages with great skill the hortatory tone, the command, from which so much bogus poetry often results.

> Come, break with time,
> You who were lorded
> By a clock's chime
> So ill afforded.
> If time is allayed
> Be not afraid.
>
> *I shall break, if I will.*
> Break, since you must.
> Time has its fill,
> Sated with dust.
> Long the clock's hand
> Burned like a brand.
>
> Take the rocks' speed
> And earth's heavy measure.
> Let buried seed
> Drain out time's pleasure,
> Take time's decrees.
> Come, cruel ease.

Notice the remarkable shift in rhythm in the last stanza, with the run-on lines that pick up the momentum of the poem. We are caught up in the earth's whole movement; I am reminded, perhaps eccentrically, of Wordsworth's

> No motion has she now, no force;
>   She neither hears nor sees;
> Rolled round in earth's diurnal course,
>   With rocks, and stones, and trees.

In this instance, I feel one poem supports, gives additional credence, to the other.

Yet Miss Bogan does not rest with that effect. There is a terrible irony in "Let buried seed / Drain out time's pleasure." Then the acceptance that all humans must make: "Take time's decrees." The last line remains for me a powerful ambiguity. Is she like Cleopatra, or Keats, asking for easeful death, or the cruel ease of unawareness, of insentience, of the relief from time that old age provides? There is, of course, no final answer, and none is necessary.

One definition of a serious lyric—it may come from Stanley Kunitz—would call it a revelation of a tragic personality. Behind the Bogan poems is a woman intense, proud, strong-willed, never hysterical or silly; who scorns the open unabashed caterwaul so usual with the love poet, male or female; who never writes a serious poem until there is a genuine "up-welling" from the unconscious; who shapes emotion into an inevitable-seeming, an endurable, form.

For love, passion, its complexities, its tensions, its betrayals, is one of Louise Bogan's chief themes. And this love, along with marriage itself, is a virtual battle-ground. But the enemy is respected, the other is there, given his due; the experience, whatever its difficulties, shared.

Thus, in "Old Countryside":

Beyond the hour we counted rain that fell
On the slant shutter, all has come to proof.
The summer thunder, like a wooden bell,
Rang in the storm above the mansard roof,

And mirrors cast the cloudy day along
The attic floor; wind made the clapboards creak.
You braced against the wall to make it strong,
A shell against your cheek.

Long since, we pulled brown oak-leaves to the ground
In a winter of dry trees; we heard the cock
Shout its unplaceable cry, the axe's sound
Delay a moment after the axe's stroke.

Far back, we saw, in the stillest of the year,
The scrawled vine shudder, and the rose-branch show
Red to the thorns, and, sharp as sight can bear,
The thin hound's body arched against the snow.

This, it need hardly be said, is typical Bogan: the concern with time, the setting put down with great exactitude, the event re-created and then looked back upon—the whole thing vivid in the mind's eye, in the memory. The details are no mere accretion, but are developed with a cumulative surprise and the power of great art.

Notice the oracular, almost Shakespearean finality of "all has come to proof"—and this, at the start of a poem. She announces boldly but not portentously, and we believe. Notice, too, the mastery of the epithet—the cock's "unplaceable cry," the "scrawled vine," the rose-branch "red to the thorns." And then the final triumph of the last image, upon which everything hinges. "The thin hound's body arched against the snow."

But what has come to proof? We are not told, explicitly, nor should we be. Invariably, the final experience, however vivid and exact the imagery, comes to us obliquely. It stays with us, can be brooded upon, and brought, finally, into our lives.

This obliquity, at once both Puritan and feminine, brings Louise Bogan close, despite differences in temperament, to Emily Dickinson and to Marianne Moore. None quails before the eye of eternity; their world is their own, sharply defined. If others enter it, the arrival, the meeting, is on their terms.

Many of the best Bogan poems in this vein are of such complexity and depth that the excerpt is virtually impossible, particularly since Miss Bogan often employs the single developed image with usually at least two levels of meaning. And often, within a very short space, she effects an almost intolerable tension, a crescendo in rhythm, as in "Men Loved Wholly Beyond Wisdom"; or builds up the theme powerfully, as in the remarkable "Feuer-Nacht," and then takes a chance with a generalization without losing the momentum of the poem:

> To touch at the sedge
> And then run tame
> Is a broken pledge.
> The leaf-shaped flame
> Shears the bark piled for winter,
> The grass in the stall.
> Sworn to lick at a little,
> It has burned all.

Some of her best pieces begin with the object perceived, as it were, for an instant, and the image remembered fixed in the mind unforgettably.

However, she is not, as I have said, a poet of the immediate moment, as say, Lawrence, but of the time after, when things come into their true focus, into the resolution, the final perspective. Listen to "Roman Fountain":

> Up from the bronze, I saw
> Water without a flaw
> Rush to its rest in air,
> Reach to its rest, and fall.
>
> Bronze of the blackest shade,
> An element man-made,

Shaping upright the bare
Clear gouts of water in air.

O, as with arm and hammer,
Still it is good to strive
To beat out the image whole,
To echo the shout and stammer
When full-gushed waters, alive,
Strike on the fountain's bowl
After the air of summer.

For me, the opening lines are one of the great felicities of our time: the thing put down with an ultimate exactness, absolutely as it is. Perhaps the two appositives "Bronze of the blackest shade, / An element man-made" in the next stanza are a bit "written"; but "gouts of water" saves everything. Nor do I care much for the evocative outcry—and the arm and hammer image. Yet the poem resolves itself with characteristic candor. We have come a long way in a short space.

I believe this poem will stay in the language: its opening alone demands immortality. Yet it exists, too, as a superb piece of observation; as a phallic poem; as a poem about the nature of the creative act in the no-longer young artist.

In the last lines of this piece, we hear the accent of the later work: a tone of resignation, an acceptance of middle age, a comment, often, on the ironies of circumstance. Of these, I believe "Henceforth, From the Mind" to be a masterpiece, a poem that could be set beside the best work of the Elizabethans:

Henceforth, from the mind,
For your whole joy, must spring
Such joy as you may find
In any earthly thing,
And every time and place
Will take your thought for grace.

Henceforth, from the tongue,
From shallow speech alone,
Comes joy you thought, when young,
Would wring you to the bone,
Would pierce you to the heart
And spoil its stop and start.

Henceforward, from the shell,
Wherein you heard, and wondered
At oceans like a bell
So far from ocean sundered—
A smothered sound that sleeps
Long lost within lost deeps,

> Will chime you change and hours,
> The shadow of increase,
> Will sound you flowers
> Born under troubled peace—
> Henceforth, henceforth
> Will echo sea and earth.

And certainly, "Song," "Homunculus," and "Kept," at the very least, are among our best short lyrics. We are told:

> Time for the pretty clay,
> Time for the straw, the wood.
> The playthings of the young
> Get broken in the play,
> Get broken, as they should.

And, in terms of personal revelation, "The Dream" might be regarded as a later companion piece to "Medusa." In some of these last poems, as "After the Persian," "Song for the Last Act," the rhythms, the music, are richly modulated, highly stylized, grave and slow. Miss Bogan is not repeating herself, but moving into another world. There is no lessening of her powers.

I find my rather simple method of "pointing out"—at which Miss Marianne Moore is such a master—has omitted or underemphasized certain qualities in Louise Bogan's work, and of necessity passed by remarkable poems.

For example, the great variety and surety of her rhythms—that clue to the energy of the psyche. Usually the movement of the poem is established in the very first lines, as it should be:

> If ever I render back your heart,
> So long to me delight and plunder,

or

> To me, one silly task is like another.
> I bare the shambling tricks of lust and pride. . . .

And she is a master of texture, yet always the line is kept firm: she does not lapse into "sound" for the sake of sound, lest the poem thin out into loose "incantatory" effects. Thus:

> Under the thunder-dark, the cicadas resound

or the grave rhythm of

> The measured blood beats out the year's delay

or in "Winter Swan":

> It is a hollow garden, under the cloud;
> Beneath the heel a hollow earth is turned;

> Within the mind the live blood shouts aloud;
> Under the breast the willing blood is burned,
> Shut with the fire passed and the fire returned.

Louise Bogan rarely, if ever, repeats a cadence, and this in an age when some poets achieve a considerable reputation with two or three or even one rhythm. The reason for this is, I believe, her absolute loyalty to the particular emotion, which can range from the wry tenderness and humor of "The Crossed Apple" to the vehemence of "Several Voices Out of a Cloud":

> Come, drunks and drug-takers; come, perverts unnerved!
> Receive the laurel, given, though late, on merit; to whom
>   and wherever deserved.
>
> Parochial punks, trimmers, nice people, joiners true-blue,
> Get the hell out of the way of the laurel. It is deathless
>   And it isn't for you.

This, for me, incorporates the truly savage indignation of Swift— and still manages to be really funny. And even in a poem on a "high" theme, "I Saw Eternity," she can say:

> Here, mice, rats,
> Porcupines and toads,
> Moles, shrews, squirrels,
> Weasels, turtles, lizards,—
> Here's bright Everlasting!
> Here's a crumb of Forever!
> Here's a crumb of Forever!

I have said that Miss Bogan has a sharp sense of objects, the eye that can pluck out from the welter of experience the inevitable image. And she loves the words, the nouns particularly, rich in human association. "Baroque Comment" ends:

> Crown and vesture; palm and laurel chosen as noble and enduring;
> Speech proud in sound; death considered sacrifice;
> Mask, weapon, urn; the ordered strings;
> Fountains; foreheads under weather-bleached hair;
> The wreath, the oar, the tool,
> The prow;
> The turned eyes and the opened mouth of love.

But let us see how this side of her talent operates when she is absolutely open, as in the deeply moving elegy "To My Brother":

> O you so long dead,
> You masked and obscure,
> I can tell you, all things endure:
> The wine and the bread;

The marble quarried for the arch;
The iron become steel;
The spoke broken from the wheel;
The sweat of the long march;

The hay-stacks cut through like loaves
And the hundred flowers from the seed;
All things indeed
Though struck by the hooves

Of disaster, of time due,
Of fell loss and gain,
All things remain,
I can tell you, this is true.

Though burned down to stone
Though lost from the eye,
I can tell you, and not lie,—
Save of peace alone.

The imagery in some of the last poems is less specific, yet still strongly elemental; we have, I think, what Johnson called the grandeur of generality. They are timeless, impersonal in a curious way and objective—not highly idiosyncratic as so much of the best American work is. Her poems can be read and reread: they keep yielding new meanings, as all good poetry should. The ground beat of the great tradition can be heard, with the necessary subtle variations. Bogan is one of the true inheritors. Her poems create their own reality, and demand not just attention, but the emotional and spiritual response of the whole man. Such a poet will never be popular, but can and should be a true model for the young. And the best work will stay in the language as long as the language survives.

[Review of *The Blue Estuaries*]   William Meredith*

There is no way to deal with Louise Bogan, one of the best women poets alive, without engaging the question of what it means to be a woman artist in a man's culture. The question underlies the accomplishment, from Sappho through Sylvia Plath.

Robert Graves would have it that a male culture is an aberration from nature: poetry, which is the divine intuition of woman, should

*Reprinted from the *New York Times Book Review*, 13 October 1968, p. 4. © 1968 by the New York Times Company. Reprinted by permission.

govern our lives. But Robert Frost has observed that in fact our culture tends to think of poetry not as a god-like intuition but as a lady-like accomplishment. "Whenever I catch a man red-handed reading my book," Frost said, "he always tells me, 'My wife's a great admirer of yours.'"

It is this ambivalent prejudice that a woman artist must face—a culture that asks her, which are you, a poetess or a goddess, a little lady poet or a great-breasted, all-knowing mother? It is a question that makes "Have you stopped beating your wife?" seem quite guileless. Like the best artists of her sex, Miss Bogan has both disdained to answer it and given the right answer: I am an observant and feeling human being.

Now that we can see the sweep of 45 years' work in this collection of over a hundred poems, we can judge what a feat of character it has been. The verse character of John Crowe Ransom is a similar accomplishment. The diction, rhythms and forms of the two poets body forth assertions of strong, but never merely eccentric, individuality.

Miss Bogan's diction, as Theodore Roethke pointed out, stems from the severest lyrical tradition in English. She uses this Elizabethan language without the irony Ransom uses to mock his own brocaded speech. With Miss Bogan it is simply a passion for grammatical and etymological accuracy. Hers is a language as supple as it is accurate, dealing with things in their own tones.

In an old quatrain called "Question in a Field," for instance, how extraordinary is her control over four heavy-scented adjectives which any sensible poet would decline to use together and straight: heart-rending, homely, horrible and beautiful. For her they define an unsentimental dialectic.

> Pasture, stone wall, and steeple,
> What most perturbs the mind:
> The heart-rending homely people,
> Or the horrible beautiful kind?

One of the 12 new poems in this collection is called "St. Christopher." In it can be seen both the stiffness and the energy of Miss Bogan's style. (The line "Strength's a derivative thereof" acts out this paradox.)

> A raw-boned and an ignorant man
> Keeps ferry, but a man of nerve.
> His freight a Child and a Child's toy
> (Which is our globe, you will observe.)
>
> But what a look of intent love!
> This is the look we do not see
> In manners or in mimicry.
> Strength's a derivative thereof.

The middle class is what we are.
Poised as a brigand or a barber
The tough young saint, Saint Christopher,
Brings the Child in to the safe harbor.

Reading this book with delight, I was struck (as Roethke must have been in 1961) by how Louise Bogan's reputation has lagged behind a career of stubborn, individual excellence. I hope "The Blue Estuaries" may set things straight.

The Distance from Our Eyes   William Heyen*

I was raised on poems—weren't we all?—that did not terrify, poems that seemed blind to experience. Really, there is nothing drearier than the leap to faith that occurs, say, in Bryant's "To a Waterfowl." I remember two other poems I once had to memorize, Longfellow's "The Reaper and the Flowers" and Leigh Hunt's "Abou Ben Adhem." In Longfellow's poem Death is an angel who takes a mother's flowers, her children, to "the fields of light above"; in Hunt's poem Abou is first among God's children because he loves men the best. And Frost's "The Tuft of Flowers" was one of my high school English teacher's favorites— I wonder if she knew "Design." And Emily Dickinson's "I Never Saw a Moor." I wonder if that teacher knew just how irreverent the Amherst virgin could be. In any case, I think that one of the things poetry ought to do is prepare us for what is ahead. This is one of the senses in which poetry is prophecy. I have to have the feeling that a poet is living in the same world I'm in, that he walks on the ground, that he knows the scenes of his own crimes and the images of his own hope, that he has been where I'm headed. Louise Bogan's poems tell me what I only half want to know. I mean this, of course, as a compliment.

Theodore Roethke, who learned a great deal from her, has written the best-known tribute to Miss Bogan. He distinguishes her from other women poets who hide "from the real agonies of the spirit," who refuse "to face up to what existence is." *The Blue Estuaries* is the portrait of a remarkable sensibility, one free from what Ezra Pound called "emotional slither," one whose constant attempt is to define and dramatize what Roethke himself called "the cold fleshless kiss of contraries" ("Her Becoming") and "the dreary dance of opposites" ("What Can I Tell

*A review of *The Blue Estuaries*. Reprinted, with the permission of the author and the publisher, from *Prairie Schooner*, 43 (Fall 1969), 323–26. © 1969 by University of Nebraska Press.

My Bones?"). In Bogan life is neither all one thing or another. The life force giveth and the life force taketh away. Here is a poetry of meditation. Where to stand in a changing world, a world in which both our desires and the objects of our desires change?—this is the question. I keep going back to "Short Summary" as one of the poems most representative of her stance and voice, and also as one of the poems that best illustrate how in Miss Bogan's work repeated readings yield layers of meaning. My mind is always on the edge of the word that will cut to the quick of this poem:

> Listen but once to the words written out by my hand
> In the long line fit only for giving ease
> To the tiresome heart. I say: Not again shall we stand
> Under green trees.
>
> How we stood, in the early season, but at the end of day,
> In the yes of new light, but at the twice-lit hour,
> Seeing at one time the shade deepened all one way
> And the breaking flower;
>
> Hearing at one time the sound of the night-fall's reach
> And that checked breath bound to the mouth and caught
> Back to the mouth, closing its mocking speech:
> Remind me not.
>
> Soon to dark's mid-most pitch the divided light
> Ran. The balance fell, and we were not there.
> It was early season; it was the verge of night;
> It was our land;
> It was evening air.

Herman Melville once wrote that "in certain moods, no man can weigh this world without throwing in something, somehow like Original Sin, to strike the uneven balance." In "Short Summary": "The balance fell, and we were not there." We disappear in the dark. This is "our land." Roethke has a poem entitled "In Evening Air." He concludes: "How slowly dark comes down on what we do." Often, Miss Bogan's vision is even harder, more austere. The universe shimmers with evil. But ultimately, perhaps, the universe is unknowable, and its mystery is her theme: the body itself is "Mapped like the great / Rivers that rise / Beyond our fate / And distant from our eyes" ("Cartography").

The great strength of Louise Bogan's poetry is its compression. No poet has been more adamant than she in demanding the uncluttered line and the precise image. Some of her early poems, I believe, blur in the mind. There is too much abstraction, too many big, bumbling nouns in "Fifteenth Farewell," "Winter Swan," and in "The Alchemist," for example:

> I burned my life, that I might find
> A passion wholly of the mind,
> Thought divorced from eye and bone,
> Ecstasy come to breath alone.
> I broke my life, to seek relief
> From the flawed light of love and grief.
>
> With mounting beat the utter fire
> Charred existence and desire.
> It died low, ceased its sudden thresh.
> I had found unmysterious flesh—
> Not the mind's avid substance—still
> Passionate beyond the will.

This is a kind of poetry I can't read. All this flesh, will, mind, passion, love, grief, breath, desire add up to an imagined garden without toads. An alchemist is speaking, of course, and his is a life of abstract speculation, but I can't pay attention to what he is saying, can't focus on the issue of his poem. But in *The Blue Estuaries* this kind of poem is certainly in the minority. At her best Miss Bogan achieves what she has described as "effects truly fitted for the condensation of language and the production of 'memorable speech.'" Consider the rhythm and imagery of this stanza from "Old Countryside":

> Far back, we saw, in the stillest of the year,
> The scrawled vine shudder, and the rose-branch show
> Red to the thorns, and, sharp as sight can bear,
> The thin hound's body arched against the snow.

Perhaps the poem in which Miss Bogan says most about what the poet and poem must be and do is "Musician." W. S. Merwin has said that part of being a poet is experiencing the despair that the miracle of a poem will not happen again. It is with this idea that Miss Bogan's poem begins. And what is finally created, it seems, is the song that was hidden in the string, the image in the stone that only needed finding. The poet here is as much of an instrument as is his instrument. The final image suggests the idea of "organicism" within traditional form: "And, under the palm, the string / Sings as it wished to sing."

The Blue Estuaries deals with our partial knowledge, our "partial strength" ("Evening Star"). These poems are strenuous, uncompromising efforts at self-knowledge and, as such, they are prophetic. It is from the poem "Night" that Miss Bogan takes her title:

> The cold remote islands
> And the blue estuaries
> Where what breathes, breathes
> The restless wind of the inlets,
> And what drinks, drinks
> The incoming tide;

Where shell and weed
Wait upon the salt wash of the sea,
And the clear nights of stars
Swing their lights westward
To set behind the land;

Where the pulse clinging to the rocks
Renews itself forever;
Where, again on cloudless nights,
The water reflects
The firmament's partial setting;

—O remember
In your narrowing dark hours
That more things move
Than blood in the heart.

This is an elusive poem. It suggests, though I could argue the opposite, that no man is as remote an island as he holds himself to be. What beats inside him is what beats out there. This is a cold, comforting poem. *The Blue Estuaries* is a cold, comforting book.

Louise Bogan: A Woman's Words   William Jay Smith*

When Louise Bogan died suddenly on 4 February 1970, at the age of seventy-two, there were many tributes to her in the press. None of these said more about her in a direct and moving way and with an economy that matched the economy so characteristic of Miss Bogan's own work than that published in *The New Yorker*,[1] the magazine with which she had been associated for some thirty-seven years:

> The first poetry review that Louise Bogan did for *The New Yorker* appeared in the issue of 21 March 1931, and the last in the issue of 28 December 1968. In this magazine, between those two dates—that is to say, for thirty-eight years—poets good, bad, and indifferent came under a perceptive and just scrutiny. Out of what they did or didn't do with language she often constructed a kind of portrait of them of lasting value. Their work was also, when this was relevant, placed in a line of descent or a tradition. Aesthetic experiments were viewed with an open mind, inflation was punctured, and entrepreneurism was put in its place. At times, the exactness and lucidity of her

*Reprinted from *The Streaks of the Tulip: Selected Criticism*, by William Jay Smith (New York: Seymour Lawrence-Delacorte, 1972), pp. 31–56, © 1972 by William Jay Smith. Reprinted by permission of the author.

criticism suggested that she was attempting to create a new kind of lyric poetry out of statements *about* poetry.

Louise Bogan was born in Livermore Falls, Maine. Both her parents were of Irish descent. Her father's father was a sea captain who sailed out of Portland. Though she returned to New England periodically, when she was tired and wanted to refresh her spirit, her home for most of her adult life was New York City. She lived quietly, almost anonymously, in Washington Heights, in an apartment full of books, with a photograph of Mozart's birthplace on one wall and, from a living-room window, a narrow view, between apartment buildings, of the Hudson River. She published six volumes of poetry and two volumes of literary criticism. A third is now in the process of being printed. She also did a number of distinguished collaborative translations, which include Goethe's "Elective Affinities" and a selection from the "Journal" of Jules Renard.

All the literary honors that *are* an honor to receive she received.[2] To say that she was one of the finest lyric poets of our time is hardly to do her justice; her best poems have an emotional depth and force and a perfection of form that owe very little to the age she lived in and are not likely to go out of style, being a matter of nobody's style but her own. She was a handsome, direct, impressive, vulnerable woman. In whatever she wrote, the line of truth was exactly superimposed on the line of feeling. One look at her work—or sometimes one look at her—made any number of disheartened artists take heart and go on being the kind of dedicated creature they were intended to be. In defense of the true artist, she wrote:

> Come, drunks and drug-takers; come, perverts unnerved!
> Receive the laurel, given, though late, on merit; to whom
>   and wherever deserved.
>
> Parochial punks, trimmers, nice people, joiners true-blue,
> Get the hell out of the way of the laurel. It is deathless
>   And it isn't for you.[3]

To certain elements of her life and work that are touched on here—and clearly by someone who knew her well both as a woman and an artist—I would like to return in a moment.

There were other tributes from poets old and young. One of the most interesting was a poem by Daniel Hoffman that presents her character in cameo; he read it at the Library of Congress shortly after her death:

THE SONNET
(REMEMBERING LOUISE BOGAN)

> The Sonnet, she told the crowd of bearded
>   youths, their hands exploring
>   rumpled girls
>   is a sacred

vessel: it takes a civilization
　　　　to conceive its shape or know
　　　　　　its uses. The kids
　　　　　　stared as though

A Sphinx now spake the riddle of
　　　　a blasted day. And few,
　　　　　　she said, who would
　　　　　　be *avant-garde*

consider that the term is drawn
　　　　from tactics in the Prussian
　　　　　　War, nor think
　　　　　　when once they've breached

the fortress of a form, then send
　　　　their shock troops yet again
　　　　　　to breach the form,
　　　　　　there's no form—

. . . they asked for her opinion of
　　　　'the poetry of Rock.'
　　　　　　After a drink
　　　　　　with the professors

she said, This is a bad time,
　　　　bad, for poetry.
　　　　　　Then with maenad
　　　　　　gaze upon

the imaged ghost of a comelier day:
　　　　I've enjoyed this visit,
　　　　　　your wife's sheets
　　　　　　are Irish linen.

Usually when a poet of Miss Bogan's distinction dies, there has already over the years grown up around his or her body of work an even greater body of fact and fiction about the poet's life. So insistent was Miss Bogan, however, on maintaining her privacy during her lifetime, so reticent about making public any of the details of her private life, that on her death there was no residue of legend for her critics to call upon in writing about her; and that is just the way she wanted it. A collection of the major part of her prose pieces was in her publisher's hands when she died and has now appeared (*A Poet's Alphabet*, New York, 1970). One of the editors of the volume, Robert Phelps, in the draft of an introduction had made a number of personal references—all very laudatory—and had included an entertaining account of a visit he and she had made to Melville's tomb in the Bronx. Louise

Bogan was adamant that the entire piece be rewritten and that all personal references be removed. John Hall Wheelock, one of Miss Bogan's oldest friends, spoke at the memorial service held for her at the Academy of Arts and Letters in New York on 11 March 1970.[4] Mr. Wheelock, quoting W. H. Auden's "In Memory of W. B. Yeats," said that on her death Louise Bogan, like Yeats, had become her poems. And yet another friend, Glenway Wescott, said to me later that it is time now that a legend begin to grow up around those magnificent poems, which seem assured of a long life and which no biographical bits of information are going to damage in any way. I hope that I may be forgiven, therefore, for mentioning first a few personal details about this extraordinary woman whom I knew for almost twenty-five years.

When I first met Louise Bogan in 1947, she was for me already a living legend. I had discovered her poetry in the middle thirties in college. It should be remembered, however, that the woman poet who was then most admired by undergraduates was Edna St. Vincent Millay. Tennessee Williams, then Thomas Lanier Williams and a friend of mine at Washington University, wrote at this time a sonnet that concluded somewhat like this:

> Sappho, O God, has gone her soundless way,
> But spare us a while our glorious Millay!

When I discovered the poems of Louise Bogan in Louis Untermeyer's anthology and in the pages of *The New Yorker*, I looked up every piece of her work I could locate and everything, then very little, that had been written about her. Official biographies said only that she was born in Maine, attended the Girls' Latin School in Boston, and married Curt Alexander, an army officer with whom she lived briefly in New York and later in the Panama Canal Zone. He died shortly after the birth of their only child, a daughter; she later married the poet Raymond Holden, from whom she was divorced after a number of years. It was the passionate intensity and control in her work that appealed to me. I remember on my first trip to New York in the summer of 1938—on my way to France for three months of study—that I wandered into Scribner's and acquired a beautiful, signed copy of *The Sleeping Fury*, which had just been published. I read that book over and over night and day and quoted from it frequently during that summer, much to the disapproval of one or two young writers I then met, who looked down their noses at Louise Bogan and had good words only for W. H. Auden, Stephen Spender, and C. Day Lewis. I gave the book later to a young lady in St. Louis with whom I thought I was in love. She had experienced, if not a passionate interest in me, a passionate interest at least in the poetry of Louise Bogan. She became, many years afterwards, a well-known writer of detective stories, and I often wonder what happened to the book. I have many signed copies of Louise Bogan's work, but I wish I had that one back.

At the time we met in the summer of 1947, Louise Bogan was greatly appreciated among poets but had no great reputation with the general public. For some years her work had been neglected or over-looked, except by a few critics such as Allen Tate and Yvor Winters. She had just been elected to the Institute of Arts and Letters, an honor long overdue. We met in Vermont at the home of Barbara Howes, who was to become my wife shortly afterwards. It was Barbara's magazine *Chimera* that had brought us together: Louise had been a contributor to that review, and a poem of mine had just appeared there. Barbara and I sat for hours at Louise's feet as she quoted poetry and regaled us with stories about the literary world—she always liked to quote Oscar Wilde's description of it as that "poisoned bowl"— that she disliked but that she knew so well. She spoke at length of the new work by her protégé Theodore Roethke, which was sure to make an impression, she said, in spite of its dependence on James Joyce.

Barbara and I left for Europe just after our marriage, and during our three years there we kept in touch with Louise. She was a marvelous letter writer. Often hers were very short letters—"very" she abbreviated as "v."—but little cameos of perceptive comment and feeling, like her poems, like her criticism. When we returned to Vermont, Louise was one of our first visitors. She came regularly, usually once in the summer and once again in the fall, and stayed never for a period of more than four days. (She liked to quote the familiar proverb that guests are like fish; after three days they stink.) We looked forward to Louise's visits; it was always a time of wonderful talk and laughter that gave us both sustenance for months afterwards. Louise was a city person—she loved New York. But the country was important to her—the New England landscape, the sea and mountains that nurtured her poems. She loved it dearly, but she had at the same time a fear of the country, a fear of being trapped there. This feeling of delight in, and terror of, the land-scape runs through all her poems. The fear of being trapped perhaps owed much to an experience years earlier when she and Raymond Hol-den were living in the foothills of the Berkshires. They drove back home one evening to find their country house burning to the ground and all her papers—her entire output since early school days—with it.

Louise did not like to walk, but she loved being driven, and we spent hours driving over the back country roads. We had a cottage on the place, and we tried for years to persuade her to walk up to see it. Ten years went by and she never got up there because we could not drive. What we did most during those days and nights was talk, and talk was always about poetry—hers sparkling with wit and studded with indignation. "Heavenly Dinah!" she would exclaim or, again, "Great God in the foothills!" And she was the only person I ever heard use those lovely expressions. She was a lapsed Catholic, but she did say strongly at times that she felt there must be some supreme power that had shaped all this universe. We always had the feeling that this power was one we could approach only in a civilized manner—in human terms—"Great God in the foothills!"

It was Louise Bogan who introduced Barbara and me to the lovely game of *bouts rimés*. This she had played with her friends Rolfe Humphries, Léonie Adams, Allen Tate, Ford Madox Ford, and others in the twenties. (*Bouts rimés*, of course, means rhymed ends: we would choose the end words, the rhyme scheme, and then as quickly as possible, each produce a poem. I understand that in some of the sessions in the twenties the poets played by the clock, seeing who could first whip off a sonnet. We were not quite that exacting about it but did try to be as quick as possible.) Louise was always fastidious about her writing. She used to say, looking over some of the surrealist rubbish that was then as now being poured out, that any one of us could write that kind of thing in the middle of the night with our hands tied behind our backs. It was wonderful to see what she could produce within a few minutes—often lines of great beauty and depth as well as ones of great wit. Somewhere among my papers I have kept the best of these *bouts rimés*; I wish I had been able to find a few examples to offer. I remember a sonnet she wrote once with amazing speed, using the absurdly difficult rhyme words we had forced upon her. Entitled "Henry James," it concluded with a line that went something like this:

He put on and took off and put on and took off his hat.

Once when Louise was with us in Vermont, she and I went into a small country store to get some supplies. She wanted to purchase some paper on which to work. I offered her what was available—a filler of looseleaf notebook paper. She turned it down firmly and rather grandly, saying, "I could never write poems on paper that has holes in it."

During the period when Barbara Howes and I lived in Greenwich Village, we saw Louise more often. She would come down to dinner on the subway from Washington Heights and then in the early morning hours take a taxi back uptown. A friend of hers and mine has remarked that as an evening of conversation went on, Louise Bogan would become increasingly Irish. She did often come up with stories about her family. She told us a number of times that for years her mother had claimed there were a number of dishes that she could not prepare because she did not possess a double boiler. "Now you know that was silly," Louise said. "Never, never in your life lead a double boiler existence!" There was in Louise Bogan's conversation the same elegance that is in her poems. I have been listening during the past few days to her recordings in the Library of Congress Archive of Recorded Poetry and Literature. With her rich contralto voice, she has the most perfect enunciation that you will encounter among poets today: every consonant, every vowel, every syllable is given its proper value, and then there are the pauses around which the poems are constructed, all carefully observed. She says in her poem "St. Christoper":

> The middle class is what we are.

And in her personal life she prided herself on her middle-class background. When she received some unexpected but deserved honor, she would often remark, but of course only to her closest friends, "Not bad for a little Irish girl from Boston."

Louise Bogan was a warm and generous person, and although she was not easy to know, how rewarding it was to those who knew her well. She was independent, and although she loved seeing people, she did not like to see them in a casual manner. After several enraged and threatening telephone calls from irate, untalented poets whose work she had dismissed in the pages of *The New Yorker*, she had obtained an unlisted phone number. (She disliked the telephone and used it rarely.) I remember that in the early years of our friendship I sometimes called her when I was passing through New York, and each time she would say at once, "I'd love to see you, I'd love to see you, but I've just had a tooth extracted. . . ." After hearing this a few times, I was tempted to say that she wouldn't have any teeth left if she kept having them extracted; but what I understood was that she did not at the moment feel up to seeing anyone, even someone she approved of. We often met for lunch at the Oyster Bar in Grand Central Station, a favorite spot of hers near the New York Public Library, where she enjoyed working, and not far from the trains she loved. (Her daughter persuaded her to fly for the first time a few years ago. I met her after her first flight and she exclaimed, "I have flown through the air like a bird!" as if flying were the most natural thing in the world to a lyric poet. She never really learned, however, to like being *inside* an airplane.) With the trains at hand she felt secure, able perhaps to make a quick getaway if something dreadful developed and in the meantime to relax and enjoy the conversation and the seafood.

John Hall Wheelock tells of meeting Louise Bogan in the twenties when Scribner's, for which he worked as an editor, became her publisher. Scribner's brought out three of her books, but after several years passed, Mr. Wheelock says, her innate distrust of publishers—a distrust shared with Lord Byron and many other poets—asserted itself. She summoned him one day to meet her at a Child's Restaurant near the publishing house. Then for several hours he was forced to listen to the most terrible accusations. She told him that she was going to leave Scribner's for another publisher. "I don't feel like quarreling today, Louise," Mr. Wheelock pleaded, "and if I did, I think I'd like to quarrel with William Carlos

Williams, perhaps, or with Wallace Stevens or someone else, but not with you." Her sense of humor, however, had deserted her, and her decision was final. The house of Scribner lost one of its most illustrious authors, but Mr. Wheelock had not lost a friend. Yet for years afterwards, he says, she would sometimes in a mischievous mood taunt him in the presence of others with what she liked to call "our old quarrel." Even a few weeks before her death she introduced Mr. Wheelock at a meeting of the National Institute of Arts and Letters to an acquaintance and described him as the man who was her publisher before their quarrel.

Allen Tate, also aware of her independent spirit, says: "Louise Bogan ignored literary fashion, went her own way, and as early as the mid-1920s was a lyric poet in the Elizabethan-metaphysical mode—traditional yet wholly original. For the originality is not in the exacerbating image, but in the subtle and elusive vision. No influences can be discerned." It is indeed difficult to point to any clearly defined influences, but it may be interesting to try to pin down one or two. Louise Bogan and I collaborated a few years ago in compiling *The Golden Journey: Poems for Young People* (Chicago, 1965), a happy and rewarding venture for us both. Of our collaboration, in an unpublished account, she had this to say, and I think her remarks may give some clues to her early reading (she said many times that she could not remember what on earth she had done before she learned to read):

> One evening, as I remember, quite casually and in a completely unplanned way, we began the game of "Do you remember?"—and we soon were surprising each other by early enthusiasms that we discovered we shared. Tennyson's "Brook," for example, the first poem which had excited me, around the age of nine or ten. Chesterton's "Song of Quoodle," more or less lost in one of his prose books. An exquisite Kipling lyric, also more or less mislaid in *Puck of Pook's Hill*. The wonderful children's verse of Christina Rossetti and Elizabeth Madox Roberts. . . . We went on and on and sometime after midnight decided that we should do the anthology together.
>
> We had other meetings—one on the outskirts of the MacDowell Colony, where we spent some mornings and afternoons surrounded by piles of books which Bill had transported thither in a station wagon— separate works, for the most part, of this poet or that—for we prided ourselves in *not* anthologizing from anthologies. We laughed a great deal; we were never for one moment bored; and we kept on "remembering."

We took our title from James Elroy Flecker, a poet we both admired. What Louise did not say here—but what she did sometimes relate to friends—was that because guests were not permitted within the Mac-Dowell Colony itself I stayed at a fine motel just below it in a room overlooking a lovely millstream. It was here that Louise joined me each day to work on our anthology. The room was equipped with two extremely large double beds which were just the right height so that we could spread out all our books and materials in front of us. And the motel was equipped with a most efficient bar from which we could order cold drinks, and so looking over the poems and out over the stream, we spent several delightful days. Louise, with her New England sense of propriety, enjoyed the rather *louche* and suggestive notion of having compiled an anthology for young people in a motel bedroom with a younger man.

For the Library of Congress Festival of Poetry held in connection with National Children's Book Week last year, Louise Bogan, on a panel with William Cole to discuss poetry for children, chose to read two poems from *The Golden Journey*. The first, "Ferry Me Across the Water" by Christina Rossetti, she said, was one that means absolutely nothing, perhaps, but one toward which she felt a shock of recognition each time she came on it anew:

> "Ferry me across the water,
>   Do, boatman, do."
> "If you've a penny in your purse
>   I'll ferry you."
>
> "I have a penny in my purse,
>   And my eyes are blue;
> So ferry me across the water,
>   Do, boatman, do!"
>
> "Step into my ferryboat,
>   Be they black or blue,
> And for the penny in your purse
>   I'll ferry you."

Louise pointed out that there are in this poem, simple as it is, overtones of death, the river of Lethe. These are the facts we realize as adults but which the little girl who is speaking does not, and implicit in it is a kind of magic. The other poem she chose to read was one more explicitly concerned with death, "The Midnight Skaters" by Edmund Blunden. In this poem skaters are described on a frozen winter pond while death watches them from the dark waters below. The poem ends:

> Court him, elude him, reel and pass,
> And let him hate you through the glass.

It is significant, surely, that Louise, who had been severely ill not long before, should choose two poems on death.

Critics usually place Louise Bogan as a metaphysical poet, stemming from the seventeenth century, but it is well to remember that as a student at the Girls' Latin School she was nurtured on the poetry of the Victorian era, and to certain Victorian poets she never lost her allegiance.

In teaching, she referred students constantly to "In Memoriam," a great poem that she felt was not sufficiently appreciated today. When asked how to get young people interested in poetry, she answered without hesitation: "Read to them until they can read themselves." There were in her day teachers—"women who were wild about poetry." She had one teacher who introduced the girls to the poetry of A. E. Housman, "who was," she said, "very hot stuff in those days." There was a good deal of nudging and giggling in the classroom, but the teacher insisted that this was *serious*. Another lesser figure whom she then discovered was Arthur Symons; and it was through Arthur Symons that she, like T. S. Eliot, discovered the French poets—Mallarmé, Laforgue, and, of course, Baudelaire. Another poem in *The Golden Journey* that she especially liked was "The Rainy Summer," by Alice Meynell:

> There's much afoot in heaven and earth this year;
> The winds hunt up the sun, hunt up the moon,
> Trouble the dubious dawn, hasten the drear
> Height of a threatening noon.
>
> No breath of boughs, no breath of leaves, of fronds,
> May linger or grow warm; the trees are loud;
> The forest, rooted, tosses in her bonds,
> And strains against the cloud.
>
> No scents may pause within the garden-fold;
> The rifled flowers are cold as ocean-shells;
> Bees, humming in the storm, carry their cold
> Wild honey to cold cells.

If we examine it alongside a poem of Louise Bogan's middle period, "Dark Summer," I think we can recognize certain parallels:

> Under the thunder-dark, the cicadas resound.
> The storm in the sky mounts, but is not yet heard.
> The shaft and the flash wait, but are not yet found.
>
> The apples that hang and swell for the late comer,
> The simple spell, the rite not for our word,
> The kisses not for our mouths,—light the dark summer.

Léonie Adams has spoken brilliantly of some of the early influences and directions in Louise Bogan's work:

> Louise Bogan's first book, which was called *Body of This Death*, had for its underlying theme the redemption of life as in art, music, poetry, and perhaps most of all in a kind of living, of choice. It appeared in 1923, almost fifty years ago, and the obituaries have all quoted poems from it—the ones I've seen. It was not then precocious to have a collection of poems at twenty-five or twenty-six although

for some it was unwise; it was precocious to have a volume in which there was almost no taint of the ungainliness of youth. . . . I met Louise Bogan at about the time of its appearance and although I was dazzled by its accomplishment, I did not then realize—and perhaps it was not until just now when I was reading over all her work and thinking of her over the years that I named to myself—what was perhaps its most extraordinary precocity, her certainty of self-discernment as poet. Perhaps she herself was not aware of it then, but had made the secret compact—as in the old legendary bonds, unbreakable though made unawares—which came to light years later in the words:

> Ignorant, I took up my burden in the wilderness.
> Wise with great wisdom, I shall lay it down upon flowers.[5]

. . . To say that the first book is still quoted from is not to say there is any lack of growth in the work. I think that each new book or portion of a book was an advance of the peculiarly living sort which becomes "apparent by invisible stages". . . I wrote a time ago and feel as strongly or more strongly now that hers was an art of limits, the limits of the inner occasion and of the recognized mode. These are formal limits; but with the discernment of which I have spoken I should say she accepted with some others of the best of her poetic generation that the generation was not to be so abundant as its predecessor, and later within her work as critic she would welcome a generation that would be more abundant again. . . . I was not then aware that *she* was so aware that she must function not only as a poet of her own time but within the limits accorded a woman poet. . . . For the poet of intensity, the lyric poet, awaiting the inner occasion, it is truly rare to manage those occasions with a continuing discretion and to work toward what is to be perfectly achieved and is in the central and tragic mode. . . . There was still at the time not a little of the Matchless Orinda syndrome in readers of women's poetry. It was easy for one of her probity to avoid the mistakes some others had made—those she used to call (after the late Clinch Calkins) the "O God, the pain girls." There could not be the confusion of the role of woman and the role of poet, or any exploitation of the role of woman. She knew, moreover, that she should not model herself upon the women she admired and who were closest to her in time. But she read good women writers, contemporaries such as Viola Meynell, who were not poets but writers of prose and noted in them a marvelous delicacy and restraint at employing the feminine sensibility for the scene. There was no need for a woman to justify this attachment by a philosophy of nature or a metaphysic of angels: she took it for granted. Perhaps to respond effectively to whatever is—the landscape, the room, the scene around—is to love it perceptively, as we love people. This was a part of the feminine way, and one could easily be quite lax and overdo it. In the writers just alluded to, such perceptions were subsidiary to the larger narrative structure, and in the poem she would make them subsidiary to the sequence of unstated statement. Thus she could achieve the lyric intensity without indulging, because it was natural to her, the true voice of woman's feeling.

Louise Bogan herself had much to say about the role of woman as poet. In 1947 she wrote in an essay, "The Heart and the Lyre":

> Certainly it is not a regression to romanticism to remember that women are capable of perfect and poignant song; and that when this song comes through in its high and rare form, the result has always been regarded not only with delight but with a kind of awe. It is a good thing for young women to bring to mind the fact that lost fragments of the work of certain women poets—of Emily Dickinson no less than of the Sappho quoted by Longinus as an example of "the sublime"—are searched for less with the care and eagerness of the scholar looking for bits of shattered human art, than with the hungry eyes of the treasure hunters looking for some last grain of a destroyed jewel. Though she may never compose an epic or a tragic drama in five acts, the woman poet has her singular role and precious destiny. And, at the moment, in a time lacking in truth and certainty and filled with anguish and despair, no woman should be shamefaced in attempting to give back to the world, through her work, a portion of its lost heart.

And in an unpublished essay,[6] written in 1962, entitled "What the Women Said" (first delivered as a lecture at Bennington College), she went into greater detail on the subject of women poets:

> To tell the truth, there is very little that one can say about women poets, past, present, and (presumably) to come. One truth about them is an open secret: when they are bad they are very, very bad, and when they are good, they are magnificent. . . . The problem of the woman artist remains unchanged. Henry James, in *The Tragic Muse*, spoke of "that oddest of animals, the artist who happens to be born a woman." Robert Graves has more recently said that women poets have a distinctly difficult problem, since they must be their own Muse. Farther back in time, in ancient manuscripts, in inscriptions chiseled into rock and marble, in ideograms, in hieroglyphics, and, of course, in print, the discussion has gone on: woman's nature, her place in society, her charm and her wiles, her physiological and economic dilemmas, her open and her hidden powers—attracting, from men and women alike (but chiefly from men), overweening praise as well as blame; temper, contempt; false and true witness; and spite. . . .

In this remarkable essay Louise Bogan discusses many aspects of women writers and calls attention in particular to certain prose writers such as Dorothy Richardson and Virginia Woolf. She has also certain sharp words for Simone de Beauvoir, in the pages of whose large book *The Second Sex* she was, she felt, at one point in her reading trapped:

> Mme. de Beauvoir cherishes, in deep recesses of her existentially trained self, a dislike, even a contempt, for the enigmatic, the intui-

tive, the graceful, the tender, the opalescent, the mercurial side of women's nature—the side that truly complements the virtues of the male. The side that has always been involved centrally in the production of women's art, the side that contributes, as one critic has said, "to the deeply feminine appeal and enchantment of Berthe Morisot's [and Mary Cassatt's] pictures"; the side upon which the great women poets have drawn; the side which sustains the great women novelists. This feeling is reinforced as, just before we close the book, we glance at its formidable index. I recommend to you, on some afternoon of rain and incipient boredom, the perusal of this index, and the ticking off of the names of women artists listed therein. The gaps and *lacunae* are shocking.

She mentions a number of them, and among the most shocking, she says, is that of Louise Labé, one of the greatest French women poets, known in the city of Lyon as *la belle cordelière*, because she was the wife of a ropemaker. Louise Labé, whom Louise Bogan very much admired, wrote some of the finest and most passionate sonnets in any language. Louise Bogan concludes with some careful admonitions:

In women's deportment, we can agree, the brutal, rough, swaggering, masculinized gesture never, somehow, works, the cigars of the young George Sand and the middle-aged Amy Lowell to the contrary notwithstanding. And in her writing, the gentle, tender, nurturing feminine nature certainly precludes ultimate coarseness and harshness, either in tone or in choice of material. Women have never succeeded, for example, in writing true surrealism, except, perhaps, in the case of Djuna Barnes (who is more Joycean than surrealist)—a style closely involved with the hallucinatory, the shocking, and the terrifying effect; with the calculated irrational and the direct or indirect erotic. A younger generation of women poets has allied itself with "far-out" poetic procedures; unsuccessfully. For (and I have looked into this subject with some care) these younger women writers, although published side by side, in anthologies and elsewhere, with their far-out brothers, cannot bring themselves to use Anglo-Saxon monosyllables of a sexual or scatological kind. They swear a little, instead—even Mary McCarthy, even Caitlin Thomas. (An exception to this rule has recently appeared in England. In her long and rather chaotic novel *The Golden Notebook*, Doris Lessing, born in Persia and brought up in Southern Rhodesia, permits herself every license of language. I recommend the results to your attention.)

Fortunately, this limitation in vocabulary does not mean that young women writers today are in any way limited in regard to subject matter. In fact, only recently a young woman of nineteen broke through several taboos formerly prevalent in the British theater. This was Shelagh Delaney, whose play *A Taste of Honey* after a great success, both in London and New York, has been made into a most poignant motion picture. "Down from Salford came this splendid young prophetess," Colin MacInnes, in *Encounter*, recently remarked.

Like all prophetesses Shelagh Delaney tells the truth—her own truth, both observed and suffered through. For in the case of the woman writer and particularly of the woman poet, every lie—every fib, even—shows, like a smutch on a child's (or on a woman's) cheek. We can, perhaps, at this point draw up a short list of tentative rules. First, in literature (or in any other art) women must not lie. Second, they must not whine. Third, they must not attitudinize (in the role of the *femme fatale* least of all). And they must neither theatricalize nor coarsen their truths. They must not be vain, and they must not flight or kite in any witchlike way. Nor, on the other hand, go in for little girlishness and false naiveté. Nor "stamp a tiny foot at the universe."

So far as form is concerned, they should consider themselves free to move about unhampered by strict rules, keeping in mind, however, the fact that women can be, and have been, superb technicians. Perhaps the long *souffle—the big machine*, as the French say—is not for them; on the other hand it may lie ahead of them, in the discernible future.

Louise Bogan adhered so rigidly and so brilliantly to her own critical principles that any poem chosen at random from her work serves as an example of her artistic probity. When she speaks of the *Don Giovanni* of Mozart as refracted "as though from a dark crystal," she might be speaking of her own poems. All the great joy of life—and its great sorrow (and there was terrible suffering toward the end)—"has been translated into treasure. . . ."[7]

Music—"speech proud in sound"—is central to her work. Barbara Howes has said of Louise Bogan that she was "so finely honed by her writing and sensitivity and lifetime of addiction to reading that she was almost a musical instrument." The poem "Musician," in both substance and form, speaks eloquently of what Louise Bogan calls elsewhere "the ordered strings":

> Where have these hands been,
> By what delayed,
> That so long stayed
> Apart from the thin
>
> Strings which they now grace
> With their lonely skill?
> Music and their cool will
> At last interlace.
>
> Now with great ease, and slow,
> The thumb, the finger, the strong
> Delicate hand plucks the long
> String it was born to know.

> And, under the palm, the string
> Sings as it wished to sing.

This poem represents one of the most extraordinary achievements of sound that I know in modern poetry. Note the vowels—the short *i* sounds throughout; and the rhythm hovering between two and three beats to the line; and then the final sense of the actual plucking of the strings. It is a poem about resonance that resounds in the mind long after it is read. And, of course, the poem is much more than just music about music; it is about the artistic process itself, which Louise Bogan examines in so many of her poems, and about the artist who has waited to return to his craft.

Another poem concerned with music is "To Be Sung on the Water":

> Beautiful, my delight,
> Pass, as we pass the wave.
> Pass, as the mottled night
> Leaves what it cannot save,
> Scattering dark and bright.
>
> Beautiful, pass and be
> Less than the guiltless shade
> To which our vows were said;
> Less than the sound of the oar
> To which our vows were made—
> Less than the sound of its blade
> Dipping the stream once more.

Of this piece Richard Wilbur says: "This poem is very lilting, very lulling; it approaches pure music, yet it contains an implicit narrative and a specific mood, which if I read it rightly is a mood of consent to passion upon whatever bitter terms may be necessary." Mr. Wilbur is right in this connection, and he is right in saying, I think, that "as a poet faithful to the theme of passion Louise Bogan is more comparable to Ahkmatova than to many Americans of her time"; and here he cites "Kept":

> Time for the wood, the clay,
> The trumpery dolls, the toys
> Now to be put away:
> We are not girls and boys.
>
> What are these rags we twist
> Our hearts upon, or clutch
> Hard in the sweating fist?
> They are not worth so much.
>
> But we must keep such things
> Till we at length begin

To feel our nerves their strings,
Their dust, our blood within.

The dreadful painted bisque
Becomes our very cheek.
A doll's heart, faint at risk,
Within our breast grows weak.

Our hand the doll's, our tongue.

Time for the pretty clay,
Time for the straw, the wood.
The playthings of the young
Get broken in the play,
Get broken, as they should.

Louise Bogan, as I said earlier, wrote little in prose of an autobiographical nature, and the autobiographical elements in her poetry are carefully objectified. There is one notable exception—a piece called "Journey Around My Room," published in *The New Yorker*, 14 January 1933. (William Maxwell read this piece at the memorial service for Louise Bogan.) She took her title, of course, from the little classic *Voyage Autour de ma Chambre* of Xavier de Maistre, the eighteenth-century French writer. De Maistre, you remember, as an officer in the army of Savoy, was confined for several weeks to his barracks, and he wrote this brilliant book during that period. He describes the objects in his room, going from dresser to table to chair to bed, and each piece has its chapter. But, of course, what he is really doing is speaking of himself. And this Louise Bogan does as she describes her room in New York:

> The most advantageous point from which to start this journey is the bed itself, wherein, at midnight or early in the morning, the adventurous traveler lies moored, the terrain spread out before him. The most fortunate weather is warm to cool, engendered by a westerly breeze, borne from the open window toward the ashes in the grate. At midnight, moonlight lies upon the floor, to guide the traveler's eye; in the early morning, the bleak opacity that serves the traveler in this region as sun brightens the brick wall of the house across the yard, and sheds a feeble reflected glow upon all the objects which I shall presently name.

And she begins to name them as she goes around the room and then tells how she happened to come here in the first place:

> The steam shrieks out of the engine and smoke trails out, into the clear morning, from the smokestack, blotting out the willows and the mill dam. The conductor lifts me up to the step. That is the reason for my presence here. I took the Boston train in March 1909.

Having almost made the circle of the room, she concludes:

> It is at this point, precisely when the end is in sight, and the
> starting point almost gained, that the catastrophe of the journey in-
> variably occurs.
>
> For it is here, as I nearly complete the circle set, that at midnight
> and in the early morning I encounter the dream. I am set upon by
> sleep, and hear the rush of water, and hear the mill dam, fuming
> with water that weighs itself into foam against the air, and see the
> rapids at its foot that I must gauge and dare and swim. Give over,
> says this treacherous element, the fear and distress in your breast;
> and I pretend courage and brave it at last, among rocks along the
> bank, and plunge into the wave that mounts like glass to the level
> of my eye. O death, O fear! The universe swings up against my sight,
> the universe fallen into and bearing with the mill stream. I must in a
> moment die, but for a moment I breathe, upheld, and see all weight,
> all force, all water, compacted into the glassy wave, veined, marbled
> with foam, this moment caught raining over me. And into the wave
> sinks the armoire, the green bureau, the lamps, the shells from the
> beach in Maine. All these objects, provisional at best, now equally
> lost, rock down to translucent depths below fear, an Atlantis in little,
> under the mill stream (last seen through the steam from the Boston
> train in March 1909).

In all Louise Bogan's poems she explores those "translucent depths
below fear." This is especially evident in the final poems of *The Blue
Estuaries*. (*The Blue Estuaries* is, of course, a brilliant title, and no one
was more conscious of titles than Louise Bogan. When Wallace Stevens
published *The Auroras of Autumn* she said to me: "Here is a word that
has been lying around for years, and no one has ever thought of using
it: auroras! *The Auroras of Autumn*. Marvelous, isn't it?" She herself
had found a word like "estuaries" that had been lying around for years
and used it most effectively.)

As an epigraph to *The Sleeping Fury* (1937), which was retained
in all her subsequent books, Louise Bogan used the lines of Rilke:

> *Wie ist das klein, womit wir ringen;*
> *was mit uns ringt, wie ist das gross . . .*
> (How small is that with which we struggle;
> how great is that which struggles with us.)

To give some sense of what a great woman has said, I will end with
her own words—with one of the greatest of her poems (I think all poets
who know her work agree that it is one that will unquestionably endure).[8] It has in it all the elements of her work; the seashell with its
resonance, the earth, the sea, the movement, the music; it is a poem
about poetry, about the poet who puts all of life, all her experience of
the earth into poetry, and in the end becomes the earth itself:

HENCEFORTH, FROM THE MIND

Henceforth, from the mind,
For your whole joy, must spring
Such joy as you may find
In any earthly thing,
And every time and place
Will take your thought for grace.

Henceforth, from the tongue,
From shallow speech alone,
Comes joy you thought, when young,
Would wring you to the bone,
Would pierce you to the heart
And spoil its stop and start.

Henceforward, from the shell,
Wherein you heard, and wondered
At oceans like a bell
So far from ocean sundered—
A smothered sound that sleeps
Long lost within lost deeps,

Will chime you change and hours,
The shadow of increase,
Will sound you flowers
Born under troubled peace—
Henceforth, henceforth
Will echo sea and earth.

Notes

1. Published anonymously, this obituary was written by William Maxwell (editor's note).

2. Louise Bogan's final book of poetry, *The Blue Estuaries, Poems 1923–1968*, received neither the National Book Award nor the Pulitzer Prize; this injustice diminished the honor of both these awards in the eyes of many of her fellow poets.

3. "Several Voices Out of a Cloud."

4. At this ceremony, at which I presided, the speakers were, in addition to Mr. Wheelock, Léonie Adams, Richard Wilbur, and William Maxwell; a statement from Allen Tate, who was unable to attend, was also read. I am indebted to the participants for their permission to quote extensively from a taping of this service, which is to be deposited at the Library of Congress.

5. "After the Persian," part IV.

6. Subsequently published in *Journey Around My Room: The Autobiography of Louise Bogan*, ed. Ruth Limmer (New York: Viking, 1980) (editor's note).

7. "After the Persian," part III.

8. Both Mr. Wheelock and Mr. Tate chose it to read at her memorial service.

Louise Bogan   **Paul Ramsey***

Louise Bogan is a great lyric poet.

Greatness in poetry is hard to discuss, especially in the lyric. It is comparatively easy to show that Bogan is a very good poet: powerful in feeling, surprising and chaste in diction, strong in structure, masterly in imagery and rhythm, important in themes; but greatness in the lyric is impact and profundity and so simple as almost to defy scrutiny. The thing happens; the note is struck; in Bogan's own language the "terrible . . . / Music in the granite hill" sounds, and there we are, where her poems arrive time and again.

Lyrics are to be judged by depth and perfecting, not range, yet the reach of her work is more than its slightness in quantity might suggest. She writes mostly on the traditional lyric subjects, themselves comprising no small range, of love, time, passion, grief, nature, death, music, stoicism, limitation, art (not overmuch), memory, dreams. She also has done some very fine light verse with its own special quartz wryness, and manages to have something to say of psychiatrists, malevolent cocktail parties, Jonathan Swift, St. Christopher.

It is the saint who is most the stranger. He is tough and able (arrived from a fresco), an infrequent sort of visitor to her poems. Religion is almost wholly lacking in her work, except in hints, including the brilliant but puzzling hints of the near light verse of "I Saw Eternity," and the spirits who do appear ("Spirit's Song," "The Daemon") are dark ones. Perhaps the lack is an ingredient in the grief which persistently and profoundly underdwells her poems.

Her unique talent is ending poems. I know no other poet who ends so many poems so well. Her endings startle and compose, in most of the poems I discuss, and in at least these others: "Betrothed," "Come Break with Time," "The Frightened Man," "Kept," "Late," "The Romantic," "To Be Sung on the Water," and "Winter Swan."

Her rhythms are brilliant, unique, and work in a variety of kinds: the short-line free verse of "The Dragonfly"; the free verse, varied in line length, often near or in rising rhythm, of "Summer Wish"; the mostly rising rhythm with five strong stresses of "Didactic Piece," one of her best poems; the long-line free verse, quite different in the two poems, of "Baroque Comment" and "After the Persian"; the special falling rhythms of "Train Tune"; and her "Poem in Prose," mostly, despite its title, in rising rhythm with some counterposing with falling rhythms.

These poems, all done well, show a very unusual range of metrical

°Reprinted, with the permission of the author, from *Iowa Review*, 1 (Summer 1970), 116–24.

accomplishment, but it is no accident that her most powerful poems are work in which, in Theodore Roethke's words about these poems, the "ground beat of the great tradition can be heard." The great tradition in English verse since the late sixteenth century is accentual-syllabics, primarily iambics, and Roethke's words are well chosen: some of her best poems are accentual-syllabic, and some are near, near enough for her pulsing variations (especially the pressure of grouped, strong accents) to be heard as changes from the norm.

The tradition is heard in other ways than metrical, in diction, image, and thought, yet always heard afresh. She does not violate the dignity of the commonplace by self-indulgent attitudes or freakish privacies, yet has something distinct to say.

She can even write greatly about emotion, a rare achievement, as in the superb "Men Loved Wholly Beyond Wisdom":

> Men loved wholly beyond wisdom
> Have the staff without the banner.
> Like a fire in a dry thicket
> Rising within women's eyes
> Is the love men must return.
> Heart, so subtle now, and trembling,
> What a marvel to be wise,
>
> To love never in this manner!
> To be quiet in the fern
> Like a thing gone dead and still,
> Listening to the prisoned cricket
> Shake its terrible, dissembling
> Music in the granite hill.

The poem says that passion is destructive and frustration terrible and fearful. These are known truths, yet only in Shakespeare's sonnets known with fiercer precision than here. The precision is reached by the images and the rhythms. The visions and tensions tell us what is felt; what is felt is the subject of the poem. Thus the poem is new knowledge of a very important kind. Of the images the staff without the banner is just and potent, requiring a moment's reflection. The other images have an immediately seen propriety yet lead to far reaches of feeling: fire, dry thickets, fern, prison, granite.

The poem is, in logical shape, a dilemma. A disjunction is offered, this or that, each alternative leading to the tragic. The poem does not say or imply whether other alternatives exist, but surely means—and says in its profound sense of closure, of completeness—there tragedy exists in any resolution of human sexuality, a truth of great moral importance.

Metrically the poem is magnificent, as are several of her poems. It is the one poem I shall discuss in some metrical detail. The principles involved apply to other poems of hers which are near traditional norms. This poem stays within hearing distance of the accentual-syllabic and turns to iambics in the last verse. The variations are more than would occur in more traditional meters but still are heard as variations. To move further from those expectancies, as much modern near-iambic free verse does, is to lose strength, the strength of vibrancy across the norm. The pattern of the poem is rising trimeter, and the following verses scan traditionally: vv. 2, 3, 4, 5, 7, 9, 10, 13. The first line scans as trochee trochee iamb trochee, but the effect is not of a falling line, because of the comparative strength of "loved" and because an iambic substitution breaks a trochaic pattern much more than a trochaic substitution breaks an iambic pattern. Shifting back and forth from rising to falling rhythm, and grouping strong stresses together often in unusual ways, are the two means by which she most frequently varies from the standard procedures of accentual-syllabic. The bacchiac (light followed by two strongs), a most unusual foot in English verse, occurs often enough in her poetry to be a singular feature. Several times in her poems the bacchiac is correct in the scansion, and the grouping more often occurs when some other scansion would apply. It occurs in verse eight, of which the best scansion is bacchiac iamb iamb feminine ending (others, acceptable foot by foot, would violate the trimeter pattern).

The sixth line scans as trochees, with iambic movement between the commas; the next to last verse scans as straight trochees, with rocking rhythm after the comma. The last verse begins falling but turns back to resolving iambs; its shape, iambic with trochee in the first place, is traditional. The struggle against the norm subsides; what is sounded, sounds.

Such rhythms are empowered by a control that subtilizes intense feeling, by passion that extends and renews form, and bear a real analogy to the subject of the poem; the contrast of, the struggle between, restraint and passion. The subject appears directly or indirectly in a number of her poems. "Ad Castitatem" deals directly with the theme. It is a good poem, well structured (parallel invocations with nice distinctions and some narrative progress) and beautiful in imagery, especially in the unforgettable "a breeze of flame." The rhythms are delicate but comparatively lax, mixing short-line free verse and iambics without achieving the intensities the kinds separately can have.

"The Alchemist" is about the passion of the mind in struggle with the passion of the flesh. The poem is in strict iambic tetrameter, except for some truncated lines, truncated iambic tetrameter being itself an important traditional measure; and once again the rhythmical changes are intense, perhaps too intensely mimetic in "ceased its sudden thresh." The poem is about the failure of the will to govern passion, yet displays, in opposition to that theme, will governing passion to a single majestic continued poetic metaphor which is the poem. Most poems—they are legion nowadays—about the impossibility of the control or understanding of our experience are, with more consistency than Bogan's poem displays, written in lax and disordered styles and rhythms, but are for the same reason much inferior to Bogan's poems.

The view of the poem is stoic, anti-rational, pessimistic, and at least approaches physicalism. If "flesh" is not the sole reality, it is the controlling one, and the mind submits. Since I believe that all four of these views have something seriously wrong with them, my admiration needs explaining. It will not do to separate aesthetics and belief, since one responds to, is moved by, the attitudes expressed in and through the forms, nor will it (simply) do to appeal to "imaginative patterns of experience" or the like as against belief, since, for one thing, some imaginative patterns of experience are more moving and more in accord with reality than others, that is, imaginative patterns themselves can be judged as better and worse. For a second thing, to insist that we are moved in poems by imaginative patterns of experience under or across beliefs is to imply that such patterns are more valid than the beliefs and that to be consistent one should reject the beliefs. Tolerance becomes a monism, and there are logical problems in belief which neither politeness nor rhetoric can dissolve.

What validates the poem is its truth, partial but relevant, and deeply seen. Passion is powerful; not all can be controlled; reasonings fail; experience can be grim and must be met honestly. That is not all there is to say; but there is that much to say, as this poem and other of her poems beautifully show.

Nor is she here offering, or necessarily exemplifying, a general truth. The alchemist in the poem is one (one individual) who seeks a passion of the mind and finds unmysterious flesh. Others may successfully go beyond the submission to passion, for instance the speaker in "Knowledge," who knows the limits of passion and its treasures, seeks to learn beyond passion and finds in the poem's success an experience which goes beyond the self.

"Knowledge" is over-structured, each verse paralleling the corresponding verse in the other stanza, but the parallelism does strengthen the impact of the last two verses "Trees make a long shadow / And a light sound." In these verses the richness of quantity and the curious grouping of accent (the simplest scansion of the next-to-last verse is trochee bacchiac feminine ending) abet the creation of the physical, literal, perfected ending which is the knowledge the poem speaks of and seeks.

"Henceforth, From the Mind" turns from the perception of nature to the strangeness of the mind's reflection of the world. It is one of her best known poems, and remains one of my favorites despite the poor second stanza. Poor writing is very rare in Bogan's work; in fact she is one of the most consistent poets in this respect since Campion and Herrick; but the second stanza of the poem is crudely written and has a bad confusion caused by syntax. In "joy you thought" the joy from the tongue is in meaning other than the powerful joy of youth—the difference is the point of the stanza—but the syntax identifies them, and the confusion damages the comparison. Shakespeare at times says more in his syntactical thickets than simple syntax could obtain; and in Bogan's "Didactic Piece" the syntax of the first stanza, especially of the last verse in it, is dislocated or else very clumsy, yet does not for me damage the emotional force of the passage. Here the syntax does harm, because Bogan says something less and more confused than she meant. The last three verses of the stanza are heavy-handed clichés, with some over-stressed alliteration.

The first stanza, however, is well written and of high generalizing power, and the last two stanzas are one of the most perfectly modulated analogies in English poetry. The image is not phenomenological, though it could have been pushed that way easily enough, since what one hears in a shell is one's blood, not the sea; but the poem has no hint of that. The mind's view of experience is strange, distant, and modified by emotion and memory, but the line to reality is still there; the echo is of truth. What is true is truly loved, even at a distance.

Love moves in grief and dreams, deeply, darkly, in many of her poems; her themes mix there. "I said out of sleeping," says "Second Song," as less explicitly say her poems often. What comes from or descends to sleeping is lucid and other. "Second Song" is a delicate farewell to passion whose delicacy is crossed by the "Black salt, black provender." The phrase may be vaginal, or anal, or for all I know or can prove neither; but to say so is not to explain the force of the phrase, since (presumably) many phrases share such sources; the power of the phrase remains literally incalculable. Its force in the poem comes in some part from its unexpectedness in context, as though she were applying her own rule in "Sub Contra" that notes should be "delicate and involute" but "Let there sound from music's root / One note rage can understand."

She asks of wine in "To Wine" to offer "All that is worth / Grief. Give that beat again." Grief is in the strength of her dreams. Dreams open on reality that the day does not reckon, reality of the mind and, as she hints once in a while, perhaps beyond. In her criticism she is sometimes for the untrammeled in art or sexuality, celebrating modernism for its freeing of the unconscious; but in her verse she never loses touch with mind's and form's lucidities even when sounding the murmurous kingdom of the undernotes. A touch of severe conscience, a passion for truth without pretension, a vested memory (I like to think) of the rockscape of her native Maine, keep her to a center where extremes meet and irradiate each other.

"Come, Sleep   .   .   ." (spaced periods hers) is about dreaming. It describes, in magnificently fresh and concise phrases, bee, ant, whale, palm, flower, grass; asks whether they dream; replies:

> Surely, whispers in the glassy corridor
> Never trouble their dream.
> Never, for them, the dark turreted house reflects itself
> In the depthless stream.

The stream is of the mind's depth and it may be deeper. Since the stream is depth-less, not to be measured, we cannot say how far it goes in or beyond the mind. The shades of voice are haunted utterance, reflective of their meaning; yet the house of the poem is well built.

Two of her best known poems, "The Dream" and "The Sleeping Fury," are imagined accounts of dreams, and "Medusa" is a retold myth, very like a dream. "The Dream" and "The Sleeping Fury," though very well done, are less successful and less dreamlike for me than other poems in which dreams flash in or cross. Perhaps the clarity of narrative development, the conscious visibility of Freudian meanings, or the not quite persuasively earned reversals get in those poems' way, or in mine.

"Medusa" perfects its motion in stillness, becoming image and example of her lyrics. Good lyrics are active objects, Bogan's especially so, steadier in shape and livelier in motion than most. She, like Medusa, fixes motion; unlike Medusa, she does not stop motion. If one fixes motion so that it stops, one has not fixed *motion*; one has usurped its place. Zeno's arrow does not fly. "Medusa," which is about the startlingness of stopped motion, is itself active and changeless, each note struck, and heard. The tipped bell does make its sound.

What the poem is about, beyond the legend, is not made clear. The legend is retold, not as allegory, although it sounds allegorical, but as private experience. One may apply analogies, to death, eternity, time, the past, the paralysis of fear, a moment of trance, but such are analogies, not given meanings, and the poem provides no bridge to any of them. Analogies are subclasses of a larger class; and subclasses are not each other's meanings, except when intentionally made so by signals. Nor are the poem's psychic sources its meaning in the way that psychic sources are part of the meaning within "The Dream" and "The Sleeping Fury." Sources and analogies help to empower the poem; but the poem does not say them. It happens; and it stops.

"Old Countryside" is of the most etched yet suggestive lyrics in the language. Its sensuous description is firm as eye can hold; what is unsaid, painfully unheard, is the silence. The impression of clarity is so final that it is startling to find surface difficulties which make the obscure silence even stranger.

The "we" is unidentified, perhaps generic: it could refer to friends, lovers, brother and sister. The time sequence is elusive. "All has come to proof" since the day remembered of the attic in the country house on a stormy day. The third stanza refers to a time between the time of the memory of stanzas one and two and the present time; since the present is "long since" that nearer time, the first time must be long long since. "Far back" from the time of the third stanza occurs the fourth stanza. The "far back" suggests space, as though the last severe images were in a place that endured "in the stillest of the year" and the stillness stops time and space, in vision. Chronologically the fourth stanza, which has snow, occurs at least one winter before the "winter of dry leaves" and could be much earlier. One cannot tell the relation between the time of the fourth and first stanzas, except that the first stanza seems earlier. It does not matter. Memory makes time past irremediably far and contemporary, as does the poem.

One detail puzzles, either an odd ellipsis or a shift to the godlike, the *we* pulling down oak leaves in a winter of dry leaves, as though they were the agents of the change. The detail in general is simply the finest I know in a lyric poem, total in the clarity of what is seen and in the integrity of what is felt: "The summer thunder, like a wooden bell, / Rang in the storm . . . ," the "mirror cast the cloudy day along / The attic floor . . . ," ". . . we heard the cock / Shout its unplaceable cry, the axe's sound / Delay a moment after the axe's stroke," and then the perfection of love and clear pain of the last stanza:

> Far back, we saw, in the stillest of the year,
> The scrawled vine shudder, and the rose-branch show
> Red to the thorns, and, sharp as sight can bear,
> The thin hound's body arched against the snow.

The rhythms are uniquely hers; the meter is conventional without variation. The poem is in the form called "the heroic quatrain." Except for four anapests, anapestic substitution being normal in much nineteenth- and twentieth-century iambics, and the graceful trimeter in stanza two, no variation occurs that one could not find in Dryden's heroic quatrains. The quatrain is traditionally used for narrative, generalizing, and explicit meditation (Dryden's *Annus Mirabilis* and Gray's *Elegy Written in a Country Churchyard*); here it is used for particularizing, and implicit meditation. Its "narration" is the narrating and relating of memories. Like much in Gray and Dryden, it focuses motion and

stillness in quietly echoing tones; and it achieves a sharpness of definition unique in the examples I know of the form, either historical or
modern.

In "Song for the Last Act," perhaps her greatest poem and certainly
the one I find most moving, her powerfully controlled energies throb
with a different resonance. Of all her poems it has the most visible frame
(a variation of the refrain verse is repeated at both the beginning and
end of each of the three stanzas) and the most radical wildness of meaning and image.

> Now that I have your face by heart, I look
> Less at its features than its darkening frame
> Where quince and melon, yellow as young flame,
> Lie with quilled dahlias and the shepherd's crook.
> Beyond, a garden. There, in insolent ease
> The lead and marble figures watch the show
> Of yet another summer loath to go
> Although the scythes hang in the apple trees.
>
> Now that I have your face by heart, I look.
>
> Now that I have your voice by heart, I read
> In the black chords upon a dulling page
> Music that is not meant for music's cage,
> Whose emblems mix with words that shake and bleed.
> The staves are shuttled over with a stark
> Unprinted silence. In a double dream
> I must spell out the storm, the running stream.
> The beat's too swift. The notes shift in the dark.
>
> Now that I have your voice by heart, I read.
>
> Now that I have your heart by heart, I see
> The wharves with their great ships and architraves;
> The rigging and the cargo and the slaves
> On a strange beach under a broken sky.
> O not departure, but a voyage done!
> The bales stand on the stone; the anchor weeps
> Its red rust downward, and the long vine creeps
> Beside the salt herb, in the lengthening sun.
>
> Now that I have your heart by heart, I see.

The first stanza is mellow description with seemingly firm shapes,
yet the firmness is in a way only a seeming. Art and nature share the
passage, and one cannot exactly visualize the relation of parts. A face
is a face in a portrait whose frame is darkened by time and itself

painted with flowers, by a window which gives on an actual garden; *or* the face is framed by a garden behind which is another garden. Neither statement quite reaches, and the small sur-rationality prepares for the second stanza.

The metaphor in the opening of the first stanza is general, "Now that I have your face by heart, I look," varied to the musical and self-inconsistent in the second stanza: "Now that I have your voice by heart, I read (the music)." To have music by heart is precisely not to read it. The music in the second stanza breaks loose beyond itself and statable meaning and returns, storming the silence of its passion. To paraphrase one needs to repeat the metaphors: the music read on the page is not for music's cage; the emblems mix with words, shake and bleed; the staves are shuttled over with silence. The general meaning, however, is in its tending clear: understanding the person addressed is like knowing musical notes and what in music reaches through and beyond the notes into love and pain and passion. To understand is to relate the formidable knowledge and the mystery, as the stanza does, in subject and feeling. The "double dream" includes the music and the silence. (The shift to the image of the stream was probably influenced by two lines from "Secret Treasure" from Sara Teasdale's book *Strange Victory*, a book praised by Bogan in *Achievement in Modern Poetry*. The lines are "Fear not that my music seems / Like water locked in winter streams." The first stanza, even more certainly, echoes some details from "In a Darkening Garden" in the same book.)

In the third and last stanza, the poem moves away from the shifting of meaning to an abundantly clear and plangent image of a port, the sea's edge as an image of oncoming death. It is a traditional image, realized with greatness, with as much beauty and regret as the first stanza's, as much strangeness of pain as the second stanza's, and as much control of the exact measure of sound touched in image on shaded meaning and feeling as that of any poem in our heritage:

> . . . the anchor weeps
> Its red rust downward, and the long vine creeps
> Beside the salt herb, in the lengthening sun.
>
> Now that I have your heart by heart, I see.

It is a great poem, and substantial to my argument. For the case for poetic greatness is always, finally, the poems. To say that some of her lyrics will last as long as English is spoken is to say too little. For since value inheres in eternity, the worth of her poems is not finally to be measured by the length of enduring. To have written "Song for the Last Act," "Old Countryside," "Men Loved Wholly Beyond Wisdom," "Didactic Piece," "Medusa," "Henceforth, from the Mind," "The

Alchemist," "Second Song," "Night," and some dozens of other poems of very nearly comparable excellence is to have wrought one of the high achievements of the human spirit, and to deserve our celebration and our love.

A Doll's Heart: The Girl in the Poetry of Edna St. Vincent Millay and Louise Bogan   Elizabeth Frank*

There are good reasons to compare the early work of Louise Bogan with that of Edna St. Vincent Millay, for it was in the work produced in their twenties that both poets used the fact of being female not merely as subject matter, but as a formal principle for invigorating and intensifying lyric speech. Through the medium of female personae, each poet developed a specific approach to the lyric past. Millay, assuming the existence of fixed conventions in lyric tradition, became virtually a crusader in the reclamation of the short lyric poem from its temporary submersion in the twin sloughs of Victorian sentiment and modernist gloom, while Louise Bogan sought in the variety, complexity, and rigor of traditional lyric versification and diction a means of forging an elemental lyric. She was from the outset of her career decidedly modernist in her commitment to reducing the lyric to its essentials, and to redefining its sources in emotion, whereas Millay intended only that her poems "measure up" to the lyric past by approximating traditional lyric uses of voice, diction, and theme. Both poets, however, were precocious adepts in the craft of lyric versification, and in the early 1920s it would have been difficult to differentiate their styles and poetic purposes.

Although the young Louise Bogan had nourished herself from late childhood with the work of William Morris, Swinburne, Dante Gabriel Rossetti, Christina Rossetti, and the French symbolists, and while in maturity she would enjoy deep poetic identification with Yeats and with Rilke, at the time that she first began to publish, in 1921, she was compelled to come to terms with the formidable presence of Edna St. Vincent Millay in order to free herself from adolescent taste and habit. The process of confrontation was neither rapid nor, from the outset, hostile. In fact, when in 1923 Edna Millay published her fourth book,

*Reprinted, with the permission of the author, from *Twentieth Century Literature*, 23 (May 1977), 157–79. All quotations of Edna St. Vincent Millay's work are from *Collected Poems*, Harper & Row. Copyright 1917, 1921, 1923, 1928, 1946, 1949, 1951, 1955 by Edna St. Vincent Millay and Norma Millay Willis.

The Harp-Weaver and Other Poems, and Louise Bogan her first, *Body of This Death*, they appeared to be members in good standing of an unbroken tradition of lyric poetry by American women beginning with Emily Dickinson and continued by Louise Imogen Guiney, Lizette Woodworth Reese, Adelaide Crapsey, Sara Teasdale, and Elinor Wylie. It extended beyond Millay and Bogan into the middle and late 1920s with the work of Louise Townsend Nicholl and Abbie Huston Evans, finally becoming something very much like major art with the work of Léonie Adams and Marianne Moore.

Arriving in New York in 1920, aged 23, and five years Millay's junior, Louise Bogan would inevitably have discovered Edna St. Vincent Millay as the contemporary standard-bearer of that tradition. Indeed, with the publication of *Renascence* in 1917, it became clear to the New York literary world that Edna Millay was preeminently the poet who offered an alternative to the "new" poetry, and whose work could serve as a rallying point for the rejection of free verse, imagism, and Prufrockian ennui. When in 1921 she made the daring announcement in *A Few Figs from Thistles* that her candle burned at both ends, she was hailed as the quintessential woman poet: high-minded and high-handed, passionate, erotic, vulnerable, yet indomitable, lodestar for post-World War I youth who, world-and-war weary as they may have been, craved intense, feelingful experience even more than bleak, sullen, or dadaist confrontation with "a botched civilization." For Louise Bogan, then as always listening for the individual voice amidst the cries of a generation, Millay must have offered through the attitudes and forms of her verse the compelling spectacle of a poet who had dared both to resist what "the age demanded" and to resuscitate such recently rejected forms as the sonnet and rhymed-stanzaic lyric from the dust of late nineteenth-century and Georgian sentimentality. In just those ballads, quatrains, rhymed stanzas, and sonnets to which Louise Bogan from childhood had been irresistibly attracted, and to whose formal demands she had made herself wholly answerable, Edna Millay was triumphant, to the immense gratitude of a popular audience desirous of impassioned feeling and a thumping beat.

In retrospect, Millay's actual achievement, which was not inconsiderable, was to conserve, in her early volumes, the melodic simplicity of the combined pastoral and personal lyric by breathing into it a hybridized diction we must ruefully call "poetic." That is, starting with her earliest verses, Millay's style was a resplendent pastiche of Sapphic simplicity, Catullan urbanity, homeless Chaucerian idiom, uprooted Shakespearean grammar, Cavalier sparkle, Wordsworthian magnanimity, Keatsian sensuousness, and Housmanian melancholy, not of course compounded all at once in a single lethal draught, but lightly dispersed here and there throughout her songs and sonnets. Such diction soon came to represent poetry at once fresh and yet "as the ancient world understood it, poetry with metaphors and phrases that were at the same time lovely and new—metaphors and phrases as like and yet as unlike those of earlier poetry as a new-springing tree is like and unlike an older one."[1] Here was no fragmented, estranged, crumbling world, which to Millay's ears and eyes seemed more depressing than it actually was in the work of Eliot, Pound, and Aiken, but a universe to which the Aeolian strings of the poet's heart could still vibrate, her fingers all the while plucking an ancient lyre:

GOD'S WORLD

O world, I cannot hold thee close enough!
　　Thy winds, thy wide grey skies!
　　Thy mists, that roll and rise!
Thy woods, this autumn day, that ache and sag
And all but cry with colour! That gaunt crag
To crush! To lift the lean of that black bluff!
World, World, I cannot get thee close enough!

Long have I known a glory in it all,
　　But never knew I this:
　　Here such a passion is
As stretcheth me apart,—Lord, I do fear
Thou'st made the world too beautiful this year;
My soul is all but out of me,—let fall
No burning leaf; prithee, let no bird call.[2]

In the long-familiar guise of the poet aching with the world's beauty, Millay uses an equally commonplace "poetic diction" of apostrophe and grammatical inversion, with touches of archaism ("thou" and "prithee") to construct a speaker at once reverent, breathless, and naïve. This persona becomes more fully rendered in the volumes following *Renascence* as the Girl, who as the analogue of the young, girlish poet herself, becomes the vehicle of the most "poetical" features of Millay's lyric diction.

By the time she came to define the lyric reaches of Millay's verse, the Girl had behind her an ancient and honorable past. She had been addressed and sometimes assumed for voice by Sappho, and had prevailed in the maiden-song of folk and ballad tradition, as the shepherdess in both high and low forms of pastoral, and in the various incarnations of Portia, Beatrice, and, especially for Millay's purposes, in the trembling virginity and mad songs of Ophelia. While Millay in both early and late verse was often to compare herself to Dido, Cleopatra, Cressida, or Elaine, these comparisons were understood as deliberate similes, obvious extravagances meant to varnish or overlay the fragile

Girl who stood as the "real" speaker of Millay's songs and sonnets, and who hovered forever between betrothal and betrayal, the promise of experience and its denouement in disillusion and despair. For the Girl, love—whether chaste or erotic, passionate or quiescent—was the whole of existence, subsuming her impetuous high-spiritedness and her thirst for intense sensation and meaning. Yet equally essential to the Girl's character was her self-abandon, and self-neglect. She would too often recklessly bestow herself upon some heartless lad who would, inevitably, betray her. Only then would she find at the very moment of heart-break, at the very crisis of anguish, a terrible strength that would allow her to grieve but not to die. This combination of weakness and strength, of erotic susceptibility and unsuspected will, provided Millay's Girl with a basic affective strategy in which disappointment could change suddenly to ennui, and high lyric lamentation to shrugging colloquial gloom. Indeed, Millay's Girl was essentially a theatrical per-sona, a medium for the expression of sudden shifts in tone and implied bodily gestures. This mercurial quality is particularly noticeable in "The Shroud," where the poet melodramatically draws attention not to her words or even to her experience as such, but to the "picture" she makes in actually uttering the poem:

> Death, I say, my heart is bowed
>   Unto thine,—O mother!
> This red gown will make a shroud
>   Good as any other!
>
> (I, that would not wait to wear
>   My own bridal things,
> In a dress dark as my hair
>   Made my answerings.
>
> I, to-night, that till he came
>   Could not, could not wait,
> In a gown as bright as flame
>   Held for them the gate.)
>
> Death, I say, my heart is bowed
>   Unto thine,—O mother!
> This red gown will make a shroud
>   Good as any other![3]

Exploiting the simplicity of ballad form not so much to ennoble the Girl's grief as to introduce the sinful symbols of red gown and red hair, the poem achieves a disarming pictorial quality that may indeed have been enhanced in oral delivery by the fact that Millay actually had red hair. The poem's real purpose is to shock and thrill the audience with sexual innuendo, not to utter a cry of the heart for lost innocence.

Through the vividly compressed ballad diction Millay's readers or hearers would discern once again the modern Girl confessing that sex has led to shame and ruin. Horace Gregory and Marya Zaturenska rightly call Millay's gifts "histrionic" in *A History of American Poetry: 1900–1940*;[4] her poetry drew attention to itself as an instrument for the swift alteration of mood, inviting swings in response from an audience thereby flattered into interpreting her volatile diction as depth of emotion. A corollary feature of Millay's theatrical mode was the power to make the audience share in the Girl's self-pity without appearing to cheapen that emotion. In "Scrub," a poem published in *The Harp-Weaver and Other Poems* (1923), the poet as ingenue views her fate as blasted and blighted, like a scrub oak destroyed by wind and storm, a stance she assumed in many other poems in which she likened her soul or her feelings to gnarled trees, budding seeds, or seasons and weathers in various stages of fervor and instability. By these means Millay's Girl bit to the core of the poet's lyric *donnée*—erotic and poetic exhibitionism—with "adorable" flair and considerable shrewdness. She spoke, that is, of her love affairs, not with Sappho's brevity, nor with Catullus's candor, but with an allusiveness indebted to both and a coyness both would have shunned. Using a rhetoric of swift changes of mood, the Girl could turn the lightsome measures of impulse and intimacy into the acrid dismissals and recriminations of scorn and ennui, becoming in the process "no mere girl at all, but a woman who had already grown weary of sin."[5]

Capable of moving readers and hearers, the skillful, charming verse through which the Girl had life was even so too dependent on implied gesture to be taken seriously as meant speech. If Millay's Girl defamed the "beautiful," or hinted at the improper, if in her excesses of feeling she occasionally rhymed bathetically or slithered around and over her meters, all it pointed to was her very modern right to say or do anything she pleased. Emancipation was a matter of mood, not conviction. Hence, in "Spring," she sulks and grumbles and finds April the cruelest month, not because it is agonizing to the torpid spirit to reawaken to life, but presumably because she has had a bad time of it romantically. In poem after poem, the formula or leitmotiv that identified Millay's Girl was the insouciant manner with which she turned grief to cynicism, often achieving a novel prestige by being the agent of the sexual rejection:

PASSER MORTUUS EST

Death devours all lovely things:
Lesbia with her sparrow
Shares the darkness,—presently
Every bed is narrow.

Unremembered as old rain
 Dries the sheer libation;
And the little petulant hand
 Is an annotation.

After all my erstwhile dear,
 My no longer cherished,
Need we say it was not love,
 Just because it perished?[6]

Coolly, cleverly, the Girl slays with a Catullan sleight of hand her own naïve romanticism and the boyfriend's too. This is Edna St. Vincent Millay's Girl at her best, the unflappable flapper whose sophistication has taken her beyond libertinage and rebellion toward an epicurean balance of urbanity and lyricism. Yet, within the volume in which it appears and in relation to the whole Millay canon, even such a polished poem as "Passer Mortuus Est" represents merely another mood-swing in the permanently inconsistent soul of the Girl. She could just as easily become the abandoned housewife, throwing off silk pajamas and donning instead a bedraggled apron:

ALMS

My heart is what it was before,
 A house where people come and go;
But it is winter with your love,
 The sashes are beset with snow.

I light the lamp and lay the cloth,
 I blow the coals to blaze again;
But it is winter with your love,
 The frost is thick upon the pane.

I know a winter when it comes;
 The leaves are listless on the boughs;
I watched your love a little while,
 And brought my plants into the house.

I water them and turn them south,
 I snap the dead brown from the stem;
But it is winter with your love,
 I only tend and water them.

There was a time I stood and watched
 The small, ill-natured sparrows' fray;
I loved the beggar that I fed,
 I cared for what he had to say,

> I stood and watched him out of sight;
>   Today I reach around the door
> And set a bowl upon the step;
>   My heart is what it was before,
>
> But it is winter with your love;
>   I scatter crumbs upon the sill,
> And close the window,—and the birds
>   May take or leave them, as they will.[7]

In this poem wistful and resigned, in another brazen and proud, the Girl sang, as Millay had her say in "The Singing Woman from the World's Edge," in the accents of "a harlot and a nun." In Millay's sonnets, especially, the Girl rode a seesaw of theatrical gestural alternation. High-mindedness turned quickly to flirtation, poetic rapture to jazzy suggestiveness. In "Oh, think not I am faithful to a vow!" and "I shall forget you presently, my dear," both published in 1920 in *A Few Figs from Thistles*, the Girl attempts a Shakespearean density of phrasing to give a "high-toned" nonchalance to the declaration of concupiscence, while in "Into the golden vessel of great song," published the following year in *Second April*, sexual passion becomes at once legitimate and trivial when regarded as the force that joins the two lovers, both poets, in the far more important ecstasy of inspiration. Most often, the Girl played upon a range of emotional extremes in those poems where, as in "Passer Mortuus Est," she coolly ended the affair. In these we see an extraordinary coordination of explicitly verbal and implicitly physical gestures. In the following sonnet, for example, the Girl dismisses and eulogizes her boyfriend, all the while smoking a cigarette (its gray rings presumably circling her bobbed red hair):

> Only until this cigarette is ended,
> A little moment at the end of all,
> While on the floor the quiet ashes fall,
> And in the firelight to a lance extended,
> Bizarrely with the jazzing music blended,
> The broken shadow dances on the wall,
> I will permit my memory to recall
> The vision of you, by all my dreams attended.
> And then adieu,—farewell!—the dream is done.
> Yours is a face of which I can forget
> The colour and the features, every one,
> The words not ever, and the smiles not yet;
> But in your day this moment is the sun
> Upon a hill, after the sun has set.[8]

It is all so staged, so visible, so temporary, and it was what the literary world into which Louise Bogan was gaining entry in the early 1920s considered rich, sustaining fare. In the first issue, in March 1921, of the "little" New York poetry magazine, *The Measure*, coeditor Frank Ernest Hill, reviewing *A Few Figs from Thistles*, called Millay "just now the most interesting person in American poetry."[9] The same issue contained work by Conrad Aiken and Wallace Stevens, and in subsequent issues work by Robert Frost, Hart Crane, Louise Bogan and Léonie Adams would also be found. While each member of *The Measure's* group of revolving editors considered himself critically autonomous, there was remarkable unanimity in the appraisal of Millay. Maxwell Anderson called her poetry "perfect" in his review of *Second April*,[10] and in a long review of *The Harp-Weaver and Other Poems*, Genevieve Taggard, one of *The Measure's* most vocal contributors, pronounced Millay "one of the poets of all time," crediting her poetry with making "all other utterance almost banal."[11]

Other members of *The Measure's* editorial core, in addition to Hill, Anderson, and Taggard, included Agnes Kendrick Gray, Carolyn Hall, David Morton, Louise Townsend Nicholl, and George O'Neil, and it was to this group that Louise Bogan firmly attached herself soon after her poems began appearing in the magazine's pages in April 1921. She eventually assumed one of its revolving three-month editorships, between December and February of 1924–25, by which time she had already published her first book of poems, *Body of This Death*, and had achieved considerable stature not only among her colleagues at *The Measure* but also at *The New Republic*, where she published verse and reviews. She had, no doubt, been attracted to *The Measure* for its determined advocacy of what Maxwell Anderson described in the first issue as "the musical and rounded forms" over "the half-said, half-conceived infantilities and whimsicalities of the dominant American school."[12] Complaining frequently of the formlessness of imagism and vers-libre, and the "negativism" of what they otherwise frankly acknowledged as the vaster ambitions of Eliot and Pound, the editors of *The Measure* upheld Edna Millay as the leading voice in the pursuit of poetic quality they believed had dwindled away from Harriet Monroe's *Poetry* as it wearily reached the end of its first decade. Anderson pointed out in his statement of *The Measure's* editorial policy that while the magazine would probably never publish a great poem, the age being inimical to great poetry,

> *Poetry*, of Chicago, has come out uninterruptedly for ten years without doing it. This is not the fault of the editors of *Poetry*. If there had been masterpieces to print they would have printed them. There have been none. But the ten years of *Poetry's* history have been useful, fruitful, interesting. Miss Monroe and her band have pioneered well, and if the near future should actually hold a poetic revival in merit as well as in bulk, it will be due largely to their efforts.[13]

Thus neither strictly *derrière* nor *avant-garde, The Measure's* editors and contributors were mustered together in the name of rhyme, meter, stanzas, lyric smoothness, pure diction, of all, in short, that they considered essential to "form." By publishing in *The Measure*, Louise Bogan identified herself with the cause of form, and thereby placed herself, deliberately or not, in Millay's league, if not on her team. In the April 1921 issue, Bogan's poem, "Words for Departure," appeared in a group of "Nineteen Poems by Americans of the Younger Generation," whose members included Robert Hillyer, David Rosenthal, Eda Lou Walton, Kathryn White Ryan, Archie Binns, Hortense Flexner, Lola Ridge, and Dare Stark. Nearly every one of these poems was short, rhymed, and stanzaic, the three keys to the kingdom currently ruled by Edna St. Vincent Millay. By her own predilection for poems in "form," by her alliance with *The Measure*, and by the linked facts of being female and a poet of immense natural gifts, Louise Bogan was virtually catapulted into an aesthetic confrontation with the imposing, slightly older poet.

That the confrontation took place, over time, there can be no doubt. It is less easy to say of what it was elemented. At first, however, from an epigram Bogan published in *The Liberator*, in 1923, it would appear to have been no less than direct imitation:

PYROTECHNICS

Mix prudence with my ashes;
Write caution on my urn;
While life foams and flashes
Burn, bridges, burn![14]

To anyone familiar with Edna Millay's "First Fig," the resemblance would have been unmistakable:

My candle burns at both ends;
It will not last the night;
But ah, my foes, and oh, my friends—
It gives a lovely light![15]

Similar echoes persisted in *Body of This Death* in poems peculiarly reminiscent in their themes and handling of certain poems of Millay's. From the outset, however, Bogan's actual workmanship differed tellingly from Millay's, and just as "Pyrotechnics" possessed a crisper, more forceful linguistic texture than "First Fig," those poems in which Bogan shared or even derived subject matter from Edna Millay turned out to be those in which she developed a wholly separate mode of diction from that of her predecessor. It was as if a fastidious younger sister had stepped into the elder's well-worn clothes, only to find them costumes of net and lace, and slightly soiled satin, with trick seams and zippers for quick changes, broad gestures, and hints of knee and breast. Even though much of Louise Bogan's early poetry took as its lyric *donnée* the experience of the Girl as Millay had defined it, it simply would not do to have it revealed through display, in the language and cadence of implied gesture and mood-change as these had characterized Millay's work. Temperamentally and aesthetically hostile to display, yet equally unwilling to refine and condense emotion into the Victorian and Georgian inanities that Millay had so effectively avoided, Bogan worked in her early poems toward a diction of extreme seriousness, in which speech was not only expressive of the moment, but binding through time. Where Frank Ernest Hill had praised Millay for being "a poet who externalized her own soul, saying not 'I shall feel thus,' but 'I shall do that,' "[16] Bogan seized not upon the theatrical occasion of that vow but upon the linguistic form of vows in themselves, and upon similiarly powerful acts made in and by language alone, as the foundation for a speech more binding, more essential, and thus more whole than that found in Millay's verbal caprice. It would be speech that contained itself without implying bodily movement, facial expression, intonation, projection, or props in a setting (such as a cigarette or red hair). The difference is clearly illustrated in the statements and sighs comprising "First Fig" as opposed to the imperatives of "Pyrotechnics." Vows, commands, promises, warnings, and other performative or approximately performative[17] expressions soon came to represent in Bogan's poetry the foundation of her lyric diction, strengthening it with the distinctive capacity to resist the ambiguity and doubtful sincerity so characteristic of Millay's verse. Moreover, when Louise Bogan occasionally did insert a dramatic antithesis or reversal into the structure of a poem, it served only to enrich the texture of speech already made firm by the logical clarity and serious purpose of explicit and semi-explicit speech acts. By contrast, the logical membrane of Millay's verse was extremely thin.

The consequence of the emerging difference in diction is that whereas Millay's lyric language continued to conjure a make-believe, theatrical world, with the poet spotlighted as mere-slip-of-a-Girl, Bogan's language was uttered by a Girl increasingly intent upon subordinating her personality and experience to the discipline of language itself. Hence Bogan's Girl began to speak more strongly, more bitterly, with greater pride and larger forgiveness than Millay's, becoming in the process a poetic persona capable of celebrating alike the piercing complexity of experience and the supple freshness of language. Where, for example, the end of the affair for Millay's Girl was reduced to the formula of a toss of the head, a curl of the lip, and a Catullan allusion, it became for the Girl in Bogan's poetry a rite de passage into the knowledge of all endings, not to be contained by a quip or defined by received wisdom, but savored, endured, and shaped through speech into dignity and finality. What is gestural, momentary, and dependent on mood in "Only until this cigarette is ended" is engraved on the mind and ennobled as ceremony in Bogan's "Words for Departure":

Nothing was remembered, nothing forgotten.
When we awoke, wagons were passing on the warm summer pavements,
The window-sills were wet from rain in the night,
Birds scattered and settled over chimneypots
As among grotesque trees.

Nothing was accepted, nothing looked beyond.
Slight-voiced bells separated hour from hour,
The afternoon sifted coolness
And people drew together in streets becoming deserted.
There was a moon, a light in a shop-front,
And dust falling like precipitous water.

Hand clasped hand,
Forehead bowed to forehead—
Nothing was lost, nothing possessed,
There was no gift nor denial.

2. I have remembered you.
You were not the town visited once,

Nor the road falling behind running feet.
You were as awkward as flesh
And lighter than frost or ashes.
.   .   .   .

3. You have learned the beginning;
Go from mine to the other.

Be together; eat, dance, despair,
Sleep, be threatened, endure.
You will know the way of that.

But at the end, be insolent;
Be absurd—strike the thing short off;
Be mad—only do not let talk
Wear the bloom from silence.

And go away without fire or lantern.
Let there be some uncertainty about your departure.[18]

Beginning with its title, the poem unfolds as an explicitly verbal act: not the hand waving goodbye, but the mind and voice together solemnizing departure. Neither disdainful nor crushed, the Girl who speaks throughout the poem evokes the scene of estrangement, summarizes the vanished richness of the affair, and goes on to issue a series of commands that, taken together, constitute an effort to establish distance, clarity, and integrity. Absent is the toying with nostalgia and cynicism so characteristic of Millay's Girl; so untheatrical, in fact, so complete is the capacity of Bogan's Girl to endure the separation that she hints that perhaps this certainty or finality itself discloses a flaw, an excessive stoicism. Thus she even counsels the lover to end his next affair with an arbitrary gesture: "Be absurd—strike the thing short off," so that the irreversibility of the formal farewell might be softened.

The middle section of "Words for Departure" is especially effective in suggesting the essential difference between Millay's superficial selection of experience as opposed to Bogan's surrender to the grain and savor of finality and limitation. Millay's Girl picks and chooses what she wishes to take from experience:

> Yours is a face of which I can forget
> The colour and the features, every one,
> The words not ever, and the smiles not yet . . .

Rejecting the involuntary impingement of memory, Millay's Girl consciously selects keepsake impressions, willfully fragmenting the past. But Bogan's yields to the past with figures of rich completeness:

> You were the rind,
> And the white-juiced apple,
> The song, and the words waiting for music.

Here are bitterness, consummation, joy, and frustration, each condensed in metaphor, each an act of memory, a recitation "by heart," as Bogan was later to call it in "Song for the Last Act," of the essence of the "erstwhile dear," as Millay's Girl would have called him. But Bogan's Girl refrains entirely from "emancipated" tones, although it is perfectly clear from the first section that the lovers have not only experienced a sexual relation, but even a degree of dissipation. A certain irony nevertheless exists that for the freedom of the poem's subject Bogan was most certainly indebted to the posturings of Millay.

As both Edna Millay and Louise Bogan no doubt keenly understood, the Girl of lyric tradition represented a figure of enchantment, poised briefly by the course of nature between maidenly hope and womanly disillusionment. In their early verse, both poets attempted that lyric set piece, the betrothal song, so familiar in both classical and European lyric tradition, with its mingling of the erotic and the elegiac. Not surprisingly, Millay points hers toward sexual innuendo and cynicism:

THE BETROTHAL

Oh, come, my lad, or go, my lad,
And love me if you like.
I shall not hear the door shut
Nor the knocker strike.

Oh, bring me gifts or beg me gifts,
And wed me if you will.
I'd make a man a good wife,
Sensible and still.

And why should I be cold, my lad,
And why should you repine,
Because I love a dark head
That never will be mine?

I might as well be easing you
As lie alone in bed
And waste the night in wanting
A cruel dark head.

You might as well be calling yours
What never will be his,
And one of us be happy.
There's few enough as is.[19]

Thinly veiling a sexual proposition in the folk accents of this bitter ballad, the poem's quaint "easing you" reduces the Girl's unhappiness to a gesture again, a seductive shrug in which she grimly offers herself to a lad she doesn't love, just as she might hope to be thus pitied by the rejecting dark-haired lover. The sophisticated, risqué pastoral barely conceals the complacent mixture of helplessness and self-pitying "toughness" that supplied the formula for so many of Edna St. Vincent Millay's lyrics of erotic disillusionment. The ballad form itself, with its capacity to achieve dramatic simplicity and pure, condensed feeling, was similarly treated as a formula in Millay's art, as the vessel into which the slightly polluted waters of Millay's lyric reservoir could be poured and made to taste like the fresh stream of English undefiled. Millay's treatment of ballad stanza and lyric diction was too often arbitrary and vehicular, rather than felt and organic. It disguised an essential vulgarity that strove for "effect" and used tradition cosmetically, as mere varnish, though it did achieve a fine simplicity. Keeping this latter virtue in mind as the chief beauty of traditional maiden-song, Louise Bogan in "Betrothed" turns an elegy for the romantic wishes of girlhood into an acknowledgment and acceptance of change and uncertainty:

You have put your two hands upon me, and your mouth,
You have said my name as a prayer.
Here where trees are planted by the water
I have watched your eyes, cleansed from regret,
And your lips, closed over all that love cannot say.

My mother remembers the agony of her womb
And long years that seemed to promise more than this.
She says, "You do not love me,
You do not want me,
You will go away."

In the country whereto I go
I shall not see the face of my friend
Nor her hair the color of sunburnt grasses;
Together we shall not find
The land on whose hills bends the new moon
In air traversed of birds.

What have I thought of love?
I have said, "It is beauty and sorrow."
I have thought that it would bring me lost delights, and splendor
As a wind out of old time . . .

But there is only the evening here,
And the sound of willows
Now and again dipping their long oval leaves in the water.[20]

Even though its syllables are, strictly speaking, arrayed in a solemn
vers-libre, in its feeling "Betrothed" is more responsive to its ancestry in
maiden-song than Millay's more explicitly musical phrasing in "The
Betrothal." In Bogan's poem, speech in the form of slow declaration
empowers the Girl to probe the rhythms of time and change that have
prompted her misgivings. She must forsake her mother, she must give
up her girlhood friend, she must question the meaning of love, even as
she savors the lover's kiss and the rich, peaceful landscape, not far from
the Claude Lorrain-inspired[21] vines and wharves of the later masterpiece, "Song for the Last Act." Bogan has sought and found in the
tradition of betrothal lyric a fusion of form and language where simplicity represents an immense compression of feeling and an effort to
overcome fear and conflict. For Louise Bogan, the balance, measure,
and above all the compressed simplicity of virtually all shorter lyric
forms were synonymous not just with high artifice, but with clarity and
integrity of attitude: the lyric was the occasion for essential speech. Her
Girl, like Millay's, finds life a bitter disappointment. But where Millay's
Girl lashes out in petulant rage, as in "Spring," or takes her revenge in
sexual cynicism varnished as Catullan irony, as in "Passer Mortuus Est,"

Bogan's girl accedes to the moment of pain as a source of mystery and of renewal, if not of complete affirmation:

KNOWLEDGE

Now that I know
How passion warms little
Of flesh in the mould,
And treasure is brittle,—

I'll lie here and learn
How, over their ground,
Trees make a long shadow
And a light sound.[22]

Turning grief away from the self, the poem affirms time, nature, and peace. In another poem perhaps more clearly competitive with Edna Millay, Bogan's Girl rejects theatrical gesture in a deliberate counter-strategy against defeat:

MY VOICE NOT BEING PROUD

My voice, not being proud
Like a strong woman's, that cries
Imperiously aloud
That death disarm her, lull her—
Screams for no mourning color
Laid menacingly, like fire,
Over my long desire.
It will end, and leave no print.
As you lie, I shall lie:
Separate, eased, and cured.
Whatever is wasted or wanted
In this country of glass and flint
Some garden will use, once planted.
As you lie alone, I shall lie,
O, in singleness assured,
Deafened by mire and lime.
I remember, while there is time.[23]

In its first seven lines the poem offers an affront to the sensibility discoverable, for example, in Millay's "The Shroud," with its melodramatic plea for death as the release from the pain of betrayal. It continues, however, not as an example of merely another style of heartbreak, but as a determined resolution to resist the "strong woman's" histrionic and self-deceiving flirtation with death. The disciplined voice in Bogan's poem vows that desire will end, with the vows themselves acting to restore the self-possession threatened with disintegration by the easier hysteria of the Millay-like scream. Then, cautious lest the series of vows become just another pose, the speaker catches herself powerfully short with the qualifying afterthought, "I remember, while there is time." Though the will can do much, it cannot do all. The voice that issues vows rather than cries tries thereby to save the endangered soul, the whole, suffering, moral self that trusts to speech and speech alone to wrench herself away from the urge toward self-destruction.

Both Bogan and Millay encouraged their Girls to play upon the strength concealed in weakness, the weakness concealed in strength. Millay's tarnished virgin could become a "tough cookie," Bogan's proud lady could become ineffably sad. Millay took the lead in using "pure" lyric diction to dissemble complex sexual ironies, but it was left to Bogan to heighten this approach by turning the innocent measures of the carol in the following poem to a darkling cry of loss:

CHANSON UN PEU NAIVE

What body can be ploughed,
Sown, and broken yearly?
She would not die, she vowed,
But she has, nearly.
        Sing, heart, sing;
        Call and carol clearly.

And, since she could not die,
Care would be a feather,
A film over the eye
Of two that lie together.
        Fly, song, fly,
        Break your little tether.

So from strength concealed
She makes her pretty boast:
Pain is a furrow healed
And she may love you most.
        Cry, song, cry,
        And hear your crying lost.[24]

Even "strength concealed" conceals from itself most dangerous sight of its own limitations. The Millay-Girl's mixture of weakness and strength, ingenuousness and shrewdness is lightly mocked, though the mockery is not lightly meant, in the trope of mutual deception, "Of two that lie together," which Bogan uses here almost exactly as she had in "My Voice Not Being Proud." By representing the Girl simultaneously summoning and denying psychic pain, Bogan implicitly alludes to a pattern occurring frequently in Millay's verse, as in "The Merry Maid," from *A Few Figs from Thistles*:

Oh, I am grown so free from care
Since my heart broke!
I set my throat against the air,
I laugh at simple folk!

There's little kind and little fair
Is worth its weight in smoke
To me, that's grown so free from care
Since my heart broke!

Lass, if to sleep you would repair
As peaceful as you woke,
Best not besiege your lover there
For just the words he spoke
To me, that's grown so free from care
Since my heart broke.[25]

The Opheliesque lightness of the heart nearly crazed with grief and bitterness in this poem is even more concentrated in the pathetic sophistry of "Chanson Un Peu Naive," while the sexual self-destruction implicit in so many of Millay's lyrics is also present when the "she" of whom Bogan's poem speaks now takes another lover, flattering him and herself with the false strength and false ardor of a heart dangerously close to having burnt itself out. The paradox is driven deeper than Millay ever cared to go: license is a lie, and the candle burning at both ends goes out in madness before oblivion.

Thus, in Louise Bogan's first two books of poems, the task of deepening and extending the implications of the Girl's experience became identical with that of defining and strengthening Bogan's range and skill as a poet. By 1929, when her second book, *Dark Summer*, appeared, Louise Bogan had completed the task of establishing her own distinctive voice. In a poem appropriately titled "Girl's Song," Bogan seems almost to have taken the refrain of Millay's "Alms," "But it is winter with your love," and transformed it into an involuted conceit that shapes the poem as the quintessential Millay-derived lyric of Bogan's early career, yet marks as well the full transition of the Girl to Woman:

Winter, that is a fireless room
In a locked house, was our love's home.
The days turn, and you are not here,
O changing with the little year!

Now when the scent of plants half-grown
Is more the season's than their own
And neither sun nor wind can stanch
The gold forsythia's dripping branch,—

Another maiden, still not I,
Looks from some hill upon some sky,
And since she loves you, and she must,
Puts her young cheek against the dust.[26]

Unlike the Girl of "The Merry Maid," who protects herself from truth with a madcap lightness, and warns the next girl of her lover's perfidy, the Girl speaking now in "Girl's Song" has completed the cycle of innocence and betrayal, and sees in the sensuous lushness of spring and in the turning of the seasons the same inexorable law by which hope is destroyed. Not as a victim, but as a witness in full possession of the bitter fruits of time does the Girl here see both herself and her rival with the clear, unavenging detachment which marks the growth beyond girlhood to maturity.

Although Millay never quite outgrew the Girl, there is evidence that she tried to put her aside. In 1928, Millay wrote curiously, in "To a Young Girl," of the emotional artifice of that creature:

Shall I despise you that your colourless tears
Made rainbows in your lashes, and you forgot to weep?
Would we were half so wise, that eke a grief out
By sitting in the dark, until we fall asleep.

I only fear lest, being by nature sunny,
By and by you will weep no more at all,
And fall asleep in the light, having lost with the tears
The colour in the lashes that comes as the tears fall.

I would not have you darken your lids with weeping,
Beautiful eyes, but I would have you weep enough
To wet the fingers of the hand held over the eye-lids
And stain a little the light frock's delicate stuff.

For there came into my mind, as I watched you winking the tears down,
Laughing faces, blown from the west and the east,
Faces lovely and proud that I have prized and cherished:
Nor were the loveliest among them those that had wept the least.[27]

It is one of Millay's stronger poems, without theater, without implicit gesture, with gentle irony toward the performing ingenue of her earlier work. Yet the poem did not mark a permanent step for Millay in the direction of reflective detachment; the persona of the Girl was outgrown more for the sake of propriety than conviction. The woman who chronicled the raptures of *Fatal Interview* in 1931 never stopped believing in the rejuvenating power of romance and passion, of simple sex and simple love for poetry's simple sake. In *Wine from these Grapes* (1934), *Huntsman, What Quarry?* (1939), and *Make Bright the Arrows*

(1940), Millay turned increasingly to set pieces, political lyrics, and love poems still composed in the Girl's pastiche diction, though too many of them failed to achieve the freshness and breadth of emotion that the Girl had provided as a symbol in her earlier efforts.

In Bogan's verse, the Girl became the Woman only to be reborn, quite suddenly, as the Child. Not satisfied with regarding the flawed world of love as an unquestionable fatality, Louise Bogan sought to discover the sources of loss and betrayal, and found them not in the pangs of adolescence, but in the obsessions of childhood, in the refusal to relinquish early wants and hungers, and in the tyranny of unacknowledged childhood memories. The Child soon became for Bogan the source of rage, both justifiable and unjustifiable, an emotion virtually absent from earlier poems which had represented the Girl as speaker. The Child lived within the adult Woman, locked away and silent, until forced by circumstances, betrayal, or time itself to disrupt, intrude, and clamor for recognition. In one of her most powerful poems, "The Sleeping Fury," published in 1937 in the book of the same title, Louise Bogan regards her tormented alter ego as just this Child, "Who, after rage, for an hour quite, sleeps out its tears," and addresses her in the seventh stanza:

> You uncovered at night in the locked stillness of houses,
> False love due the child's heart, the kissed-out lie, the embraces,
> Made by the two who for peace tenderly turned to each other.

And in the last stanza:

> Beautiful now as a child whose hair, wet with rage and tears
> Clings to its face. And now I may look upon you,
> Having once met your eyes. You lie in sleep and forget me.
> Alone and strong in my peace, I look upon you in yours.[28]

The Child, with its desire for justice, its supreme vulnerability, its unanswerable demands, had to be reclaimed and integrated within the self of the Girl if she were to achieve the wholeness, strength, and renewal of maturity. Yet the Child could not be allowed to tyrannize the process of growth. Thus, in "Kept," Bogan puts to rest the clamoring, unsatisfied Child, substituting once again command for cry:

> Time for the wood, the clay,
> The trumpery dolls, the toys
> Now to be put away:
> We are not girls and boys.
>
> What are these rags we twist
> Our hearts upon, or clutch
> Hard in the sweating fist?
> They are not worth so much.

But we must keep such things
Till we at length begin
To feel our nerves their strings,
Their dust, our blood within.

The dreadful painted bisque
Becomes our very cheek.
A doll's heart, faint at risk,
Within our breast grows weak.

Our hand the doll's, our tongue.

Time for the pretty clay,
Time for the straw, the wood.
The playthings of the young
Get broken in the play,
Get broken, as they should.[29]

Having been fully experienced, both Child and Girl are effectively silenced, not to emerge again for nearly thirty years when, in "Little Lobelia's Song," written late in Louise Bogan's life during a period of extreme emotional pain, the Child cries out to become once again part of the whole person:

Each day, at dawn,
I come out of your sleep;
I can't get back.
I weep, I weep.[30]

To go this deeply, this painfully into the psyche Millay was unwilling and unprepared. Yet without the precedent, and the challenge of Millay, Bogan might not have gained access to her full resources as a poet as swiftly, as assuredly, and as powerfully as she did. As Bogan and Millay discovered, the Girl was a lie, a doll, yet one essential to poetic identity and growth. The Child was more enduring, though finally peace, reconciliation, honor, and even joy came only to the Woman, the adult who had fought her way clear to detachment, and, no longer "faint at risk," had put her dolls away.

Writing to Edmund Wilson, in May of 1923, after Wilson had left some of Bogan's poems with her, Millay asked:

Who is this person? I never even heard of her. I was quite thrilled by some of the poems. Isn't it wonderful how the lady poets are coming along? "Votes for women" is what I sez![31]

In 1951, a year after Millay's death, Louise Bogan wrote in *Achievement in American Poetry* that Millay

formulated for a new generation of young women a standard of sexual defiance and "heroism" which, in spite of its romantic coloring, was marked by truth and pathos. A certain hampering nihilism, as well as a close attachment to literary fashion, apparent in Miss Millay from the outset, prevented her from breaking through to impressive maturity; but even her later work is filled with distinguished fragments. She often succeeded in transcending her worst faults. Many of her sonnets are in the great tradition; and that she was, by nature, a lyric poet of the first order, is an incontestable fact.[32]

The little petulant hand had become an annotation—mere footnote to the era that had taken her for text.

Notes

1. Elizabeth Atkins, *Edna St. Vincent Millay and Her Times* (Chicago: Univ. of Chicago Press, 1936), p. 113.

2. Norma Millay, ed., from *Renascence* (1917) in *Collected Poems* (New York: Harper, 1956), p. 32. All subsequent citations of poems by Edna St. Vincent Millay are from this edition.

3. *Ibid.*, p. 43.

4. Horace Gregory and Marya Zaturenska, *A History of American Poetry: 1900–1940* (New York: Gordian Press, 1969), pp. 265 ff.

5. *Ibid.*, p. 268.

6. Millay, from *Second April* (1921) in *Collected Poems*, p. 75.

7. *Ibid.*, p. 88.

8. *Ibid.*, p. 575.

9. Frank Ernest Hill, rev. of *A Few Figs from Thistles*, by Edna St. Vincent Millay, *The Measure*, No. 1 (Mar. 1921), p. 25.

10. Maxwell Anderson, rev. of *Second April*, by Edna St. Vincent Millay, *The Measure*, No. 7 (Sept. 1921), p. 17.

11. *The Measure*, No. 38 (Apr. 1924), pp. 11–12.

12. *The Measure*, No. 1 (Mar. 1921), p. 23.

13. *Ibid.*, p. 25.

14. Louise Bogan, "Pyrotechnics," *The Liberator*, Ser. 61, 6, No. 5 (May 1923).

15. Millay, from *A Few Figs from Thistles* in *Collected Poems*, p. 127.

16. Hill, p. 26.

17. I use the term *performance* as it occurs in J. L. Austin, *How To Do Things with Words* (New York: Oxford Univ. Press, 1965), to mean acts actually constituted in and by language.

18. Louise Bogan, *Body of This Death* (New York: Robert M. McBride & Co., 1923), pp. 10–11.

19. Millay, from *The Harp-Weaver and Other Poems* (1923) in *Collected Poems*, pp. 173–74.

20. Bogan, *Body of This Death*, p. 9.

21. I am indebted for this insight to William Jay Smith, "The Making of Poems," in *The Streaks of the Tulip: Selected Criticism* (New York: Delacorte Press, 1972).

22. Bogan, *Body of This Death*, p. 13.

23. *Ibid.*, p. 16.

24. *Ibid.*, p. 28. Line 15 in this edition contains a misprint, "Plain," corrected to "Pain" in later editions.

25. Millay, from *A Few Figs from Thistles* in *Collected Poems*, p. 145.

26. Louise Bogan, *Dark Summer* (New York: Scribner's, 1929), p. 9.

27. Millay, from *The Buck in the Snow* (1928) in *Collected Poems*, p. 238.

28. Louise Bogan, *The Sleeping Fury* (New York: Scribner's, 1937), pp. 27–29.

29. *Ibid.*, pp. 38–39.

30. "Little Lobelia's Song," in "Three Songs," *The Blue Estuaries: Poems: 1923–1968* (New York: Farrar, Straus & Giroux, 1968), pp. 132–33.

31. Allan Ross Macdougall, ed., *Letters of Edna St. Vincent Millay* (New York: Harper, 1952), p. 173.

32. Louise Bogan, *Achievement in American Poetry* (Chicago: Henry Regnery Co., 1951), pp. 79–80.

Music in the Granite Hill:
The Poetry of Louise Bogan
Deborah Pope*

In an early essay, appearing in a volume titled *First Impressions*, the critic Llewellyn Jones went straight to the heart of Louise Bogan's poetry.[1]

> [Louise Bogan presents] a picture of the spiritual situation in America today of the young, sensitive, self-conscious woman—of such a woman in a civilization which has theoretically made room for her as a person, but practically has not quite caught up to her yet—which does not understand her. . . . It is the poetry of struggle against . . . the pettiness that haunts the footsteps of love, especially against the limitations, imposed and self-imposed, on women. . . .

His insight is all the more remarkable since he had only the evidence of her first book to go on, but his view that she took as her starting point the difficult emotional, sexual, and spiritual experience of women is a view critics and readers are only recently coming to fully grasp. Although her lyrical intensity and formidable precision of form have long been recognized and admired, the impeccably sculpted container has tended to obscure its volatile contents. Both thematically and stylistically, Bogan's poetry must be understood in terms of her unique experience of gender, examined anew in directions set out by the far-sighted Jones over fifty years ago. Bogan was indeed aware of, and compelled by, the restricting power of the few social roles available to women. She was also aware of how women themselves perpetuated their situation by low aspirations, mistaken obedience, fear, ignorance, and lack of imagination; but most often she believed they fell prey to romantic illusions in the sway of physical passion. In the power of such forces, the women Bogan repeatedly portrays in her poetry are always unequals in emotional relationships, victimized by their lack of power or inner control. Their experience of love is inevitably bitter and destructive.

*This essay was written for this volume and appears with the permission of the author.

Consequently, the need for control emerges as a major aspect of her work, closely aligned with the need for a strong sense of self as a means of emotional protection and counterbalance in intimacy. However, while women in the poems variously struggle to establish a sense of selfhood and control over their emotional and social environments, those very emotions and environments constantly operate to defeat them. Even the natural world, through the forces of fertility, time, and change, inexorably asserts its power over the self. Rather than the proximity and kinship women may be supposed to feel for natural cycles and procreation, Bogan sees these as threatening. Characteristically, there is an enormous amount of tension in her poetry as physical self squares off against spiritual self and reality attempts to face down illusion. The emotional tenor of the writing resembles nothing so much as an embattled stand-off, often internalized within the woman-speaker herself. The result is a poetry dominated by the impulse of rejection, as nature and the sexual and emotional demands of human ties become synonymous with the loss of power, freedom, and selfhood.

Throughout her work, her most frequent objective correlative for rejection is her obsession with the barren, withered landscapes of late fall and winter. Nature, like the human relationships enacted against its backdrop, is overwhelmingly sterile and static. The invulnerability of the self in such a landscape, devoid of change and emotion, serves her concept of the stoic, disillusioned self. Yet coupled with this rejection is a corollary longing for escape, both impulses clearly signified by the startling epigraph from St. Paul which opens her first book, *Body of This Death*: "Who shall deliver me from the body of this death?" Of all Bogan's work, this collection remains the most compelling, the most fruitful for close reading, not only in the richness and durability of the poems, but in its poignant and relatively unguarded cry against gender and its youthful determination to evade life's traps. This early collection establishes the foundation of all her work, a stance and style underlying and illuminating what is, above all, a study of female isolation, of women isolated from major aspects of human existence—the natural world, social interchange, their physical bodies, time. Bogan's term for this isolation is, fittingly, "death"; the diminishment and circumvention of the self results in a spiritual and even literal death from which the speaker seeks escape and freedom on new terms.

More explicitly and movingly than any subsequent collection, in both individual poems and the arrangement of the volume as a whole, *Body of This Death* explores the meaning of "death," the means of deliverance, and the role of the body in its own oppression and release. One of the most prominent exemplifications of this theme is the fact that a remarkable number of the women in the poems are bound, trapped, prone, immobile, or dead, figuratively or actually unable to express physical or emotional freedom. In poems like "Medusa," "The Frightened

Man," "Knowledge," "Portrait," "My Voice Not Being Proud," and "Statue and Birds," a speaker's static outer state corresponds to an inner paralysis of will and selfhood, both symptom and cause of her isolation.

The first reach is toward the environment, as four of the opening five poems present experiments in landscape: the desert in "A Tale," the jungle of "Decoration," the mythical realm of "Medusa," and the New England countryside in "A Letter." Escape through another person, indicative of the emotional environment, is explored in such poems as "The Frightened Man," "Betrothed," and "Words for Departure,"[2] but similarly fails. At the heart of the collection, "Men Loved Wholly Beyond Wisdom" and "Women" resolve to the utterly bleak proposition that women are by gender unable to love, to move, to be free, that it is neither landscapes, partners, nor roles, but women's very selves that are ultimately "the body of this death." This clearly marks the nadir of Bogan's search. Yet in the remaining poems of the book a new energy and capacity for escape emerges. The impact of "Women" is to bring about the final abandonment of hope for deliverance from the outside. The "who" of the epigraph can only be answered in the first person. The ultimate supportability or even accuracy of this premise is severely tested in Bogan's life and work, as well as by the powerful poems which precede this revelation in *Body of This Death*. Nevertheless, the final poems evince a determination for positive action and responsibility that the earlier, static poems do not. Immobilization characterizes the speakers before "Women," while movement and spatialization characterize most of those following it.

The youth of the opening poem, "A Tale," is an early version of the characteristically trapped and enclosed Bogan persona. This poem also establishes the motif of the inner journey, or quest, which reappears in subsequent poems, and is suggested by the overall arrangement of the volume itself. Here the metaphoric movement to the interior underlies the literal geographic progression from the sea inland to a rocky desert, signaling the youth's rejection of the familiar world of time and motion in an attempt to locate a permanent, unchanging self.

> This youth too long has heard the break
> Of waters in a land of change.
> He goes to see what suns can make
> From soil more indurate and strange.
>
> He cuts what holds his days together
> And shuts him in, as lock on lock:
> The arrowed vane announcing weather,
> The tripping racket of a clock;
>
> Seeking, I think, a light that waits
> Still as a lamp upon a shelf,—

> A land with hills like rocky gates
> Where no sea leaps upon itself.

The forces frustrating him—weather, time, tides—are the stuff of dailiness, but drive him to seek a radical reordering of landscape. What is unusual is that these conventional symbols of mundanity, dullness, and sameness are not eschewed for something more vital and lovely, but are themselves associated with other conventional symbols of fertility—water, change, sound. All are rejected in favor of silence, sterility, and absolute still-ness—a desert where "no sea leaps upon itself." I would suggest that this is in fact the encoded wish—encoded in the use of the male subject and the landscape projection—of a female persona who ambivalently re-gards the body, the fertile environment, as an oppressive force and who can only imagine release in terms of an utterly unproductive landscape. Yet the youth's goal emerges not as release but as death. Short of this finality of stasis, all "he" will ever find is an opposition in the self that is both ambiguous and "dreadful."

> But he will find that nothing dares
> To be enduring, save where, south
> Of hidden deserts, torn fire glares
> On beauty with a rusted mouth,—
>
> Where something dreadful and another
> Look quietly upon each other.

At the center of the landscape is an embattled deadlock between the "fire" of the inner self and the "beauty" of the physical self in which the world would imprison one. This final alignment comes off less power-fully and directed than it might because Bogan lapses into vague, im-precise language, diminishing what should be strong, dramatic closure. The weak use of "something," "another," "each other," undercuts the revelation of meaning, just as her use of the masculine figure and the third-person narrator obscure her personal stake in the poem. Her own participation in the experience becomes clearer in the poem which functions as a sequel to "A Tale."

This poem, "Medusa," continues "A Tale"'s final image of a static, unproductive landscape dominated by forces "looking quietly upon each other." In order to create the ideal environment the youth sought, Bogan turns to the figure of Medusa, whose mythic power stops time and process, seeking out the goddess the way the youth seeks for his desert:

> I had come to the house, in a cave of trees,
> Facing a sheer sky.
> Everything moved,—a bell hung ready to strike,
> Sun and reflection wheeled by.
>
> When the bare eyes were before me
> And the hissing hair,

> Held up at a window, seen through a door.
> The stiff bald eyes, the serpents on the forehead
> Formed in the air.

After this apparition, the speaker is frozen in a landscape that categorically evades the death-wish of the youth by virtue of its water and foliage; yet, through the agency of Medusa, any threatening process is also evaded. In this fantastic realm, the speaker has it both ways, much like the figures adorning Keats' Grecian urn. There is fertility (water, grass, hay) without the corruption of it (the water does not fall, nor the hay get mown).

> And I shall stand here like a shadow
> Under the great balanced day,
> My eyes on the yellow dust, that was lifting in the wind,
> And does not drift away.

This paradox of stasis and motion is not "dreadful" to the speaker as are the opposing forces of "A Tale." In fact, here all has come to a "great balanced day." The drawback is that this balance is only possible through the intervention of the supernatural. At this point Bogan cannot appropriate for herself the feminine power embodied in Medusa, and so remains still and passive in the "dead scene."

"Betrothed," a beautiful, complex poem, successfully moves away from the depersonalization and encoding of "A Tale" and "Medusa" in the continued search for a personal landscape, incorporating an exploration of personal relationships and conventional gender ties. The speaker, a young woman on the verge of marriage, mourns the estrangement from her mother and her girlhood friend that her new status seems to demand. Her rite of passage into womanhood is connected with the loss of bonds to other women, yet it is these relationships, rather than the prospective male lover's, which are positively associated in her mind with discovery, sensuality, and freedom. Significantly, the speaker envisions her impending separation from her friend as a change of landscapes:

> In the country whereto I go
> I shall not see the face of my friend
> Nor her hair the color of sunburnt grasses;
> Together we shall not find
> The land on whose hills bends the new moon
> In air traversed of birds.

The young girl hears in her mother's emptiness and bitter memories a curse on her own future in a similar role. The male lover does not compensate the speaker for her real and projected losses. Their attitudes together are stiff and formal, their landscape negligible and dim. Further, the girl's perception of her lover is disoriented; he is not seen as a totality, but rather as a set of disembodied features. Bogan accomplishes this depersonalization through redundancy and deliberate phrasing:

> You have put your two hands upon me, and your mouth,
> You have said my name as a prayer.
>
> . . . .
>
> I have watched your eyes, cleansed from regret,
> And your lips, closed over all. . . .

By contrast, the friend is perceived as a whole, rather than a collection of separate features, and it is with her the speaker achieves intimacy and communication, while the conventions of romantic love prevent any realistic exchange with the man. Yet this recognition ultimately leaves her no less passive and imprisoned than earlier speakers, since she capitulates to the predicted course, her romantic illusions interweaving with her resignation. Isolated from her lover and her sex, at odds with the landscape of her new role, she is isolated as well from time, already seeking to recover events from the past—"lost delights," "Old time"— already investing her happiness in the memory of a time that will quickly become as illusory as her expectations for the future. The poem closes with the darkening image of the young girl under the weeping willow— almost as if she has passed already into the ironic imprisonment of a sentimental pose—the leaves suggesting powerlessness and passivity:

> But there is only the evening here,
> And the sound of willows
> Now and again dipping their long oval leaves in the water.

The autobiographical dimension of "Betrothed" and four of the poems following it cannot be denied. They combine with others published contemporaneously in little magazines and journals to frankly and compellingly document the emotional turmoil of Bogan's own early marriage in 1916, when she was barely nineteen, and its subsequent breakdown.[3] The legacy of this early marriage informs much of the pain and disillusionment of her portrayal of relationships. Bogan's collected letters, which begin in 1920, after the marriage had ended, make rare references to this period. The marriage was, however, a disaster, as Bogan acknowledged: "I was the highly charged and neurotically inclined product of an extraordinary childhood and an unfortunate early marriage, into which state I had rushed to escape the first."[4]

Her memories of the poverty-stricken milltowns like Livermore, Milton, and Ballardvale where she spent her youth echo the barren, wasted landscapes that fill her poetry: "Terre Vague—uncultivated land, filled with 'chance vegetation.' The unbuilt lots of my childhood, filled with tansy and chicory; sometimes with some scrub trees. . . . The edge of things; the beaten dead end of nature, that fascinated me almost with a sexual fascination."[5] The strange resonance of "the beaten dead end of nature," so strong in Bogan's poetry, comes out of her own early identification with physical and psychic abuse, almost certainly at the hands of her mother, and helps account for the destructive sense of gender and love Bogan carried into her poetry and own emotional relationships.

Arguably, Bogan's strong emphasis on control and order in her poetry grew out of her great aversion to the unpredictability and chaos of her early emotional and domestic environment. Throughout her life she was impressed by examples of orderliness and efficiency, which she first experienced as a child during a stay with a family named Gardner. Bogan writes recurringly and extensively in her journal, even from the distance of more than fifty years, of the nearly epiphanic impression made on her by Mrs. Gardner, a woman who seems to have been the exact opposite of Mary Bogan. What so awed and impressed the young Louise Bogan were the neatness, the tidiness, above all the order, of Mrs. Gardner's household. This order remained inextricably linked in Bogan's mind to the absence of fear and vulnerability. The lesson of Mrs. Gardner becomes an ethic for Bogan's poetry; order, precision, and attention to form become ways of managing fear and disruption.

Bogan, however, was just a young girl when she escaped from the turbulence of her family life into a marriage she must have almost immediately regretted. In the December 1917 issue of *Others*, along with "Betrothed" appeared a companion poem, "The Young Wife." This latter poem, left out of *Body of This Death*, explicitly details the painful death of a naive, romantic attachment and in its place the beginnings of estrangement and resentment. The poem specifically addresses the disillusionment and betrayal felt by the sexually inexperienced girl at the easy knowledgeability of the male. Not only does she lose her feeling of uniqueness in the relationship, but her lover's previous partners have hardened into a perfected memory of sexuality and femininity that she, as a real woman, cannot equal. Thus the impotence and despair in "Betrothed" are dramatically developed and climaxed through the marriage tableau formed by four poems which follow it, "Words for Departure," "Ad Castitatem," "Knowledge," and "Portrait." These move eloquently from the ominous ambivalence of the young girl on the verge of commitment, through the breakdown of the relationship and a poignant, aggrieved separation ("Words for Departure"), to a bitter renunciation of sexuality altogether ("Ad Castitatem"), to a more stoic but nonetheless radical resignation to celibacy ("Knowledge"). Each step is a further armoring against the pain and betrayal of sexual commitment, concluding in the most extreme withdrawal of all—death ("Portrait").

Like the later "Men Loved Wholly Beyond Wisdom," "Ad Castitatem" is a violent, extravagant poem renouncing sexuality by an admittedly sexual woman. The Latin title, the ritual of invocation ("I make the old sign / I invoke you"), the gesture of the sign, suggest the vows of the nun, as if Bogan is entering a celibate sisterhood in retreat from the destructive passions of the world. There is a strong sense underlying the poem of the speaker using a special kind of spell, availing herself of an ancient rite in order to ward off evil. The evil is human passion, which appears in the poem as a destroying flame that has "withered" nature indiscriminately and "ravaged" and "blackened" her own heart. The infertile landscape, the bitter tone, and imminent isolation are true Bogan, as is the resort to sacrificial measures in order to obtain control. In important ways, this poem is a companion to "Medusa." In fact, the personified figure of Chastity is Medusa in another guise, a variation on a type who appears throughout Bogan's work under several names. This powerful figure, while at times ominous, is essentially protective in her ability to arrest time and change. She is Medusa, Chastity, the Sleeping Fury, the interceding woman in "The Dream," and ultimately the force of poetry itself, representing the human-controlled frame where time is stopped and process formalized. From her early work on, Bogan returns again and again to the lure of a power-ful, mythic female who embodies inviolability, sanctuary, and control. (It is interesting to note that Bogan liked to identify herself with strong women in history and myth. Replying to a scholar's query about her family origins, she once said, "It is my firm belief that I was Messalina, the Woman of Andros, . . . Boadicea, Mary Queen of Scots, Lucrezia Borgia, the feminine side of Leonardo . . . Saint Theresa of Avila . . .").[6] Yet the Chastity Bogan invokes is not without cost, bringing but a pyrrhic peace. She is, finally, "beautiful" but "futile."

The passionate disavowals of "Ad Castitatem" are spent in the Oriental mysticism of "Knowledge," where another prone speaker dedi-cates herself to solitary, spiritual repose, suggestive of death. This figure is more fully revealed in "Portrait," where the betrayed woman has moved beyond the painful reach of love and time altogether, by actual or spiritual death, to a sterile landscape reminiscent of "A Tale"'s:

> She has no need to fear the fall
> Of harvest from the laddered reach
> Of orchards, nor the tide gone ebbing
> From the steep beach.

The title calls attention to her literal still-life. The poem implies that alive, the woman had "need to fear" the "ravage" brought by change and love, "ravage" echoing the same threat in "Ad Castitatem," and like the speaker in the earlier poem, this woman could only survive by turning "stern and savage." Yet the elegaic, quiet tone of "Portrait" (a poem with curious parallels to Wordsworth's "A Slumber Did My Spirit Steal") suggests that only death brings the desired quittance of grief and alarm. Neither physical separation, chastity, nor stoic retreat have sufficed to ward off the "ravage" of being "loved by men."

Yet, as elsewhere in *Body of This Death*, the impression lingers in "Portrait" that the "death" may be an outer pose disguising an inner, fiery life. Like the fixed, formalized surface of a painting, the woman has a certain flat presence with others, a "glass" onto which they (presumably the men who love her) project their own conceptions, while her real life continues elsewhere, out of "reach." This tension, this paradox, between inner and outer selves becomes startlingly objectified in the figure of the statue in one of Bogan's finest poems, "Statue and Birds." Here, a marble girl stands at the heart of an empty winter arbor, the last human trace in a decaying formal scene. Her mind and exterior, like those of other personae, are grotesquely at odds. She is a type familiar from myth, a young girl transformed into a tree, or stone, or constellation, to escape the violence of men or gods; her violation is prevented, but her escape is too, and a panicked, vital consciousness lives on imprisoned. The statue becomes as well the literal woman on a pedestal, a marble symbol for the conditions restricting all women. Thus the opening lines compare her to "the arrested wind," a free, natural force held in check. Similarly, the landscape surrounding her is a largely artificial one where natural forces have been formalized and diverted. The leaves and vines have been "woven" into a "pattern"; the water is made to rise through the mechanical devices of a fountain; even the birds do not fly, but walk "closed up in their arrowy wings, / Dragging their sharp tails." The very mannered, restrained scene is designed to set off the central feature, the statue, which is, paradoxically, charged with an intensity of volition and gesture unmatched by anything around her. Her arms are "flung out in alarm / Or remonstrances," "her heel is lifted,—she would flee,—." The punctuation of the last phrase emphasizes its sharpness and tension and builds a sense of terror and desperation that is not fulfilled by the brief, muted closure: "the whistle of the birds / Fails on her breast." The descending sound of the phrase, the complexity of the word "fails" when the ear echoes "falls," beautifully achieve the doom of hope and escape.

Symbolically, the marble girl is representative of women fixed by art as well as by artificiality, unable by "definition"—that is, statue, myth, pedestal, art—to express themselves. Inside the immobilizing form of marble or sexual / social roles, such women are psychically and physically isolated. Even the girl's inner refusal, her gesture of alarm and remonstrances, ironically takes the shape of what the outside world sees as art or a pose. Because she is a statue, she cannot act or will; because she is a woman, she is trapped and isolated.

In poems following "Statue and Birds," this theme of the pain of gender intensifies. Paralysis and radical emotional denial impel the speaker of the well-known poem "Men Loved Wholly Beyond Wisdom." Here Bogan specifically resists the prodigal nature of women's love, so compulsive it burns like a fire in a thicket, totally consuming and destructive. Such love can be terrible in the homage it exacts, "the love men must return." Yet the alternative, to refuse to love at all, is equally grim, resulting in the emotional death of the woman:

> Heart, so subtle now, and trembling,
> What a marvel to be wise,
> To love never in this manner!
> To be quiet in the fern
> Like a thing gone dead and still,
> Listening to the prisoned cricket
> Shake its terrible, dissembling
> Music in the granite hill.

The image of the "prisoned cricket" exemplifies the irreducible feminine state, trapped and alone. The sounds that come from her are "terrible" and "dissembling," rigidly controlled by the "granite hill" of personal and stylistic discipline.

"The Crows" continues the mood of self-disgust present in "Men Loved Wholly" while looking back to "Statue and Birds" for important image parallels, most clearly in the winter setting and the dramatic use of birds.

> The woman who has grown old
> And knows desire must die,
> Yet turns to love again,
> Hears the crows' cry.

The speaker, like the statue, is trapped in a recalcitrant body while inwardly she teems with life and desire; however, it is not marble, but her own physically aged body that restricts her. Both the statue and this woman would flee their barren, withered world; for the latter, turning to love again is made to appear as futile as the former's lifted heel.

The collection's two central emotions—fear and denial—reach their nadir in the poem "Women."[7] Whereas speakers in previous poems found it possible, even convincing, to place responsibility for isolation on forces such as tradition, magic, various male figures, and age, the voice in "Women" totally internalizes the enemy and turns on her own feminine self. The identification of the "body of this death" becomes her own female body. The poem's unrelieved bitterness toward gender epitomizes the worst kind of isolation, extending to encompass both the outward and inward world. Women are excoriated as stunted, constricted creatures, senselessly paralyzed and paralyzing:

> Women have no wilderness in them,
> They are provident instead,
> Content in the tight hot cell of their hearts
> To eat dusty bread.

Hermetic, ingrown, they have sensuousness neither in themselves nor in their perception of the varied world about them:

> They do not see cattle cropping red winter grass,
> They do not hear
> Snow water going down under culverts
> Shallow and clear.

Unable to build or create, they only destroy. Everything they do suffocates; life itself is a mistake for these eternally blundering women.

> They wait, when they should turn to journeys,
> They stiffen, when they should bend.
> They use against themselves that benevolence
> To which no man is friend.

> They hear in every whisper that speaks to them
> A shout and a cry.
> As like as not, when they take life over their door-sills
> They should let it go by.

The encompassing nature of the attack is clear from the bluntly inclusive title and the rapid, accusatory "They's" with which half the lines begin. The women are composite reductions of previous personae, isolated from nature, the material world, productive social interchange with either sex, and isolated from themselves.[8]

Yet, strangely enough, the catharsis of "Women" is tremendously freeing. In terms of the opening epigraph, it faces squarely and summarily every aspect of gender that frustrates deliverance and admits death, while it simultaneously abandons hope for a third-party rescue. Underlying its leaden charges is the awareness that only the self can alter the self. Thus it is fascinating, in the context of the bitterness of "Women," to read the poem Bogan placed immediately following it. "Last Hill in a Vista" can be interpreted as almost a point by point reversal of the indictments just leveled. From the opening lines it is as if, miraculously, the women of the previous poem have escaped from their "tight hot cells" into the expansive landscape and freedom suggested in the title word "vista." Indeed, the first word of each stanza is the imperative "Come":

> Come, let us tell the weeds in ditches
> How we are poor, who once had riches,
> And lie out in the sparse and sodden
> Pastures that the cows have trodden,
> The while an autumn night seals down
> The comforts of the wooden town.

The call "let us" is a radical break from the distancing of the cumulative "they" in "Women" and marks only the third use of the inclusive first-person plural in the first twenty poems of the collection; indeed, it is one of the rare expressions of fellowship with others in all of Bogan's work. After poems of singularity and entrapment, this Fergus-like voice comes suddenly advocating a disregard of convention in favor of a journey under the stars. Throughout, the poem records an affinity to the natural world and the elements that was specifically denied women in the previous poem. In fact, these women much prefer the hills and fields to the "comforts of the wooden town," a phrase which suggests a limiting propriety and domesticity, much like the subsequent "with stiff walls about us." They risk cold and danger for a physical and psychic freedom. The realities of their new condition make their act courageous and determined, but the most crucial words are "we / Chose." The overriding trait of the previous speakers has been their lack of choice. They evince little control over the often horrific circumstances of their lives; the positive action here is revolutionary. The closure of "Last Hill" does not conclude or frustrate process, but rather opens uniquely outward.

The importance of this change in the sense of movement is seen by comparison with earlier poems where stasis is structurally reinforced by an ambivalence in poetic closure that is a signature of *Body of This Death*. Repeatedly poems fail to achieve any sense of completion because of the alignment of phrases and images which act to cancel each other out. This effect often occurs internally as well, revealing seeming alternatives of action to be but means to the same end. This structural neutralization is itself a correlative of thematic immobility and futility; for example:

> Where something dreadful and another
> Look quietly upon each other. ("A Tale")

> The water will always fall, and will not fall,
> And the tipped bell make no sound. ("Medusa")

> To escape is nothing, not to escape is nothing. ("A Letter")

> In fear of the rich mouth
> I kissed the thin,—
> Even that was a trap
> To snare me in. ("The Frightened Man")

> Nothing was remembered, nothing forgotten.
> .   .   .   .
> Nothing was accepted, nothing looked beyond.
> .   .   .   .
> Nothing was lost, nothing possessed. ("Words for Departure")

> Alike upon the ground
> Struck by the same withering
> Lie the fruitful and the barren branch. . . . ("Ad Castitatem")

Over what yields not, and what yields,
Alike in spring, and when there is only bitter
Winter-burning in the fields. ("The Crows")

Their love is an eager meaninglessness
Too tense, or too lax. ("Women")

Unlike any poem in the volume before it, "Last Hill" is the voice of rebellion and community, raised by women determined to free themselves mentally and physically from an environment which oppresses. They have simply pulled up stakes and left, preferring the challenge of a risky liberty to the deceptive comfort and safety that diminish their vitality and maturity. The remaining poems should be read in light of this change. For example, "Stanza," which was first published alongside "Last Hill" in *Measure*, focuses on mythical women figures who were raped by men, and who are now alone, going about their lives, refusing to be imprisoned in memory or trauma. Their attitude is one of self-sufficiency and specific indifference to the sexual impact of men on their lives:

Leda forgets the wings of the swan,
Danaë has swept the gold away.

Similarly, "The Changed Woman" takes for its subject a woman striving to live positively alone, which is a marked change from the behavior of earlier personae:

The light flower leaves its little core
Begun upon the waiting bough.
Again she bears what she once bore
And what she knew she re-learns now.

The cracked glass fuses at a touch,
The wound heals over, and is set
In the whole flesh, and is not much
Quite to remember or forget.

"The cracked glass" suggests a split in the self, a duality existing in some previous state, while "the wound" seems to be a familiar, negative metaphor for sexual experience. Both are now "fused," "healed," and set "In the whole flesh." The male / female tension is emphasized in the third stanza by two patently phallic images and two female images—"Rocket and tree, and dome and bubble"—which are, to the speaker's mind, images of treachery. Yet having "changed," the woman "need not trouble" with them any longer. The negative parts of her life belong to the past—"cracked glass," "wound," "treachery," "trouble"—while the fusing and healing belong to the present. The "unwise, heady / Dream" seems to be her desire to live independently without the internal divisions brought on by insufficient sexual relationships. Here, "unwise" sounds a commendation, since we have seen in poems such as "Knowledge" and "Men Loved Wholly" the desolation of wisdom. Yet the woman's life remains uneasy. Elsewhere the dream is "ever denied" and she fears she will "never . . . be forgiven" for her choice.

The poem following "The Changed Woman" is the curious "Chanson un peu naïve," curious because the naive, childish singer seems out of context with the emerging, toughened women of the final poems. The style imitates the riddle songs of folk ballads, and the riddle in this case comes close to a parody of the volume's epigraph:

> What body can be ploughed,
> Sown, and broken yearly?
> She would not die, she vowed,
> But she has, nearly.

The answer to the riddle, the female body in childbirth, literally exemplifies broader discoveries the poems have been making about the vulnerabilities brought on by gender. The stanzas trace a girl's illusions about childbirth and love, as she gradually answers the riddle, but evades its implications. All that "flies free" is her naiveté, and that is lost in cries. She undergoes no effective revelation, capable of only "a pretty boast" to conceal her pain and bafflement.

What emerges more subtly than the girl's plight, and what perhaps explains the poem's placement at this stage, is the altered voice of the speaker. There is an undertone of mockery, amplified by the affected French title, the nursery rhyme meter, and the pathetic rendering of the girl, that measures the distance between this unenlightened figure and the more complex initiated Bogan. Positively construed, the suggestion of parody is a mile-marker of the one voice's comparative security, a flexibility and even self-wit. Yet the tone is still disturbing, for it hints at an as yet unresolved disgust of gender that will continue to appear in Bogan.

Body of This Death, however, closes out on the new upsurge of freedom and self-reliance. The penultimate poem of the volume, "Fifteenth Farewell," suggests by its title a move often attempted but never fully made, until now when the poem finally carries through the break between a woman and her lover. As the speaker explains, she regards the move as a matter of her own survival, fearing her selfhood will be buried under the man's domination. She refuses to comply with her psychic extinction, "covering all that was" (her past life) "with all that will be" (her future with her lover):

> You may have all things from me, save my breath.
> The slight life in my throat will not give pause
> For your love, nor your loss, nor any cause.
> Shall I be made a panderer to death,
> Dig the green ground for darkness underneath,

> Let the dust serve me, covering all that was
> With all that will be?

While fully admitting the inevitable loneliness, she has significantly re-defined it; it is wrong to imagine loneliness as a physical setting, an absence of people, or any tangible emptiness. Rather it is the unbridge-able separateness of an unequal human relationship: "Loneliness was the heart within your side." One can adjust to "simple empty days," but not to the paralyzing alienation of "that chill / Resonant heart [striking] between my arms/ Again." The poem closes in a mood and setting similar to that of "Last Hill." The first crucial liberating steps have been taken, but the consequences remain untracked and darkness is closing in.

> Now that I leave you, I shall be made lonely
> By simple empty days,—never that chill
> Resonant heart to strike between my arms
> Again, as though distraught for distance,—only
> Levels of evening, now, behind a hill,
> Or a late cock-crow from the darkening farms.

Clearly, "Sonnet" deserves special attention as the concluding poem of *Body of This Death*, and the highmark of the book's movement.[9] Like "Last Hill" and "Fifteenth Farewell," "Sonnet" is a poem of separation and independence; however, it turns more on "Fifteenth Farewell" 's sense of pain and uncertain future:

> Since you would claim the sources of my thought
> Recall the meshes whence it sprang unlimed,
> The reedy traps which other hands have timed
> To close upon it. Conjure up the hot
> Blaze that it cleared so cleanly, or the snow
> Devised to strike it down. It will be free.
> Whatever nets draw in to prison me
> At length your eyes must turn to watch it go.
>
> My mouth, perhaps, may learn one thing too well,
> My body hear no echo save its own,
> Yet will the desperate mind, maddened and proud,
> Seek out the storm, escape the bitter spell
> That we obey, strain to the wind, be thrown
> Straight to its freedom in the thunderous cloud.

In a crucial shift, the poem's focus is specifically on the entrapment of the mind, while the majority of previous personae have also expressed an entrapment of the body. Here it is the will, the power of independent thought, that drives the speaker to a "desperate" revolt against the "reedy traps" and "nets" of others, presumably here her lover. The distance traveled from the first poem of the volume with its motive of escape and this final poem is remarkable. The former is vague, third-person, reactionary, motivated primarily by romantic escapism, while the latter is disciplined, courageous, first-person, and charged with a strong sense of self. The direction of deliverance moves figuratively from the earth/body toward the sky/spirit.

This orientation toward the last preserve of the self signals the emphasis of much of Bogan's subsequent work, yet the concluding sestet of "Sonnet" is a curious blend of the pride and madness of her pursuit. The liberation is seen in violent, reckless terms; there is danger equal to triumph in the mingled sense of exhilaration and sacrificial release.

Behind Bogan's struggle is the specter of an even greater isolation, a solipsism that is potentially more enclosing than the state she seeks to escape. After *Body of This Death*, her fears did in very real ways come true. She did "learn one thing too well," and her poetry often seems to have heard "no echo save its own." Her distrustful, cynical perspective built on a reduction of the human and natural landscape becomes habitual and predictable. What hope for freedom the concluding poems of her first volume may imply solidifies in subsequent collections into an isolation and suspicion that are profound. In *Dark Summer*, her second book, one comes upon the familiar stretches of barrenness set against fall, winter, night, and inclement days. The atmosphere of impending catastrophe is registered by the volume's title. Modulations in theme and tone occur mostly in the new determination to survive and maintain, rather than to solve or change.

The use of nature as an emblem of rejection diminishes with the later poems of *The Sleeping Fury* (1937), *Poems and New Poems* (1941), and *The Blue Estuaries* (1968), although it remains important in her images. The significant change is Bogan's increasing dependence on the mental and creative process as a sphere of selfhood and control. Poetry itself emerges as the containable, acceptable landscape of the self. The shift seems to come out of a motive of self-protection, moving away from the risk and tension of struggling with the human and physical. In *The Sleeping Fury*, poetry is clearly given the burden of assuming the fulfillment and constancy unobtainable in human relationships. She reaches the point of reduction where only her own inner mental discipline and poetic skill provide a bulwark against the external world's betrayal, and her style is the direct expression of the extremity of emotion she felt alone led to legitimate poetry. In "Springs of Poetry," an early essay contemporaneous with *Body of This Death*, Bogan described the impulse to write:

> When [the poet] sets out to resolve, as rationally as he may the tight irrational knot of his emotions, the poet hesitates for a moment. Unless the compulsion be absolute, as is rarely the case, the excitement of the resolution sets in only after this pause, filled with doubt and terror. He would choose anything, anything, rather than the desperate

task before him: a book, music, talk, and laughter. Almost immediately the interruption is found, and the emotion diverted, or the poem is begun, and the desperation has its use. . . . Few poems are written in that special authentic rage because even a poet has a great many uses for grief and anger, beyond putting them into a poem. The poem is always a last resort.[10]

In her poetic, there was little room for meditative, exploratory vehicles; with a few rare exceptions, such as the lovely valedictory "After the Persian," there is no sense in Bogan's work of recollecting in tranquillity. Rather her poems are essential speech under the stress of the moment, creating what Marianne Moore called a "forged diction," where every thought and phrase is "compactness compacted."[11]

Subordination of the external to the service of an interior necessity results in a poetry of aftermaths, summations, epitaphs, offering a minimum of context or circumstance. Her artistic fidelity is less to actual nature than to the inner world of the psyche, colored by emotional and psychological response. The insularity of situation and response is an indication of the need to control, through her poetry, the literal and emotional aspects of her landscape. What results is not a Faustian or Adamic power, but an even greater powerlessness and rigidity dependent upon the exclusion and suppression of any nature and life that does not fit her frame. What seems least to fit is the female body itself, the "body of this death." Isolating herself from time, nature, the human, from the cathartic release of emotion itself, Bogan's persona is a desperate, rigid figure. The conditions of her life and the perceptions of her poetry are perhaps expressed in her own words to May Sarton:

> I have been *forced* to learn to wait, to be patient, to wait for the wheel to turn. . . . I have been *forced* to find a way of loving my destiny; of not opposing it too much with my will. I have been forced "to forgive life" in order to get through existence at all. . . . My "peace" and "calm" are, as I have said again and again, too hard won to be lightly tossed aside.[12]

The extreme self-discipline and suppression that enabled her to survive emotionally and practically a difficult girlhood, marital failures, mental breakdowns, lifelong struggles with her muse and her own nature come out in a style and stance pared to the bone: the granite hill that is both imprisoning and terrible.

Notes

1. Llewellyn Jones, *First Impressions: Essays on Poetry, Criticism and Prose* (New York: Knopf, 1925), pp. 112, 118.

2. Poems in *Body of This Death* were included in the subsequent collections *Poems and New Poems*, *Collected Poems*, and *The Blue Estuaries* with the excep-

tion of the following, which were never reprinted: "Decoration," "A Letter," "Words for Departure," "Epitaph for a Romantic Woman," and "Song."

3. Poems which most certainly center on Bogan's marriage and early widowhood not collected in *Body of This Death* (or elsewhere) are "The Young Wife," *Others* (December 1917); "Survival," *Measure*, No. 9 (November 1921); a series of five poems published under the title "Beginning and End," including "Elders," "Resolve," "Leavetaking," "To a Dead Lover," and "Knowledge" (which alone of these was reprinted in *BD*), *Poetry* (August 1922); "The Stones," *Measure*, No. 28 (June 1923).

4. Letter to Morton D. Zabel, 11 June 1937, in *What the Woman Lived: Selected Letters of Louise Bogan 1920–1970*, ed. Ruth Limmer (New York: Harcourt Brace Jovanovich, 1973), p. 6, n. 2. All subsequent letters refer to this volume, unless otherwise noted.

5. *Journey Around My Room: The Autobiography of Louise Bogan*, ed. Ruth Limmer (New York: Viking, 1980), p. 20. Strengthening this association is the passage several passages later, "The incredibly ugly mill towns of my childhood, barely dissociated from the empty, haphazardly cultivated, half-wild, half deserted countryside around them. Rough stony pastures, rugged woodlots, lit up and darkened by the clearly defined, pale, lonely light ..." (*Journey*, p. 23).

6. Letter written 1 May 1939, in response to a research student who had the temerity to send her a lengthy questionnaire; the letter was never sent. See *What the Woman Lived*, p. 189.

7. Bogan had a special fondness for the poem "Women," and had it privately issued as a reprint (Pasadena: Ward Ritchie, 1929).

8. Bogan's ambivalent tone of anger and grief directed against the stolid, numb, constricted, helpless female figures in "Women" appears again very sharply in the essay "Art Embroidery," *New Republic*, 21 March 1928, p. 156.

9. "Sonnet" was the only poem Bogan chose to have printed in italics, as it appeared at the conclusion of *Body of This Death*. This form was dropped in subsequent printings. Bogan apparently had some thought of printing "Song for a Lyre" in italics as the final poem of *The Sleeping Fury*, but this was not carried out.

10. Louise Bogan, "The Springs of Poetry," *New Republic*, 37 (5 December 1923), Supp. 9.

11. Marianne Moore, "Compactness Compacted," in *Predilections* (New York: Viking, 1955), p. 130.

12. May Sarton, *A World of Light: Portraits and Celebrations* (New York: Norton, 1976), pp. 227–28.

Circumscriptions   Ruth Limmer*

Louise Bogan, born in 1897 and dead in 1970, was the author of six books of poetry, five books of translation, two volumes of criticism, and one anthology of poetry for children. Since her death there have been three more books: One, *A Poet's Alphabet*, is a collection of critical articles. Following it came a volume of her letters, running from

*This essay appears here for the first time, with the permission of the author.
© 1977, 1984 by Ruth Limmer.

1920 to 1970, published under the title *What the Woman Lived*. Both are out of print. In 1980 came the "mosaic autobiography" *Journey Around My Room*, which brought together journals, notebook entries, short stories, published and unpublished poetry, and a variety of fugitive pieces written over a lifetime. Despite these many books, despite her winning all but one of the poetry awards offered in America, and despite the fact that for some thirty-seven years she was the by-lined poetry reviewer for the *New Yorker*, what was true back in 1936 remains true today. In that year Bogan complained to her publisher that she was the one poet in America with a "definite note" who was almost unknown.

What can that fact, more than forty years true, tell us about Bogan's life and art?

Let me begin to answer by quoting a poem called, unoriginally but with sharp purpose and poignant result, "Portrait of the Artist as a Young Woman." It was probably written in 1940 (this guess is Bogan's not mine), when she was forty-three years old. It was copied and re-written sixteen years later, and a dozen years after that, when she came to put together her final collection—*The Blue Estuaries*—it was still not one of the poems she wished to include.

PORTRAIT OF THE ARTIST AS A YOUNG WOMAN

Sitting on the bed's edge, in the cold lodgings, she wrote it out on her knee
In terror and panic—but with the moment's courage, summoned up from God
    knows where.
Without recourse to saints or angels: a Bohemian, thinking herself free—
A young thin girl without sense, living (she thought) on passion and air.

The winds struck her; she flew abroad; what is this land wherein she wakes?
The armoire broods and the bed engulfs; the cafe is warm at ten;
The lindens give out their scent, the piano its scales; the trams rumble; the
    shadows in the formal garden take
The half-attentive gaze of the still-young woman, who will grieve again.

Everything falls to pieces once more; and the only refuge is the provincial stair;
People without palates try to utter, and the trap seems to close;
A child goes for the milk; the library books are there,
Generous to the silly young creature caught again in the month of the rose.

Is there a way through? Never think it! Everything creaks.
And here once more is the cold room, between thin walls of sadist and lout.
But at last, asking to serve, seeking to earn its keep, about and about,
At the hour of the dog and the wolf, is it her heart that speaks?
She sits on the bed with the pad on her knees, and writes it out.[1]

We recognize the poem as Bogan's by its risk-taking meter, by its form, and by its language. "This land wherein she wakes," the piano and the scales, "everything creaks," "the hour between the dog and the wolf"—these are her turns of speech, of sight, and of sound. And the meter—the impossible and dangerous hexameter—might easily be hers; unlike many poets she continually dared varieties of meter and was astonishingly successful with them.

But without the internal evidence, one would not take Bogan for the author. The content is wrong. The poem tells too much, too openly. Almost by definition, a Bogan poem is one in which experience is refined, disguised, transmuted alchemically into a different substance. She even wrote a poem called "The Alchemist":

> I burned my life, that I might find
> A passion wholly of the mind,
> Thought divorced from eye and bone,
> Ecstasy come to breath alone.
> I broke my life, to seek relief
> From the flawed light of love and grief.
>
> With mounting beat the utter fire
> Charred existence and desire.
> It died low, ceased its sudden thresh.
> I had found unmysterious flesh—
> Not the mind's avid substance—still
> Passionate beyond the will.[2]

What event does that poem describe? Who is the speaker? Where? Under what specific pressure? We don't know. We are not meant to know. Her poems are based, she told an inquirer, "on some actual occasion, some real confrontation," and we see for ourselves that they are filled with palpable objects: mirrors, anchors, apples, mansard roofs, porcupines. . . . But these are never the curtains and bushbeans of direct autobiography; her poems are written under high pressure, and a symbolic hand is upon them. No "actual occasion" ever appears.

Her "Portrait of the Artist" is unBoganish precisely because the transmutation has *not* fully taken place. The brooding armoire and the provincial stair, yes, perhaps they are sufficiently distanced, but the "young thin girl" remains identifiable as an actual actor in a temporal room, seated on a bed in which and on which her life and her art are played out. No wonder then that she never sent the poem out for publication. After nearly thirty years, it had still not given up its autobiographical immediacy.

Why must it? Because Bogan required of herself and, I propose, of all women poets that they disappear behind the work, as the ancient Greek actor disappeared behind the mask. However strong and identifiable the voice, the person of the actor was in that way safe from recognition. Masking gives freedom. And importantly, it frees the poem itself from narrowing and limiting associations.

Bogan wanted poetry to be timeless and, in a very real sense, personless. No biographical note need accompany "Western Wind, when will thou blow the small rain down can rain? Christ, if my love were in my arms and I in my bed again." Similarly, Bogan's poetry tried for and often reached the permanence of the always existent. Her "Portrait of the Artist" would not and could not.

Why so strong an emphasis on anonymity? As I move toward an answer, let me take up another fact: Bogan, who was a wise, appreciative, and vastly knowledgeable critic, had remarkably little regard for most of the women poets of her time.

Of her forebears, she deeply valued Sappho, Louise Labé, Christina Rossetti, Emily Dickinson. Of her near-contemporaries, she championed Abbie Houston Evans and Marianne Moore, and did much to make the latter's reputation. She also admired the work of Léonie Adams, especially when they were both young together. Among those somewhat younger than herself, she thought Elizabeth Bishop "greatly gifted" but reviewed her, I believe, only once, and among her juniors she was strongly supportive of Barbara Howes, May Swenson, Jane Cooper, and other fine if uncelebrated poets. But on the whole, and notwithstanding her long guiding friendship with May Sarton, Bogan was generally cool toward women poets. Her greatest enthusiasms, where 20th century women were concerned, were for English and European prose writers: Viola Meynell, Isak Dinesen, Colette.

Let me be clear. I very much admired Louise Bogan as a critic, and many of my own tastes were shaped by her. I do not basically disagree with her critical positions. Nevertheless, I think it is significant that she who could come up with so many deep admirations for male poets—for Yeats, Rilke, Mallarmé, Eliot, Valéry, Lowell, Wilbur—and with so many judicious and close-to-the-bone evaluations of male poets who she thought were less than first rate . . . that she often did not give to female poets the same warmth of consideration in her criticism. I think, for example, of her ignoring the fine work of Maxine Kumin and her total dismissal of Denise Levertov.

It would be easy enough to explain it by saying "jealousy": the excellent but little-known poet harboring resentments against those smaller talents who have captured attention. In part that is true. But anyone who is familiar with the quality of Bogan's published criticism must sense that jealousy is the smallest part of the explanation. Nor does it seem likely, as was once suggested by Gloria Bowles, that Bogan adopted a "masculine" critical position which required her to denigrate and mis-value women's experience.

No, hers was not, I think, a "masculine" position, but it *was* a non-feminist one. To begin with, she believed strongly that men and women differed in their natures and talents, and she would not have it otherwise. She once made the point that homosexuality was simply dreary: men with men, women with women. . . . "They're so *on* to each other," she said; "no surprises. How boring it must be."

As she made clear in a lecture published as chapter 13 of *Journey Around My Room*, from which I paraphrase, men could, if they wished, be totally abandoned, directly destructive, give themselves to sustained play in life and in art, throw reason to the winds. Women, whose nature, she felt, was to be practical, nurturing, tender, could do none of these things, or do none of them well. Women could not successfully imitate men's rough ways. Harsh eroticism, shock, and a coarse way with language were not women's metier.

Those who tried? It was *they* who were imitating men. Did she in this way limit women's possibilities? Most certainly. She chose to set limits to women's artistic behavior much as we choose to limit behavior of all sorts—perjury, brutality, child molestation—because we disapprove of it. The examples are strong; Bogan felt strongly, and disapproval can be as strong in art as in ethics.

To be a woman poet and let self-pity creep into the poem was not acceptable; to be lachrymous, pious, naive, preening, affected—I am using her language—also not acceptable; to act out, to self-dramatize, was not acceptable. Why? A matter of taste. An old-fashioned belief in dignity or standards or, one might say, an old fashioned notion of the sacredness of art, except that "sacredness" implies solemnity and Bogan's critical muse embraced laughter and vulgarity and full-bodied earthiness such as Molly Bloom's while it rejected middle-class refinement—oh, how she despised and feared middle-class refinement!

What Bogan refused to poetry by women was complaint and confession, poems that say: "My life is wretched. I deserve better." Perhaps so, but about pain and injustice, Bogan's daemon said, "*Why not?* It said, *Once more.*" That is pride speaking, and hard-won knowledge, the voice of someone who has fought alone, against terrible odds, for her own freedom. She knew, of course, that freedom was not there for the winning in all times and places, but it could be won in America, in the 20th century. She knew because she had done it. To *complain* that it was very, very hard struck her as puerile and unworthy. Women must be above that.

Because her lines of permissible conduct in poetry were drawn so sharply, and because great talent for poetry is a rare commodity at best, she necessarily had little regard for most women poets. Additionally, because she had a strong preference for form (in life and in all the arts), the women poets who yearned humorlessly around in a free-versey way were dismissed. So too the poets of either sex who thought poetry a vehicle for political statement.

All of this makes Bogan sound like the most ferocious of critical dragons and the most circumscribed of personalities. Those familiar with her work know how far off the mark that is. But it is certainly true that she presented herself in public in a most formal and reserved way. Accounts of her reading poetry even back in the Bohemian 1920s describe her non-giving ways. Unlike Edna Millay, for example, who created a vivid persona, we're told Bogan looked disdainful of the audience, of the poetry, of herself for reading it. The audience got the poem or it didn't. Normally, Bogan provided no help except exquisite diction. Even her photographs seem posed to keep the reader at arm's length. Nancy Milford, in her review of *What the Woman Lived* in the *New York Times*, describes how, when looking for "a face to match my own," she saw Bogan in a photograph, wearing, she tells us, "a buttoned suit with perhaps a brooch fastened high on a soft collar." Said Milford, "She was no fiery lady to pattern myself on."

It's a strange business. In *The Golden Notebook*, Doris Lessing writes: "Are you saying there haven't been artist-women before? There haven't been women who were independent? There haven't been women who insisted on sexual freedom? I tell you, there's a great line of women stretching out behind you into the past, and you have to seek them out and find them. . . ." Bogan stood in the van of Lessing's line; no question about that. But for reasons of her own, she made the search as hard for others as she could. She simply wouldn't deliver herself up— not to audiences, not to readers, not to the publicity offices of the publishers.

Her letters, published posthumously, allow us to come closer, of course, but even in them we hear a voice whose enchanting range is limited not by what it can say but by what it will say. We also have from her pen, her private pen as it were, the extended excerpts from notebooks and journals published in *Journey Around My Room*. Mostly they are about the past and about how, in maturity, one comes to deal with it. Even there, where she is struggling to explain herself *to* herself, we hear the voice of restraint. Even at the furthest end of her tether, she is in absolute control: the walls of the permissible are not breached.

In these days, when almost all writers except Pynchon and Salinger seem to serve as their own public relations agency and Masters and Johnson report, Bogan's reserve is magnificently welcome. But it can be argued that her reticence had two deplorable effects: one, that it alienated the larger audience which, not entirely without reason, wants access to its poets; and two, it had the effect of circumscribing her talent.

If everything were not required to be transmuted, I think Bogan not only could have written more poetry, but she could have extended her poetically creative life to the end, for the process of alchemy requires powerful magic, as it were—enormous energy not often available to lyric poets after their youthful years. And if she had allowed the "unworthy" emotions and experiences to be material for her poetry, then, obviously, she would have had a much wider range of subject matter on which to draw. But it was never to be. Once, referring slightingly to a new volume of poetry, she wrote: "I am really v. envious of [her] ability to express—to have emotions regularly and suitably and mirthlessly. It is all so noble and so—respectable somehow.... Should I write some imitation poems of this experiential kind? No, no."[3]

One might well ask then whether Bogan *had* won the freedom she prided herself in achieving. To answer that, I think one must weigh against her undeniable independence the fact that in her last two decades she wrote almost no poetry whatever. Obviously she didn't lose her talent, as one might an umbrella. The talent remained, but she had so hemmed it in that translation and criticism finally became almost her only creative outlet.

We might argue that you can't have it both ways. Either you have Bogan's pure and tensiled poetry—for the alchemist actually did find gold—or you have the looser, the unbuttoned, the confessional tell-all. But even as we set up the polarities, we recognize their falsity. Among others, Yeats had both; Robert Lowell had both. Bogan did not. For some reason, she put a stop to her own freedom. This far, she said; no further.

Was it fear? When you fear excessively, as Bogan did, middle-class refinement, perhaps it is because it has some hold over you. In any event, her strictures kept her from the range of expression that many men, neither more nor less talented, have been able to achieve.

In the course of working through this essay, I have come to entertain the possibility that the grief and frustration that absorbed her last years may have had their origin in her chosen circumscriptions; and that what I will continue to call dignity, taste, and a belief in the (qualified) sacredness of art—*but which may also be called a fear of revealing oneself*—kept her from full creative freedom.

And just what is there to be revealed? Bohemianism? Sure. Heterosexuality? You bet. Pre-marital sex? Yes. Adultery? That too. A certain ruthlessness in her escape to freedom? Unquestionably. But if there is anything more, anything seriously worth concealment, I've yet to discover it.

In this context, her "Portrait of the Artist as a Young Woman" becomes almost unbearably poignant, because we find that at least twice in her life, this genuinely courageous woman confronted her fear and tried to record it nakedly—not, as in "Medusa" or "The Dream," for example, in highly symbolic form.

"The young thin girl" of the poem had no exemplars and knew little yet of the "great line." That she found a "moment's courage" at all, no less than for three decades, speaks to us of human triumph and of a creative spirit that will not be stilled. But then, something happened. Call that something the impact of life itself, for which one pays; call it the overburdening demands for renunciation, and control; call it cumulative silences.

It is instructive at this point to pair two of her published poems. The first was written when Bogan was no more than twenty-five years old and defiant as hell.

SONNET

Since you would claim the sources of my thought
Recall the meshes whence it sprang unlimed,
The reedy traps which other hands have timed
To close upon it. Conjure up the hot
Blaze that it cleared so cleanly, or the snow
Devised to strike it down. It will be free.
Whatever nets draw in to prison me
At length your eyes must turn to watch it go.

My mouth, perhaps, may learn one thing too well,
My body hear no echo save its own,
Yet will the desperate mind, maddened and proud,
Seek out the storm, escape the bitter spell
That we obey, strain to the wind, be thrown
Straight to its freedom in the thunderous cloud.

The second poem was written and published when she was sixty-nine.

LITTLE LOBELIA'S SONG

I was once a part
Of your blood and bone.
Now no longer—
I'm alone, I'm alone.

Each day, at dawn,
I come out of your sleep;
I can't get back.
I weep, I weep.

Not lost but abandoned,
Left behind;
This is my hand
Upon your mind.

I know nothing.
I can barely speak.

But these are my tears
Upon your cheek.

You look at your face
In the looking glass.
This is the face
My likeness has.

Give me back your sleep
Until you die,
Else I weep, weep,
Else I cry, cry.

What spirit weeps, what "child ghost" cries? It is easy to oversimplify, but might it not be the voice that was never permitted to speak in public and was hardly ever allowed to utter even in private?

Had Bogan not so severely limited the scope of female expression—if she had allowed women the license she permitted to men—might little Lobelia have sung a somewhat less despairing song? We cannot know. But it is a question to explore as we ponder, for our own purposes, the dialogue between the woman poet's life and her art.

Notes

1. Published posthumously in *Journey Around My Room* (New York: Viking, 1980; rpt. New York: Penguin, 1981).

2. First publication in 1922, in the *New Republic*.

3. Letter to Ruth Limmer, 11 February 1966, previously unpublished.

The Problem of the Woman Artist:
Louise Bogan, "The Alchemist"

Diane Wood Middlebrook*

To tell the truth, there is very little that one can say about women poets, past, present, and (presumably) to come. One truth about them is an open secret: when they are bad they are very very bad, and when they are good, they are magnificent. . . . The problem of the woman artist remains unchanged. Henry James, in *The Tragic Muse*, spoke of "that oddest of animals, the artist who happens to be born a woman." (Louise Bogan, "What the Women Said," lecture at Bennington College, 1962)[1]

*This essay appears here for the first time, with the permission of the author. Portions originally appeared in *Worlds into Words: Understanding Modern Poems* (New York: Norton, 1980), and are used with the permission of the author.

Louise Bogan is one of a generation of distinguished American woman poets born between 1885–1900 whose art expresses a felt contradiction between writing and living a woman's life. The milieu of the early twentieth century—thanks to the recognized genius of Bogan's contemporaries Yeats, Eliot, Pound, Stevens, and Williams—saw a genuine cultural renaissance of poetry. But women writers remained marginal to this renaissance. The list of Bogan's female peers would include Elizabeth Madox Roberts, Elinor Wylie, H. D., Edna St. Vincent Millay, Genevieve Taggard, Babette Deutsch, Léonie Adams, and Marya Zaturenska, and among fiction writers, Katherine Anne Porter and Janet Lewis. Each is an impeccable stylist highly respected by fellow artists. Yet all worked in a climate of awareness that a woman must, as Léonie Adams said of Louise Bogan, "function not only as a poet of her own time but within the limits accorded a woman poet. . . . There could never be any confusion of the role of woman and the role of poet, or any exploitation of the role of woman. She knew, moreover, that she should not model herself upon the women she admired or who were closest to her in time."[2]

Bogan rarely wrote directly about her mistrust of the origins of her poetry in a specifically female experience of the world. But her collected poems, *The Blue Estuaries: Poems, 1923–1968*, contains a handful of poems on this theme which gives us what might be described as a private mythology constructed to account for her creativity. Bogan did not, in these poems, analyze her cultural situation; rather, she reflected its influence in a body of symbols that express the contradiction woman/artist in other bipolar metaphors: flesh/breath, low/high, earth/heaven, silence/voice. Central to the symbolisms of this mythology are, on the one hand, anxiety about aspects of the self which cannot be controlled; on the other hand, reverence for the mind and its powers. "The Alchemist," "Cassandra," and "Fifteenth Farewell" are among the poems which elaborate this myth. In them art is viewed as the product of both a freedom and a control hard to attain within the limits of a woman's mind, which Bogan viewed as sometimes helpless, often under domination by unconscious forces. Woman, in this mythology, is carefully distinguished from artist.

"The Alchemist"—written by the time Louise Bogan was twenty-five—displays her characteristic strength: a skilled formalism in which the syntax is simple and straightforward ("I broke my life, to seek relief"; "I had found unmysterious flesh"). And in it she addresses symbolically the problem of "that oddest of animals, the artist who happens to be born a woman."

In "The Alchemist" the contradiction between woman and artist is an implication latent within the explicit subject of the poem: the desire to attain self-transcendence through brutal self-control.

I burned my life, that I might find
A passion wholly of the mind,
Thought divorced from eye and bone,
Ecstasy come to breath alone.
I broke my life, to seek relief
From the flawed light of love and grief.

With mounting beat the utter fire
Charred existence and desire.
It died low, ceased its sudden thresh.
I had found unmysterious flesh—
Not the mind's avid substance—still
Passionate beyond the will.

Alchemy—one of the earliest efforts to develop an exact science that would combine philosophy and technology—regarded gold as the most spiritual metal. Bogan's poem is about an analogous quasi-scientific quest for purity. Her alchemist is a metaphor for the human type, frequently regarded as heroic, who seeks spiritual transcendence through esoteric study requiring rejection of the common life. Poetry is full of such heroes: Shelley's Alastor, Byron's Manfred, Arnold's Scholar Gypsy. The narrator in Yeats's "Sailing to Byzantium" offers a close analogy to the speaker in "The Alchemist," for he too is a being "sick with desire" seeking the relief of a wisdom that can only be secure when he has attained a condition wholly of the mind. "Consume my heart away," he appeals, embracing like Bogan's alchemist a refining, intellectual fire. He too desires a form of existence divorced from eye and bone: "Once out of nature I shall never take / My bodily form in any natural thing." Bogan's poem, however, rejects the idea affirmed in "Sailing to Byzantium" that a world of pure spirit exists beyond the sphere of physical existence, to be attained by deserting or destroying the physical. The alchemist does indeed find in the crucible something in a pure form, but it is not "the mind's avid substance." It is "unmysterious flesh— still / Passionate." The creative mind may only deny, it may never escape, its dependence on tormented sensuous existence.

"The Alchemist," then, can be interpreted as a critique of a romantic theory of art. The meaning of the poem changes, however, if we view the alchemist not as a symbol for the romantic poet heroically bent on defying nature—Shelley, Byron, Yeats—but as a *woman* poet hopelessly defying the social significance of her femininity.

From this perspective, the will to deny the body expressed in "The Alchemist" grows poignantly comprehensible. For the metaphorical gold she seeks—"passion wholly of the mind," "Thought," "Ecstasy come to breath"—are attainments essential to creativity; but in Western culture they have always been regarded as "masculine" attainments. Throughout her long career, Bogan's poetry reflects ambivalent acquiescence to the stereotype that makes aspiration to intellectual power a contradiction of the "feminine." This contradiction is rarely expressed in direct statement; rather, it infuses most of the poems that, like "The Alchemist," deal with a conflict between mental power and sexual passion. It is expressed in metaphors where "flesh" and "breath" form fateful polarities. "Flesh" is mortal, dumb, blind, hopelessly instinctual; it is low, associated with darkness and the earth, and it is feminine. "Breath," by contrast, is the medium of inspiration, speech, music—high achievements, not associated with the feminine sphere. This polarity is the explicit theme of a powerful poem, "Cassandra," in which Bogan imagines Cassandra's clairvoyance as a consequence of liberation from feminine roles:

> To me, one silly task is like another.
> I bare the shambling tricks of lust and pride.
> This flesh will never give a child its mother,—
> Song, like a wing, tears through my breast, my side,
> And madness chooses out my voice again,
> Again. I am the chosen no hand saves:
> The shrieking heaven lifted over men,
> Not the dumb earth, wherein they set their graves.

Cassandra's fate as seer tragically ignored by the princes of Troy was the punishment Apollo ordained when she withheld promised sexual favors. She paid a high price for her ascent from femininity. In this respect, "Cassandra" is typical, for in Bogan's vision woman is frighteningly bound to and by her sexuality. It brings her low. In "The Crows," for example, Bogan likens an old woman who is still full of sexual passion to a harvested field, in which "there is only bitter / Winter-burning." The girl in "Chanson un Peu Naïve" is a "body . . . ploughed, / Sown, and broken yearly." Another, in "Girl's Song," lies with her lover in a field as on a grave: "And, since she loves [him], and she must, / Puts her young cheek against the dust."

Identification of the feminine with fields, seasonal cycles, and mortality has other implications in Bogan's poetry. The field is not only a fertile space, it is space enclosed for others' use. The gate to its enclosures is the awakening of sexuality. Before love, the girl in "Betrothed" has roamed freely with other maidens "In air traversed of birds"—"But there is only evening here, / And the sound of willows / Now and again dipping their long oval leaves in the water." The feminine personae in Bogan's early poems are as fatally determined as heroines in Hardy—and by the same rural and sexual cultural conventions. As Bogan writes in "Women":

> They cannot think of so many crops to a field
> Or of clean wood cleft by an axe.

Their love is an eager meaninglessness
Too tense, or too lax.

They hear in every whisper that speaks to them
A shout and a cry.
As like as not, when they take life over their door-sills
They should let it go by.

In these lyrics, Bogan is working with stereotypes of the feminine from which she, as author, maintains a knowing distance. These are *some* women, *other* women. Yet the same conflicting opposites—low/high, flesh/breath, feminine/masculine—furnish the imagery in which Bogan speaks as "I" describing her own creative powers. In these poems, as in "The Alchemist," the speaker seeks to purify herself of personal history, to become "thought divorced from eye and bone."

"Fifteenth Farewell" is a pair of sonnets in which the speaker wills a commitment to "breath"—identified with both life and art—as an escape from an unmanageable and painful sexual passion:

I

You may have all things from me, save my breath,
The slight life in my throat will not give pause
For your love, nor your loss, nor any cause.
Shall I be made a panderer to death,
Dig the green ground for darkness underneath,
Let the dust serve me, covering all that was
With all that will be? Better, from time's claws,
The hardened face under the subtle wreath.

Cooler than stones in wells, sweeter, more kind
Than hot, perfidious words, my breathing moves
Close to my plunging blood. Be strong, and hang
Unriven mist over my breast and mind,
My breath! We shall forget the heart that loves,
Though in my body beat its blade, and its fang.

II

I erred, when I thought loneliness the wide
Scent of mown grass over forsaken fields,
Or any shadow isolation yields.
Loneliness was the heart within your side.
Your thought, beyond my touch, was tilted air
Ringed with as many borders as the wind.
How could I judge you gentle or unkind
When all bright flying space was in your care?

Now that I leave you, I shall be made lonely
By simple empty days,—never that chill
Resonant heart to strike between my arms
Again, as though distraught for distance,—only
Levels of evening, now, behind a hill,
Or a late cock-crow from the darkening farms.

In the first sonnet, "You" is unmistakably a lover. But "you" also denotes in both sonnets the power of the masculine over the feminine as these two abstractions are consistently rendered in Bogan's poems, where "he" is nearly always either a voice or a pair of censorious and faithless eyes. This man, Bogan says, has always been in some sense beyond her, or at least beyond what she could gain by touching him physically. She could not apply ordinary value judgments ("gentle," "unkind") to one whose thought and ambition appeared boundless. Nor could she approach his mind by holding the man in her arms. Rather, his heart delivered blows and taught her by example to be definitively alone. "Fifteenth Farewell," part II, also makes use of the polarities described above, which place the feminine in the context of "forsaken fields" rather than "bright flying space," of "levels" rather than "tilted air," of a loneliness which is willed rather than sought. The masculine is above and beyond the imperiousness of flesh and seeks a noble though desperate distance from it.

Yet, if the masculine is identified with "air" in this elevated, authoritative sense, air is not exclusively the domain of men. This is the theme of "Fifteenth Farewell," part I, explicitly a rejection of suicide. The tone of triumph is almost militant and comes, significantly, from the speaker's recognition that she possesses "breath." Not merely ongoing life, "breath" is a creative power, like the "air" of thought in the second sonnet. It flows coolly in the throat, above as well as "close to" that source of "hot, perfidious words," the plunging blood; it appears to be the breath which shapes from active pain a formal art, "The hardened face under the subtle wreath." This is the kind of transformation which may be won by denial of the feminine, the body in which beat "love's blade and its fang."

All these poems may be seen to bear upon the project undertaken in "The Alchemist" to separate flesh from breath, to break one's life in order to attain a mental ecstasy, to transmute base metal into gold. At the opening of the poem the alchemist seems to think that if she could purge her passionate thought of any trace of its origins in a (female) body, she might ascend to that high plane occupied by the greatest spirits. But at the end of the poem, the "utter fire" of acute intelligence illuminates the absurdity, even the unworthiness, of such a goal. Hence, failure of the alchemist may be interpreted as a liberation of the woman as artist. The poem ends on a note of self-mocking relief, wry rather than bitter: "I had found unmysterious flesh." Explicitly, she denies a distinction between matter and spirit. Implicitly, she accepts her sex as a fundamental basis of her art. Implicitly, too, she challenges the long tradition in which the woman artist seems, in James's phrase, "that oddest of animals." While in her life Bogan never conquered the ambivalence toward the woman artist that colored her cultural milieu, "The Alchemist" in its technical and spiritual confidence testifies eloquently to the power of the female imagination. Further, it foreshadows the project of contemporary literary criticism to expose the cultural biases of the ahistorical ideologies of the early modern poets, as well as the project of contemporary women poets to transform art by asserting the validity of their subjectivity. In retrospect, Louise Bogan emerges as an unknowing precursor of those women poets who write today liberated from many constraints of that old contradiction—liberated, that is, from all but the inescapable constraints of poetry itself.

Notes

1. *Journey Around My Room*, ed. Ruth Limmer (New York: Viking Press, 1980), pp. 135–36.

2. Quoted in William Jay Smith, *Louise Bogan: A Woman's Words* (Washington, D. C.: Library of Congress, 1971), p. 13.

Form, Feeling, and Nature: Aspects of Harmony in the Poetry of Louise Bogan
Carol Moldaw*

Like T. S. Eliot, and unlike William Carlos Williams, in answer to whom she wrote the essay "On the Pleasures of Formal Poetry,"[1] Louise Bogan believed that verse is never free. For her, the music and meaning of a poem are indissoluble, and the experience which inspires a poem must be transformed in order to become a work of art:

> "unadulterated life" *must* be transposed, although it need not be "depersonalized." Otherwise you get "self-expression" only; and that is only half of art. The other half is technical, as well as emotional, and the most poignant poems are those in which the technique takes up the burden of feeling *instantly*; and that presupposes a practised technique.[2]

*This essay was written for this volume, and appears here with the permission of the author.

Bogan felt that her own work expressed her personal experience without betraying it; experience pervades the poems, but is disguised. As she wrote in her journal, and to an admirer, respectively:

> The poet represses the outright narrative of his life. He absorbs it, along with life itself. The repressed becomes the poem. Actually, I have written down my experience in the closest detail. But the rough and vulgar facts are not there.[3]

> with my work . . . you are dealing with emotion under high pressure— so that *symbols* are its only release.[4]

Autobiographical veracity does not consist of "rough and vulgar facts"— these are replaced by, or released in the form of, symbols. Furthermore, "technique takes up the burden of feeling." In a sense this is incontrovertible, for emotion is always conveyed through the textures of the surface. But Bogan's phrase also signifies that feeling is problematic, a "burden," which it is technique's vital function to express successfully. She has no sympathly for technique for technique's sake: "The fake reason, the surface detail, language only—these give no joy."[5]

To describe what, beyond technique, a poem requires to be emotionally effective, Bogan used the term "the breath of life,"[6] which connotes both vitality and the rhythmic basis of human nature. In "The Pleasures of Formal Poetry," Bogan traces the pleasure of rhythmical utterance to physical activities, and finally to the human body and breath itself:

> I want to keep on emphasizing the pleasure to be found in bodily rhythm as such. . . . We think of certain tasks, the rhythm of which has become set. Sowing, reaping, threshing, washing clothes, rowing, and even milking cows goes to rhythm. . . . Hauling up sail or pulling it down; coiling rope; pulling and pushing and climbing and lifting, all went to different rhythms; and these rhythms are preserved for us, fast or slow, smooth or rough, in sailors' songs.
>
> How far back can we push this sense of time? . . . It certainly springs from the fact that a living man has rhythm built in to him, as it were. His heart beats. He has a pulse. . . . and man shares with the animals not only a pulse, but an attendant rhythm: his breathing.[7]

Focusing on language as an accompaniment to and preserver of the rhythms of physical acts imparts an importance to form—sound, rhythm, rhyme—that is not dependent on words. Poetry's primary distinction here is that it combines words (descriptions, meanings) with rhythms which in themselves are firmly rooted in the human psyche.

Bogan often expresses her predilection for the rhythmical aspects of poetry through the metaphor of music. Music was one of Bogan's great loves. She once wrote, "you can have anyone who writes 'odic poems.' I'm going right back to pure music: the Christina Rossetti of

our day, only not so good. My aim is to sound so pure and so liquid
that travelers will take me across the desert with them. . . ."[8] Music
is the central image of many of Bogan's poems. The titles reflect this:
twelve poems are called songs, and other titles include "The Drum,"
"M., Singing," "To Be Sung on the Water," "Musician," and "Train Tune."
Bogan also weaves sound into other images, often describing a motion
along with its sound, as in "Betrothed":

> But there is only the evening here,
> And the sound of willows
> Now and again dipping their long oval leaves in the water.

The image of willows "dipping their leaves" creates a continuum of
rhythmical motion while it refers to, and is meant to evoke, the sound
which accompanies this motion. Further, the sounds of the words create
the melodious sounds they invoke. In "Old Countryside" we experience
the various seasons primarily through sounds:

> The summer thunder, like a wooden bell,
> Rang in the storm above the mansard roof,
>
> . . . .
> . . . wind made the clapboards creak.
> . . . .
> . . . we heard the cock
> Shout its unplaceable cry, the axe's sound
> Delay a mome.tt after the axe's stroke.

The correlation between the rhythmical natures of the aesthetic
and natural worlds and the human psyche is at the heart of Bogan's
poetry. To a large extent the poems are about poetry and the aesthetic
process. Many images central to the poems are of sound and rhythmical
motion, two fundamental elements of poetry which also emphasize its
connection with human life. The poems most expressive of spiritual
peace, like "Song for a Lyre" and "Night," are those in which images
of natural rhythms dictate emotional rhythms. The awe and harmony
embodied in these poems emanate from a vision of the natural and
changing world, and the poems end with a declaration drawn from
human experience. The appeal is to a world in which rhythms and form
embody otherwise inexpressible emotions. The most peaceful world is
neither rigid, with too much form, as in "Sub Contra," nor chaotic, as
in the beginning of "Baroque Comment," but fluid, ordered to the point
where patterns are discernible.

"Sub Contra," which uses as metaphors the techniques and forms
of music, expresses the desire for a pattern that will fulfill passionate
demands. The poem exists in an aesthetic vacuum, without a surrounding
world. No person is explicitly present: the ear, brain, heart, and rage
take the place of an individual. The poem asks technique to "take up

the burden of feeling," but technique alone, "like mockery in a shell," is inadequate, until the emotions provide impetus and direction. "Sub Contra" is about the discovery that a good poem "cannot be written by technique alone. It is carved out of agony, just as a statue is carved out of marble":[9]

> Notes on the tuned frame of strings
> Plucked or silenced under the hand
> Whimper lightly to the ear,
> Delicate and involute,
> Like the mockery in a shell.
> Lest the brain forget the thunder
> The roused heart once made it hear,—
> Rising as that clamor fell,—
> Let there sound from music's root
> One note rage can understand,
> A fine noise of riven things.
> Build there some thick chord of wonder;
> Then, for every passion's sake,
> Beat upon it till it break.

The desire for "One note rage can understand" is initially countered by a dispassionate tone and an emphasis on a controlled, contrived aspect of music. The first five lines describe the formation and reception of music's sound simply and meticulously, first deviating from exposition with "whimper," which is affective. "Whimper" usually suggests a quality of emotion emanating from the source of the sound—for instance a child whimpers to convey a need. Bogan, however, inverts this. The notes themselves do not whimper, the ear perceives the sound as such, and the passive construction of "Plucked . . . under the hand" de-emphasizes the musician's role. This inversion conveys the idea that the listener infers, or passively creates, the tremor of the emotional. The ear, "delicate and involute," appears more complex than the music.

Next, the notes are compared to "the mockery in a shell." The metaphor, predicted and supported by "involute," which suggests the shape of a shell as well as the ear, conveys both the emotionally neutral sense of being imitative, and the sense that the music is hollow, without real inspiration. The implication is that this music, like the sound of the sea heard from a shell, is not authentic.

Dissatisfied with this state of things, the poem from here on is exhortative, asking for a note, then a chord, then a rhythm, to inspire the brain in the way the heart once did. Although the music so far has been unsatisfying, the exhortation implies the heart's present inability to inspire the brain without assistance.

As the poem redefines the musical process outlined at its beginning, and shifts from "the frame of strings" to "music's root," the music evolves until it becomes adequate first to the demands of rage, and finally, "for every passion's sake." "One note" and "a fine noise of riven things" expand into "some thick chord of wonder"; and "beat," which suggests a drum, not a stringed instrument, replaces "plucked." The rhythm of the poem also becomes more insistent: the last two lines both begin and end on a strong stress. The hortatory subjunctive, "let," demanding something from no one in particular, delays the necessity of direct address until, at the poem's end, "build" and "beat" demand action from the musician, who had been portrayed as passive. Whereas the music at the beginning was only a mockery, this is meant to be emotionally authentic.

It is the demand, "Then, for every passion's sake, / Beat upon it till it break," which reinvigorates the poem and allows, finally, a cathartic release. The poem's frustration stemmed from its own inabilities—technique alone was inadequate, as was the heart. Only in combination, with directives from the emotions and ability from technique, can the poem achieve its desired resolution.

"Sub Contra" expresses the desire for an aesthetic form which will exemplify, or even create a heightened state of emotion. In contrast, "Baroque Comment" embraces the world and its aesthetic creations and embodies the human desire for harmony. Its theme is the already resolved coexistence of the world, form and symbolic expression.

> From loud sound and still chance;
> From mindless earth, wet with a dead million leaves;
> From the forest, the empty desert, the tearing beasts,
> The kelp-disordered beaches;
> Coincident with the lie, anger, lust, oppression and death in many forms:
>
> Ornamental structures, continents apart, separated by seas;
> Fitted marble, swung bells; fruit in garlands as well as on the branch;
> The flower at last in bronze, stretched backward, or curled within;
> Stone in various shapes: beyond the pyramid, the contrived arch and the
>   buttress;
> The named constellations;
> Crown and vesture; palm and laurel chosen as noble and enduring;
> Speech proud in sound; death considered sacrifice;
> Mask, weapon, urn; the ordered strings;
> Fountains; foreheads under weather-bleached hair;
> The wreath, the oar, the tool,
> The prow;
> The turned eyes and the opened mouth of love.

Unlike any other poem by Bogan, "Baroque Comment" has facets which recall Whitman: parallelism, long lines, and the listing of images. And, unlike many of Bogan's poems, this one contains no "I." Any emotive powers seem to emanate not from the viewer, but directly from that which is viewed.

In the first stanza the images reflect the chaotic organic world and the human destructive forces. Immediately, with the preposition "from," the poem asserts that this organic chaos is the origin of something else, the nature of which is not yet specified. The adjectives emphasize the natural chaos and lack of proportion. Sound, not merely present, is "loud." Chance, in direct contrast, is "still"—perhaps because it is abstract and insubstantial. The earth, "mindless," cannot function as the controlling center; nor can the "tearing" beasts, or the "kelp-disordered" beaches. Both "mindless" and "disordered" are privative, pointing to the lack of control, the lack of human influence, and indirectly introducing the idea of form.

The distinctly human faculties, "the lie, anger, lust, oppression, and death in many forms," each imply a morally antithetical partner. Without the existence of truth, calmness, spiritual love, justice, and natural death, there would be no vocabulary for the other; they *are* only in the context of what they are not. The line, which begins "Coincident with," also affirms that the aesthetic, spiritual creations which follow in the second stanza neither arise from, nor exclude, the humanly created chaos.

The second and last stanza presents that which emerges from the chaos; it does not ask how the transformation, or the impulse to transform, occurs. "Ornamental structures, continents apart, separated by seas" arise as if by a natural extension of human existence. They are the expression and symbol of the ordering human.

For the poem as a whole, what must be noted, besides the absence of the "I," is that the poem does not contain a complete sentence. The presence of a verb would presume to solve the question of how aesthetic objects or symbols are derived from the chaotic earth. Its absence avoids the question, and precludes the formation of a time sequence. The earth precedes aesthetic creation, but the process may have always been, and may still be occurring. The world is not devoid of disorder; "the lie, anger, lust . . ." have not been purged even though there are "palm and laurel chosen as noble and enduring." The relationship is posited as continual, and the transformed does not replace either its antecedent or that which is antithetical. However, out of the natural disorder, as though requiring it, comes that which is distinguished by harmony and form.

Some of the aesthetic images are in fact related directly to particular images in the first stanza. "The pyramid" inhabits an otherwise "empty desert"; "the named constellations" contrast with the "kelp-disordered beaches"; the leaves, "palm and laurel chosen as noble and enduring," give "mind" to the "mindless earth, wet with a dead million leaves"; "fruit in garlands as well as on the branch" also contrasts with the leaves' decay. "Speech proud in sound" gives dignity and order to "loud sound," as "death considered sacrifice" does to both "still chance" and "death in many forms."

These images harken to a sense of reason, harmony, and fulfillment: they order, elevate, and immortalize the natural world. The flower is "at last" in bronze—safe from death, consecrated in full bloom or in bud. The phrase "at last" is the most explicit hint of the all but untraceable tone of relief and peace which nevertheless dominates the stanza.

The images loosely follow a progression from the created objects to the implements of creation (themselves created) to the final declaration of the human, portrayed as one passionately receptive. But the nouns are generic, visually accessible only through their universality, and the adjectives and adjectival clauses do not help us see the images. Instead they stress the artifice, the difference between the humanly created and their organic counterparts. The adjectives are all participles, invoking the unmentioned creative force: "*fitted* marble," "*swung* bells," "*contrived* arch," "*named* constellations," and "*ordered* strings." Thus, while the created objects refer to the organic world, they have new symbolic connotations, as the fruit of the human impulse and ability to create, to shape objects of beauty and order.

The last five lines, shorter and more sparse, move in quick succession through the images (eight of them are nouns without qualifiers), and thus accentuate the fact that the objects are listed without explicit purpose. At the same time their simplicity deemphasizes the baroque quality of the list and slows the pace. It is in these lines that the human figure is introduced, and the objects ("Mask, weapon, urn . . . / . . . / The wreath, the oar, the tool, / The prow") are closer to the human world. The centrality to human endeavours clarifies what the previous images only suggest: design and pattern, ordering and naming, are expressions of the human desire for harmony and for self-realization.

The ending line, "The turned eyes and the opened mouth of love," indirectly addresses the question of how the transformation from disorder to harmony occurs. As in "Sub Contra," authentic expression can originate only in the emotions. Love, at once spiritual and sexual, is the apex of humanness. The most natural of the poem's images, the eyes and mouth can be seen as the essential link between the natural world and aesthetic creations. It is typical of Bogan that the sensuous image, "opened mouth," also suggests the imminent acts of speech, song, or prayer: the beginnings of expression.

"Baroque Comment" acts as an elaborate reminder. As if arguing by example, it transmits, through images and abstract ideals, a vision of harmony. Unlike "Sub Contra," which arises from dissatisfaction and demands something missing from the poem, "Baroque Comment" posits no dissatisfaction. Lacking a verb, an explicit argument, and a specific persona, the poem affirms a world in which symbols "take up the burden of feeling instantly."

Like "the turned eyes and the opened mouth of love," many of the images which end the poems are of things caught in the midst of incipient, or endlessly recurrent, motion. This is another way that Bogan's poems convey the rhythmic and the emotional together: the motion symbolizes the point of change in both nature and the emotions; in itself it captures the essence of a situation.

"Winter Swan" and "Old Countryside" both end with images of arrested motion. "Winter Swan," which contains the challenge, "But speak, you proud!," poses the "leaf-caught world once thought abiding" as a "dry disarray and artifice," and ends with "the long throat bent back, and the eyes in hiding." "Old Countryside" recounts change in the guise of prophecy "come to proof." The last image, seen "far back . . . in the stillest of the year," is "the thin hound's body arched against the snow."

Like aesthetic objects, the stilled images bring the world into focus. Each image can be thought of as stilled only by the perceptions of the poems themselves. In the reality of the past they continue—the swan to sing its death song, the hound to leap, the human being perhaps to kiss— but in memory they are caught, and become significant, in these postures of incipient motion. They are cathartic because they direct the reader to the point of change.

Whereas a sense of freedom, or eternity, results when the stilled images seem to be part of a continuum, other images seem frozen in stasis. Stasis is the result of fear, and occurs when the elements of the self and the world cannot be integrated, as in "Medusa," or when the persona is stymied by her inability to perceive and feel fully, as in "Henceforth, from the Mind." These poems, and some of the early embittered love poems, disclose an imbalance between the elements of the self and the world—a desire to escape into a world wholly formalistic, without the dangers inherent in the chaotic physical world. The result is akin to the musical and emotional rigidity in "Sub Contra," which that poem ultimately overcomes.

"A Tale," the first poem in Bogan's first, fourth, fifth, and sixth books, ends with an image of the double. It initially presents the impulse to go past the contrived signs of change ("The arrowed vane announcing weather, / The tripping racket of a clock") and then to escape from the transitory altogether ("Seeking, I think, a light that waits / Still as a lamp upon a shelf"). The last two stanzas suggest that the end of the youth's journey is to be very different from the peaceful and domestic light he seeks:

> But he will find that nothing dares
> To be enduring, save where, south
> Of hidden deserts, torn fire glares
> On beauty with a rusted mouth.—
>
> Where something dreadful and another
> Look quietly upon each other.

The language describing the landscape indicates nothing in reality, but instead a mythic, or inner landscape—the dark regions of the self. Though the double figures confront each other "quietly," it is with the quiet of terror. Stillness is not, the youth discovers, synonymous with peace.

The confrontation of the selves, inescapable and uncontrollable, can lead to spiritual death. Things are stilled, but this does not lead to an aesthetic focusing: stillness becomes their nature. Bogan returns to the double in "Medusa," "The Sleeping Fury," "The Dream," and "The Meeting." Like "A Tale," these poems do not exist in the natural world; they are part of myth, or abstract and symbolic. "Medusa" exemplifies the entrapment that results from confrontation with the other self. In the poem it is not, as in the myth, just the viewer who turns to stone; the entire perceived world is paralyzed:

> And I shall stand here like a shadow
> Under the great balanced day,
> My eyes on the yellow dust, that was lifting in the wind,
> And does not drift away.

Only in the poems "The Sleeping Fury" and "The Dream," where the speaker faces the double with "control and understanding," is the paralysis circumvented, and does "the terrible beast . . . put down his head in love."[10]

"The Alchemist," "Henceforth, from the Mind," "Summer Wish," "Spirit's Song," and "Little Lobelia's Song" also embody the double theme. In these poems the persona is split, implicitly or explicitly, into two irreconcilable selves, usually a physical and spiritual self. "The Alchemist" relates the futile attempt to transmute the substance of the baser self into "A passion wholly of the mind" and finds

> . . . unmysterious flesh—
> Not the mind's avid substance—still
> Passionate beyond the will.

The rigidity in these poems stems from a denial of the natural—an asceticism or romanticism which will not, or cannot, accept the dangers perceived in the physical world. As in the beginning of "Sub Contra," the persona is resigned, or even wants, to exist in a circumscribed world. In "Henceforth, from the Mind," "joy, you thought, when young, / Would wring you to the bone, / Would pierce you to the heart" has as little effect as "shallow speech alone." In "Little Lobelia's Song," which is written from the perspective of a spirit "not lost but abandoned," the spirit wants to, but cannot, reenter the "blood and bone."

The only double which is positive for Bogan is that which reflects and expresses the real, as an aesthetic image does. The divided self is built upon fear and depends upon emotional barriers; the aesthetic object, like the images of things caught, focuses. It comes out of the natural world but creates something more and connotes peace and permanence. In "Division," the aesthetic double, the "replica," is the tree's shadow, and it is the shadow, not the tree itself, which is "woven in changeless leaves" and "clasped against the eye."

"Baroque Comment" is a full expression of the world divided into itself and its aesthetic reflection. Its underlying assumptions—that natural disorder contains the kernels of order, that the human destructive forces are akin to the creative forces, that created order referring back to the natural world epitomizes harmony—also underlie Bogan's life-affirming poems, such as "Song for a Lyre" and "Night," which address the problem of form in experience itself.

Emotions and insights, like aesthetic objects, and like the images of things caught, focus and order the world. Conversely, the world itself can be a source of inner exhaltation and freedom. Bogan broaches this in a letter to Morton Zabel:

> concerning the heightening which comes to the artist when he acquires the habit of regarding life as mythical and typical. That's only another way of saying that when one lets go, and *recognizes* the stream on which we move as the same stream which moves us within—that it is time and the earth floating our blood and flesh, floating its own child—and stops fighting against the kinship, the light flows in; peace arrives.[11]

In Bogan, the desire to duplicate things through description is countered by the stronger desire to duplicate and evoke responses to the things perceived. Thus, the poems are often written in the past tense, from the specific viewpoint of memory, and the claims which the past makes upon the present are equaled by memory's reevaluation of the past. Throughout there is a tension between sensuous particulars and the abstract.

In both "Song for a Lyre" and "Night" the speaker gathers strength from the rhythms of nature which, though not all exclusive to night, are perceived as night phenomena. Neither poem emphasizes the speaker's experience until the last stanza, but both return to the human element, with a clear sense of renewal that is caused by the *perception* of natural, continuous rhythms.

In "Song for a Lyre" the images of the leaves, the stream, sleep, and dream are repeated incrementally. The setting of night exists primarily on two levels—the night as present, and the night as future. The shift into the future is subtle: only the modal auxiliary "must" and the repeated adverb "soon" reveal the future tense. It is as if night is so completely imagined, and so like past nights of the same season, that it is present.

SONG FOR A LYRE

The landscape where I lie
Again from boughs sets free
Summer; all night must fly
In wind's obscurity
The thick, green leaves that made
Heavy the August shade.

Soon, in the pictured night,
Returns—as in a dream
Left after sleep's delight—
The shallow autumn stream:
Softly awake, its sound
Poured on the chilly ground.

Soon fly the leaves in throngs;
O love, though once I lay
Far from its sound, to weep,
When night divides my sleep,
When stars, the autumn stream,
Stillness, divide my dream,
Night to your voice belongs.

Here the moments of summer's passing and autumn's return revitalize both the world and the speaker. The recurrence of change is shared: the speaker "again" is in the particular landscape; summer "again," and inevitably, turns to autumn. The change cleanses and lightens the world: the "thick, green leaves" disperse; the "shallow autumn stream" awakens; the speaker is reunited with the memory of her lover.

The speaker's relation to this world is not as a participant, and not even fully as a witness, but as an *anticipant*—renewed by the signs of approaching change. Furthermore, the speaker is moved not only by the coming transformation of the earth, but by her awareness of the transformation; because the natural changes are foreseen, they occur first within the speaker's mind. Though the images refer to the landscape, they have their origin and effect almost equally in the imagination.

This imagination, however, is not severed from the world, but attuned to it; part memory, it needs only the intimation of seasonal change to infer the rest. The first inference occurs with the change from the present tense ("The landscape where I lie") to the future ("all night must fly"). The landscape is abstract to the point of being nondescriptive; suggesting only that the speaker is outdoors, it in fact encourages the idea that she is being metaphorical, and actually may be indoors. The full phrase ("Again from boughs sets free / Summer") inverts our usual conception of the relationship between the land and the season. Normally, the season is imbued with the power to affect and dominate the land; here it is the land which discards, "sets free," the season. Only with the shift to the future tense, "the thick, green leaves" which the imagination foresees, does the language become more descriptive.

The second stanza further emphasizes the description's imaginative qualities: night becomes "the pictured night," which suggests both night imagined and a night of dreams. The metaphor of the dream "left after sleep's delight" is extended to the stream, "softly awake," as if while dry it too had been asleep. As in "Betrothed," it is the sound that signals the stream's movement and motivates the more visually descriptive language of the "shallow autumn stream" and the "chilly ground."

Although the poem so far indicates the imagined and remembered aspects of experience, it is the external world which has been described, and described in terms of its motion. In the last stanza, the speaker is more prominent, as the awareness of the natural world and the continued remembrance of the lover inspire her.

Many of the images in the last stanza echo images in the first two stanzas, but they are woven together, and not merely reiterative. Even the repetition of "soon" is altered, by the lack of a comma, as if what was soon to arrive had drawn nearer; and that image itself, "fly the leaves in throngs," draws us deeper into autumn than does the similar image in the first stanza. "O love, though once I lay / Far from its sound, to weep," echoing the poem's first line, "The landscape where I lie," introduces the emotions directly, in the past tense.

The object to which "its sound" refers may be either the autumn stream or all the sounds of night. But revealing that the speaker had wept, and in her sorrow had excluded the world, the stanza concludes by capsulizing her revelatory experience. We are first given the conditions ("When night . . ." "When stars . . .") that evoke the lover's voice, and not until the last line are we introduced to love, the catalyst that brings the speaker out of herself and allows her to experience the world.

That the effect of the repeated images in the last stanza differs from their effect in the preceding stanzas is due partially to the introduction of the lover, and partially to the interweaving of images. The freed leaves, the returning stream, the stars and stillness are integrated to create a night fuller and more real. The images of sleep and dream, metaphorical in the preceding stanza, also now inform the speaker's reality. The poem has come full circle; from an emphasis upon a reality which the speaker creates, or anticipates, it moves to a reality which is bestowed.

The sense of fullness in this stanza also results from its formal divergence from the first two. It contains one additional nonrhymed line, and a different rhyme pattern, *a b c c d d a*, rather than *a b a b c c*. "Stream" and "dream," rhymed in the second stanza, are here a couplet, accentuating their partnership, while the last line's rhyme with the first envelops the two adjacent couplets.

"Song for a Lyre," initially describing seasonal change, ends with the correlation between the perception of the elements and the vivid remembrance of the lover. As such, the poem affirms the soothing power of evocation even as it affirms the soothing power of love.

A later poem, "Night," makes a similar correlation among the elements, perception and the human heart. In "Night," however, the speaker is not explicitly present, and the experience of renewal is more implicit in the imagery itself. Not written in a set stanzaic form, the overall construction relies, as it does in "Baroque Comment," on the suspension, finally the omission, of the main clausal verb. Like "Song for a Lyre," "Night" makes manifest the recurrent, eternal, and healing qualities of rhythmic motion:

NIGHT

The cold remote islands
And the blue estuaries
Where what breathes, breathes
The restless wind of the inlets,
And what drinks, drinks
The incoming tide;

Where shell and weed
Wait upon the salt wash of the sea,
And the clear nights of stars
Swing their lights westward
To set behind the land;

Where the pulse clinging to the rocks
Renews itself forever;
Where, again on cloudless nights,
The water reflects
The firmament's partial setting;

—O remember
In your narrowing dark hours
That more things move
Than blood in the heart.

The first three stanzas form the beginning of a periodic sentence that is never concluded. Because the poem's substance resides in the description of ongoing motion, the missing verb (which would act definitively) becomes superfluous. The parallel construction of the adjectival clauses, connected by "where," and the unremitted use of the present tense, indicate the continuity which informs the poem's peaceful mood.

Sensuous particulars relieve the initial abstractness of the landscape; the "cold remote islands" become accessible through images signifying recurrent motion—the "restless wind" and the "incoming tide"—which form the basis for the equally rhythmical, but more detailed, images in the following stanzas. Ending a line with the repetition of "breathes" (the two "breathes," with the pause between them, occupy over half the line, and all of its metrical stress) suspends the poem's motion. The following line, particularly in its lighter sounds and its more visual image, relieves the suspension, and, by giving the verb an object, unexpectedly carries the image forward. This pattern, which recurs in the next two lines (where "drinks" echoes "breathes" and "incoming tide" echoes "wind of the inlets"), evinces a calm, rhythmical, life-imbued landscape.

The expansiveness suggested in the first stanza is reinforced now by more specific images, each of which revolves around the tide or the moving stars. The poem embodies the idea of movement: nothing is static; no motion is concluded; the scene is not limited to any specific night, but is ever-present.

The insistence upon continuing motion is emphasized by the rhymes and sounds which reverberate throughout the poem. The irregular meter rests upon iambs and anapests; many lines end on a falling rhythm (islands, estuaries, inlets, westward, forever, setting, remember), intimating the next strong beat of the iamb. Within stanzas, and from one stanza to the next, words echo each other in sound. In the second stanza, for example, s's, w's, and strong open vowels are repeated, and there is one internal rhyme, "nights" and "lights," in the middle of consecutive lines. The words "wash," "stars," "weed," "swing," "set," and "behind" are echoed by "water," "dark" (and "heart"), "wind," "inlets," and "tide."

By the last stanza, rhythms, sounds, and images, focused on the recurrent motions of the sea and the night sky, have cumulated to the single effect of tranquillity. With the last stanza the poem interrupts itself, breaking the adjectival clause, and the poet addresses herself.

The last stanza brings the poem, for the first time, to the human world, only to remind us that the human being is enriched and strengthened by attending to the natural world. The underlying connection between "blood in the heart," which moves, and the seascape, its essence also expressed as recurrent motion, is that all life, and in particular the salt blood of the human being, originated in the sea. In asserting that to look beyond oneself is more self-sustaining than to dwell, in one's "narrowing dark hours," on "blood in the heart," the poem also suggests that it is the life-sustaining rhythmical forces which connect us to the origins, the essences, of our lives. Implicated in this scheme is poetry; its essence also rhythmical recurrence, it too unites the human with the fundamental forces of life.

Bogan called poetry "the heart's cry"[12] and said that it "gives reality freedom and meaning."[13] She made these aesthetic principles her subject, and took on the double task of "going back to pure music" and expressing "what I have become and what I know."[14] One feels that the endeavours are not separable, but become part of each other in a given poem. Through image, sound, and rhythm, the poems express the desire for and the discovery of natural and aesthetic forms that uplift human consciousness.

Notes

1. Letter to Morton Zabel, 24 October 1948, in *What the Woman Lived: Selected Letters of Louise Bogan*, ed. Ruth Limmer (New York: Harcourt Brace Jovanovich, 1973), p. 263.

2. Letter to May Sarton, 17 March 1955, in *Letters*, p. 296.

3. *Journey Around My Room*, ed. Ruth Limmer (New York: The Viking Press, 1980), p. 72.

4. Letter to Sister M. Angela, 5 July 1969, in *Letters*, p. 92, n. 3.

5. *Journey Around My Room*, pp. 173–74.

6. "The Pleasures of Formal Poetry," in *A Poet's Alphabet* (New York: McGraw Hill, 1970), p. 150.

7. *Ibid.*, p. 152.

8. Letter to Theodore Roethke, September 1937, in *Letters*, p. 163.

9. Letter to Roethke, 23 August 1935, in *Letters*, p. 97.

10. "The terrible beast . . . / . . . put down his head in love" is from "The Dream." In 1954 Bogan wrote to May Sarton, " 'The Dream,' by the way, is a poem of victory and release. The terrible power, which may v. well be the psychic demon, is tamed and placated, but NOT destroyed; . . . something was done about control and understanding" (*Letters*, p. 369, n. 2).

11. Letter to Morton Zabel, 10 August 1936, in *Letters*, p. 136.

12. *Journey Around My Room*, p. 97.

13. *Ibid.*, p. 114.

14. *Ibid.*, pp. 161–62.

"The Repressed Becomes the Poem": Landscape and Quest in Two Poems by Louise Bogan

Sandra Cookson[*]

Louise Bogan was an intensely personal poet whose poems were made from the most intimate material of her life: love, death, the mysteries of the unconscious, the terrors of mental illness, the ponderings of a subtle and analytical mind on the nature of life and art. But she was a personal poet who rejected direct autobiographical statement

[*]This essay was written for this volume, and appears here with the permission of the author.

in her poems, except rarely and in the earlier work, and employed instead the obliquity of image used as symbol; who relied upon a symbolic language and the combined power of sound and rhythm and rhyme—form, in short—to convey meaning and emotion.

Although her poems are formal and symbolic structures, they cannot be separated from the most intimate psychological events of her life. For instance, in her poems that explore the unconscious in dream or vision and in her poems about sexual passion, images of a ravaged or hellish landscape symbolize the devastation of the psyche from assaults upon it by violently disruptive feelings which Bogan identifies as rooted deeply in her childhood. Archetypal images of the Medusa and the Furies, as well as a small gallery of more private myth figures, personify the poet's deepest fears and impulses. Thus, contrary to what one might expect from a poet who relies upon generalizing images such as these archetypal ones, and upon formal and traditional poetic structures, the urge toward the personal is always powerfully felt in Bogan's work. Her own brief remarks from a journal entry written late in life are of interest as the poet's view of the uses she made of her experience: "The poet represses the outright narrative of his life. He absorbs it, along with life itself. The repressed becomes the poem. Actually, I have written down my experience in the closest detail. But the rough and vulgar facts of it are not there."[1] The poet's conviction of absolute fidelity to her experience, although she has transformed "the rough and vulgar facts" of it, is a traditional aesthetic position, with moral overtones, of formalist lyric poets. Bogan's notion that "the repressed becomes the poem" is a kind of twentieth-century commentary on Wordsworth's idea of the poem as experience "recollected in tranquillity."

The remark further illuminates the unique power of Bogan's poetry by providing an insight into her belief that the repressed material of her life was her true poetic raw material, that therefore true poetry comes from the unconscious, a belief she stated many times in reference to her poems. Bogan spent many years of her life in psychotherapy, but her greatest poems bear out the implication that her true access to "repressed" material remained largely a mystery of the poetic process.

Bogan's life and her poems are marked by two obsessions. The first is her preoccupation with a childhood full of half-remembered scenes of violence between her parents, which she focuses upon her mother. The second is her marriage to the poet and novelist Raymond Holden. Bogan left Holden in 1934 and divorced him in 1937, but his presence persisted in her poems. Both the poems and journal entries written late in life suggest that while Bogan probably succeeded in freeing herself from the Holden obsession, the terrors of her childhood remained with her to her death.

From her earliest poems to her latest, Bogan's landscapes and seascapes represent the poet's mental universe. Often they are the settings for journeys into the darkest regions of the self, undertaken in order to achieve peace through understanding. Understanding, Bogan hoped, would allow her to exorcise her personal demons, which she identified as hatred and sexual jealousy. Two of Bogan's most distinguished poems, "Putting to Sea" (1936) and "Psychiatrist's Song" (1967), complement each other as poems of quest and reconciliation. "Putting to Sea" concerns liberation from the violence of sexual jealousy and the rage which were exacerbated by the last years of the Holden relationship. "Psychiatrist's Song," looking back on that struggle from a distance of thirty years, celebrates the achievement of psychic equilibrium. Yet it still contains the haunting image of the damaged child, the victim of experiences too painful ever to fully come to light.

The sea voyage is the mode of these psychological and spiritual journeys, and Bogan signaled its importance in her work when she chose "A Tale" (1921) as the opening poem in her collected poems, *The Blue Estuaries* (1968). "A Tale," though it is not chronologically the book's earliest, is Bogan's prototypical voyage poem. In it, a "youth" prepares to relinquish the everyday world of time and flux ("the break / Of waters in a land of change") in search of something enduring, "a light that waits / Still as a lamp upon a shelf." The ideal country which he seeks will be an austere place "where no sea leaps upon itself."

The poet, however, tells us that the youth's journey will not bring him wisdom attended by peace and steadiness of spirit. If, indeed, he does journey far enough to find the truth, it will be just the opposite of what he has hoped for:

> But he will find that nothing dares
> To be enduring, save where, south
> Of hidden deserts, torn fire glares
> On beauty with a rusted mouth,—
>
> Where something dreadful and another
> Look quietly upon each other.

At the center of his universe, the youthful voyager will find nameless terror, corrupted love, and presences monstrous beyond his comprehension. This hellish landscape, populated by demons, will recur throughout Bogan's poetry as the terrain of the unconscious.

In "Medusa," written at about the same time as "A Tale," the speaker, paralyzed by the monster's gaze, finds herself suspended in a vast surreal landscape where she is condemned for eternity to watch "the yellow dust" rising in the wind. Another version of this hell is depicted in "M., Singing," written about fifteen years later, in which the song of a young girl releases the demons of the unconscious, "Those beings without heart or name," permitting them to "Leave the long harvest which they reap / In the sunk land of dust and flame."

Bogan was remarkably consistent in her use of a particular land-scape with its cluster of images to signify an emotion or state of feeling. In the poems of her first book, *Body of This Death* (1923), passion is the "breeze of flame" ("Ad Castitatem") that consumes the field set afire and burned back to stubble after harvest. The image may originate in the agricultural practice of slash-and-burn, common in some tropical countries. The youthful Bogan lived in Panama for about a year with her first husband, and must have seen on many occasions whole fields set alight, the flames racing over the dry stalks. "Feuernacht" (1927) is a remarkably faithful depiction of such an event, while at the same time it clearly suggests the all-consuming power of sexual passion.

The blackened stubble which remains after the fire has burned itself out is a recurring image in these early poems, and signifies the woman's sexuality depleted by the fires of passion. The image belongs to Bogan's youth, and it disappears from her poems after the beautiful lyric of 1930, entitled "Song," in which the speaker attempts to renounce an impulse to sexual passion, claiming that she has long since paid her dues to it.

> Years back I paid my tithe
> And earned my salt in kind,
> And watched the long slow scythe
> Move where the grain is lined,
> And saw the stubble burn
> Under the darker sheaves.

Though it appears to have been Bogan's unhappy first marriage that gave expression to the pain of passion, the image of the young woman's sexuality as a "ravaged country" ("Ad Castitatem") carries over into the Holden years, where it is transformed into another tortured sexual landscape, the obscene and sterile tropical country of "Putting to Sea." Thirty years later in "Psychiatrist's Song," the same landscape recurs, but it is merely a dim shape on the horizon to the voyager now freed of the torments which it represents in the earlier poem.

In "Putting to Sea," the sea-voyage metaphor symbolizes the under-taking of a journey into the deepest self ("the gulf, the vast, the deep"), with the specific purpose of freeing the voyager from the obscenity of hatred. To accomplish this, she must confront it, and reject its tempta-tions, which take shape in the poem's unnatural tropical landscape. "With so much hated still so close behind / The sterile shores before us must be faced. . . ."

The voyager, first of the poem's two speakers, is the conscious self and controls the narrative. "Who, in the dark, has cast the harbor chain?" she asks, as if the journey were compelled by a force beyond her will. The land she is leaving is the everyday world described in natural, cycli-cal images, which connect it to sensual experience, as these lines suggest:

"Sodden with summer, stupid with its loves, / The country which we leave. . . ." Its counterpart in the unconscious is the tropical land, described by the poem's second speaker, the voice of the treacherous unconscious. The voyager, shunning all inducements toward the tropical shore, must journey into an awesome moral proving ground, the "bare circle of ocean," which is deep as heaven's height and "barren with despair." Later in the poem, the landscape of the quotidian, the sea, and the tropical shore will be joined by a fourth psychological country, which suggests the tender promise of childhood left unfulfilled.

The voyager understands that the second speaker's tantalizing descriptions of a gaudy and exotically flamboyant artificial land where "love fountains from its deeps" are meant to seduce her with false promises of love and fulfillment. The sly tone of this voice is supposed to conceal from her the true hideousness of the landscape:

> "O, but you should rejoice! The course we steer
> Points to a beach bright to the rocks with love,
> Where, in hot calms, blades clatter on the ear;
>
> And spiny fruits up through the earth are fed
> With fire; the palm trees clatter; the wave leaps.
>
> Fleeing a shore where heart-loathed love lies dead
> We point lands where love fountains from its deeps.
>
> Through every season the coarse fruits are set
> In earth not fed by streams."

The voyager is not taken in. She knows that this is really the landscape of madness. It is fiend's country, far more dangerous than the everyday world she has fled "where heart-loathed love lies dead." Bogan's specific reference is to the failure of her second marriage, to Raymond Holden, for which she was later to blame herself as a "demon of jealousy."[2] In 1936, she wrote her friend and editor at Scribner's, John Hall Wheelock, that this poem would "sum up the Holden suffering, endured so long, but now, at last, completely over."[3]

With the resumption of the narrative by the first speaker, following the passage just quoted, a new landscape enters the poem.

> . . . Soft into time
> Once broke the flower: pear and violet,
> The cinquefoil. The tall elm tree and the lime
>
> Once held out fruitless boughs, and fluid green
> Once rained about us, pulse of earth indeed.

The "birth" of flowers, emblematic for Bogan of New England where she was born and raised, suggests her own "early time." These limpid and tender lines also contrast with the harshness of the preceding images. Moreover, "fluid green" and "pulse of earth" suggest a primordial condition that is full of promise, teeming with life, but unformed.

The potential of this tender land is not to be realized, however. With the contrasting landscapes as her psychological terrain, the first speaker traces the seeds of her destructive impulses back to her childhood: "There, out of metal, and to light obscene, / The flamy blooms burn backward to their seed." Childhood is a land of promise, but within its tender depths anything can take root. In her view, the compulsion from which the voyager now seeks catharsis stems from this time of unformed life, from her childhood.

The poet-voyager has set herself a hard task. Lacking even the celestial guides of the mariner, she wonders at the necessity of this dark and perilous journey:

> The Way should mark our course within the night,
> The streaming System, turned without a sound.
> What choice is this—profundity and flight—
> Great sea? Our lives through we have trod the ground.
>
> Motion beneath us, fixity above.

"Putting to Sea" derives its power from the depiction of this moral/ psychological deep. The descriptions of the great mythic sea and the stars have a silent and formidable grandeur, evoked equally by the bare, grand simplicity of the adjectives and the vibrations of a long tradition they set in motion. A line like "The streaming System, turned without a sound" is so suggestive that, while it is describing the absence of stars in the heavens, it evokes their presence by the infusion of light "streaming" produces. At the same time, the void and utter silence of these disturbed heavens must recall, in "turned without a sound," the ancient music of the spheres, so out of place in this poem where the heavens themselves conspire in the voyager's bafflement.

In the same letter to Wheelock, Bogan remarks on the poem's provenance. "I know what it's about, with my upper reason, just a little; it came from pretty far down, thank God."[4] Bogan's comment states her conviction of the poem's origin in her subconscious, but it also suggests why "Putting to Sea" has such power; for in it resound echoes of the great mythic voyages which preceded it. The most reverberant of all is the quest of Odysseus. Dante provided Tennyson with the model for his Ulysses, and the opening lines of Bogan's last stanza suggest the spirit and tone of Tennyson's version of Ulysses' speech to his mariners:

> There lies the port; the vessel puffs her sail:
> There gloom the dark broad seas. My mariners,
> Souls that have toil'd, and wrought, and thought with me—

Bogan addresses her "mariners" with similar gravity: "Bend to the chart, in the extinguished night / Mariners! Make way slowly; stay from sleep."

Bogan may also be indebted to Baudelaire, if not for the actual sea-voyage metaphor, at least for certain aspects of its treatment in "Putting to Sea." Bogan's voyager has a specific moral purpose for her journey into the unknown, while Baudelaire's persona is a restless seeker after experience. Yet both poets share the belief that truth may be found in the search for the self. Bogan's final line, "And learn, with joy, the gulf, the vast, the deep," is almost an imitation of the last two lines of Baudelaire's "Le voyage": "Plonger au fond du gouffre, Enfer ou Ciel, qu'importe? / Au fond de l'Inconnu pour trouver du *nouveau!*" While Baudelaire exhorts his voyager to experience for its own sake, Bogan urges the striving for understanding. Her final line reaffirms her conviction that suffering can be surmounted as well as endured.

The most contemporary voyage which "Putting to Sea" recalls is the brief echo of "Sailing to Byzantium" heard in the second line. The voyager wonders at the extraordinary journey she is about to undertake. "This is no journey to a land we know," she says, echoing Yeats, who also rejects the everyday world, remarking of it, "That is no country for old men." Each of these poems partakes of the common impulse to represent the human journey as a sea voyage. In "Putting to Sea," Bogan both epitomizes that tradition and creates a poem uniquely her own.

Early in 1967, thirty years after the publication of "Putting to Sea" and just three years before her death, Bogan sent three "songs" to *New Yorker* poetry editor Howard Moss, with the note that they "seem to go together...[as poems] of dream and aberration."[5] A way to read the shifting and merging voices in "Psychiatrist's Song" is in the light of dream logic, in which identities are often fluid and interchangeable. Moreover, in the course of the long journey which psychotherapy was for Bogan, perhaps psychiatrist and patient each take on attributes of the other.

In a typescript of the poem, the only draft extant, the title reads "Psychiatrist's Recitative and Aria."[6] The published version retains the same stanzaic divisions. In the poem's opening section, which would be the recitative, the psychiatrist begins his monologue, musing in a general way upon the persons who have played crucial roles in the lives of his patients, but of whom "they" (the patients) cannot speak directly: "Those / Concerning whom they have never spoken and thought never to speak...." In spite of the psychiatrist's hint that patients deliberately conceal things, we may infer that the reason they do not have access to the whole narrative of their lives is that much of what is crucial has been repressed, and remains hidden in the unconscious:

> That place
> Hidden, preserved,
> That even the exquisite eye of the soul
> Cannot completely see.

From that generalized and somewhat rambling diagnostic beginning, the psychiatrist's attention soon settles upon particulars, and we realize that he must now be thinking of one patient:

> But they are there:
> Those people, and that house, and that evening, seen
> Newly above the dividing window sash—

At this point the narrative intensifies. Another voice enters, and from this moment to the end of the poem, the voice of the psychiatrist contains the voice of the patient. The sudden shift from generalities to particular details—"that house . . . that evening . . . the dividing window sash"—and the personal cry of anguish in the lines that follow, indicate that the point of view has shifted to that of the patient; yet there is no break in the narrative:

> The young will broken
> And all time to endure.

> Those hours when murderous wounds are made,
> Often in joy.

The images of the damaged child and the treacheries of passion recall major themes in Bogan's poems. As the recitative, providing exposition or background for the rest of the poem, this opening section, with its merging voices of psychiatrist and patient, is a poetic statement of the psychological traumas for which the journey of the next section was undertaken.

The second section, the aria of the typescript, begins with the line "I hear." The merging voices of psychiatrist and patient acknowledge the warning contained in the last line of the preceding section about the treachery of passion. The narration of the journey is taken over by the patient, whose voice dominates from now on, though the guiding presence of the psychiatrist is felt in the poem until the final stanzas. Since the patient is also the poet-voyager of "Putting to Sea," thirty years after, this "I" stands for the several selves of the poet. That she has absorbed the psychiatrist persona completely by the end of the poem suggests, perhaps, the health of the psyche achieved.

Although the old temptations to the evils of fiend's country are recalled in the opening lines, this tropical landscape is "far away" and no longer threatens the voyager. The old motif of sexual jealousy echoes mockingly in the three repetitions of "man"-words, probably a play on the free-associative technique often used in psychotherapy: "the *mango* trees (the *mangrove* swamps, the *mandrake* root...).” The reminder of the “clattering” palms from “Putting to Sea” fixes the identity of this receding landscape, hazy now, having lost its clear sense of evil. The voyager “watches” the thicket of palms—not even sure anymore that they are palm trees, “as though at the edge of sleep.” Indeed, the narration of this section has the dream character of a perfectly sequential and straightforward presentation of fantastic events.

The voyager has now achieved such control and certainty that she can journey toward the once disastrous landscape represented by the palms “in a boat without oars, / Trusting to rudder and sail.” The idea that the voyager is in control of the journey contrasts with the formidable voyage of “Putting to Sea.” Moreover, the whole landscape has been scaled down from the enormous and overpowering sea and sky of the earlier poem to a size more manageably human. She now leaves the boat and walks “fearlessly” to shore. Previously, even the ripples of the shallows might have been full of peril, for the sea has, until now, been an awesome and uncharted place. The lines that suggest control over a sea which will bring the speaker to a place of repose are reminiscent of Eliot’s “*Damyata*: The Boat responded / Gaily, to the hand expert with sail and oar,” from part 5 of *The Waste Land*, in which the rain brings with it the possibility of the renewal of life and hope.

The dangerous landscapes of ocean and palm trees recede, and the voyager finds herself “on firm dry land,” with the solidity of earth all around her. The last stanza banishes the old terrors of “flesh and of ocean” that were given full expression in “Putting to Sea.” If the last stanzas also evoke death in images of imminence, darkening, and silence, it is death welcomed, celebrated even, as the final healing. We need not be troubled by the implication that the cure for human suffering is death. Bogan was sixty-nine years old and in failing health when she wrote “Psychiatrist’s Song.” It is nearly her last poem, and marks the very last time she would use the voyage metaphor to set down in a poem the long struggle with her private demons. The truce between them was always, at best, a “troubled peace.”

Bogan places a great deal of the burden for making the poem intelligible upon the reader. In “Putting to Sea” the poem’s two voices were clearly separated. The voice out of fiend’s country spoke a different language from that of the voyager or conscious self in the poem, and her speeches were set off from the voyager’s narration by quotation marks. Bogan’s decision to remove the recitative and aria directions from “Psychiatrist’s Song” suggests a lightening of the poet’s hand, a willingness to let the narrative take its own way.

Bogan takes more chances with language and form than she has done previously, and can risk beginning the poem with the halting awkwardness of a slightly pedantic and visually ungainly line. The play on "man" in "mango," "mangrove," and "mandrake," and the many irregularities in the free-verse line indicate greater flexibility and the freedom to experiment with the line and with the rhythms of common speech. The third line of the second section, with its truncated thought, "And the thickets of—are they palms?" is an illustration. And in the simple but strung-together statements of the line, "Coming to the shore, I step out of the boat; I leave it to its anchor," Bogan risks a kind of austere prosiness. In addition to its echoes of *The Waste Land*, "Psychiatrist's Song" is reminiscent throughout of Eliot's later poems of the 1930s, in particular "Marina" and "Coriolan."

The classical and formal Bogan still dominates in "Psychiatrist's Song," but her willingness to chance being prosaic places in relief the more poetically gorgeous phrases, such as "the exquisite eye of the soul," and the line with which she bridges the poem's two major sections, "Those hours when murderous wounds are made, / Often in joy." The elevated simplicity of the penultimate stanza is due in part to the extreme economy of the spare, predominantly one-syllable words. The luminosity of another late major poem, "After the Persian" (1951–53), glows for a moment in the final stanza. In the hortatory tone that is reminiscent of part 5, the "farewell" section of that poem, Bogan sounds again the note of sage or prophet, which is the final expression of her lifelong consciousness of herself as poet. Like "Putting to Sea," "Psychiatrist's Song" closes with an exhortation. But Bogan lowers the tone, and the moving prayer to earth, "Heal and receive me," ends the poem in an affecting combination of dignity and vulnerability.

Notes

1. *Journey Around My Room: The Autobiography of Louise Bogan*, ed. Ruth Limmer (New York: Viking Press, 1980), p. 72.

2. *What the Woman Lived: Selected Letters of Louise Bogan, 1920–1970*, ed. Ruth Limmer (New York: Harcourt Brace Jovanovich, 1973), to May Sarton, 28 January 1954, p. 282.

3. *Ibid.*, p. 132.

4. *Ibid.*, p. 133n.

5. Letter, 25 January 1967, in *Letters*, p. 371. The other two poems are "Little Lobelia's Song" and "Masked Woman's Song."

6. Bogan Papers, box 11, folder 56, Amherst College Library, Amherst, Massachusetts. This title is written at the top of the page in Bogan's hand, and is enclosed between quotation marks. The typescript is dated 14 December 1966.

INDEX